Programming Our Lives

Television and American Identity

Walter Cummins and
George Gordon

Westport, Connecticut
London

Library of Congress Cataloging-in-Publication Data

Cummins, Walter M.
  Programming our lives : television and American identity / Walter Cummins
and George Gordon.
      p. cm.
  Includes bibliographical references and index.
  ISBN 0–275–99020–6 (alk. paper)
  1. Television broadcasting—Social aspects—United States. I. Gordon, George
G. II. Title.
  PN1992.6.C863 2006
    302.23'450973—dc22   2006008232

British Library Cataloguing in Publication Data is available.

Library of Congress Catalog Card Number: 2006008232
ISBN: 0–275–99020–6

First published in 2006

Praeger Publishers, 88 Post Road West, Westport, CT 06881
An imprint of Greenwood Publishing Group, Inc.
www.praeger.com

Printed in the United States of America

The paper used in this book complies with the
Permanent Paper Standard issued by the National
Information Standards Organization (Z39.48–1984).
10 9 8 7 6 5 4 3 2 1

To the families with whom we first watched.

Contents

Contents

Preface

For Americans today, television is a fact of life, a given of our daily existence, like indoor plumbing, central heating, and self-service supermarkets. The majority of the population was born after TV sets entered our living rooms at the end of World War II and has never known a home without one. Even for those who were alive in the mid-1940s, six decades of viewing have made the time before TV a distant memory. But because the screen is now a ubiquitous presence, we take television for granted and don't consider how the existence of the medium has changed our daily lives, our culture, and our relationship to the institutions and systems around us.

This sense that TV has always existed makes it difficult to sit back and determine the role it has played in causing or contributing to the ways our society has changed in the past sixty years. Some of those changes are obvious and can be documented by facts and figures—the average hours of daily viewing and the impact on how we spend our leisure time, the costs of election campaign commercials, the applications of TV in education, and the growing prominence of highly televised sports like professional football and NASCAR racing. Yet the deeper effects of such changes and the simply overwhelming amount of other influences, including many of the most significant, tend to be overlooked, and many of the most important questions go unanswered. Watching the screen has become as natural to us as sitting down to eat a meal. In fact, now that we are living in a time of dietary awareness, many of us spend much more time pondering what we ingest in our dietary systems than we do thinking about the images and information that enter our consciousness.

Clearly, certain areas of TV content have been subjects of contention and have been studied, debated, and even legislated. The Janet Jackson Super Bowl nipple incident led Congress to toughen broadcast "decency" laws. Interest groups have complained about the correlation between junk food commercials and childhood obesity. A myriad of researchers have investigated the potential cause-effect relationships of TV violence and juvenile crime with inconclusive results.

Although we note such issues in this book, our object is not to revisit what has already been said, but rather to go beyond that and consider the broader consequences for Americans living in an age of television—personally, socially, and politically. Although some of our conclusions are based on concrete evidence and the tabulations of others, many are our own interpretations. However, we attempt to support most of these interpretations with references that consider some aspect of the subject, linking and extrapolating to see the bigger picture.

A fundamental question that we pondered many times was whether television was a primary source of significant change or just a component of larger movements. Definitive cause-effect relationships are difficult to prove conclusively, and separating one social phenomenon from a host of influences may be impossible. But even if television were not the primary cause of change, it has served as the messenger and supporter of ideas and movements, sometimes overtly and knowingly; many other times TV has had consequences that were unintended, unstated, and even unknown to those involved in its programming. Indeed, the history of television's influence is more a history of unanticipated side effects than it is of predictable outcomes. Thus, we find that, among other things, TV serves as a clear example of society's inability to foresee the actual consequences of a new technology.

The fact that the great majority of the influences we discuss were unintended makes them subjects for inference and speculation and therefore, in some cases, debatable. For us, agreement with any of our specific conclusions is a less important matter than raising the questions and trying to determine TV's larger impact.

That impact often bears a tangential relationship to assumptions about television's role and purpose in our society. It was on May 9, 1961, that Newton Minnow, then chairman of the Federal Communications Commission, delivered his now-famous "vast wasteland" speech to a meeting of the National Association of Broadcasters. In that speech he called for television to act in the public interest. Quoting the president of the association, he agreed that the term "public interest" encompasses "the building of the character, citizenship, and intellectual stature of people." To act on the public's behalf in all these regards was surely a tall order for any of society's institutions.

For Minnow, television had the responsibility to be educational and even uplifting. The wasteland he found lay in TV's content, programs that failed to fulfill this responsibility. A contrasting perspective is that of Marshall McLuhan, who said, "The medium is the message," meaning that the fact of television in our homes mattered much more than the content of those broadcasts. An analogy might be to say the widespread existence of telephones is that medium's real importance in transforming society, rather than what is said in people's conversations.

Our own analysis does not choose either extreme. Certainly, just the presence of television sets in almost every American home would have in itself been the source of many changes in our lives. But what appears on the screen is not neutral filler. The programs, the performers, the commercials, the political ads, and the delivery of the news all infuse our consciousness and leave their mark.

The nature of that mark in its many manifestations is our subject in this book, one we believe is vital to explore because the findings are so central to how we and our society function today, more than a half-century into the television age.

We would like to thank Dan Harmon and Gail Chalew for their valuable editorial suggestions. Thanks also to Renée Ashley for her meticulous proofreading.

Introduction:
The Dominant Medium

It's 1950, it's Tuesday night, and a group of people are seated around the TV watching Milton Berle take yet another pie in the face, his dress splattered with filling. They are gathered in the living room of one of the few families on the street that owns a television set (a seven-inch screen in a console cabinet that stands about three-and-a-half feet high and two feet wide)—friends, relatives, and a few neighbors together to share in the laughs. In 1950, it was not unusual to consider the Milton Berle show a special event because there were few shows on the air and Berle was clearly the "king" who could attract practically the entire viewing public for his weekly hour.

For a population that had grown up on radio, television was mesmerizing just because it existed, actually bringing active pictures—gray and blurry though they might have been—into our homes. It's difficult for anyone born in the second half of the twentieth century to appreciate this transformation of people's lives brought about by television. For them, TV has always been around, a given of their surroundings, with TV sets in dens, kitchens, bedrooms, and now even in the palms of their hands. Possibly the most dramatic cultural fact that separates the experience of the baby boomers and later generations from those preceding them is that the former grew up never knowing a world without television. As a result, many activities, beliefs, and institutions that are taken for granted by one generation mean radical change for the other. This book investigates television's effects on a variety of institutions and processes important to life in the United States.

In reality, the roots of TV's influence go back as far as the invention of the printing press, which became the basis of the first medium of mass communication in human history. Printing resulted in the development and dissemination of newspapers, books, and pamphlets that enabled society to experience a very broad and pervasive exchange of ideas and information. When Pittsburgh's KDKA began regular broadcasting in 1920, this centuries-old print monopoly was challenged by radio, which involved our sense of hearing rather than sight, and also provided a more immediate access to information than was available from even a newspaper's special edition.

At about the same time, another new medium, moving pictures, appeared on the scene. This medium had the advantage of being seen as well as eventually heard, and even more dramatically, the action involved continuous movement, a quality that was sure to hold our attention. But because of the time required for production and the infrequency with which people went to the movies, the lag between the occurrence of any event and the screen's ability to deal with it was much longer than with either radio or newspapers.

However, although the motion picture medium may have lacked immediacy, it had the very powerful capacity to present a strong visual image that could move emotions, thoughts, and desires. One only need look at such works as *The Great Dictator*, *Yankee Doodle Dandy*, *The Purple Heart*, or *They Call Me Mr. Tibbs* to realize the potential effect motion pictures could have upon our attitudes and the way in which we viewed the world. But despite the potential power of the movies, and even though eventually newsreels were commonly shown with the features, newspapers, books, magazines, and radio remained the primary sources for news and entertainment.

It would seem that the immediacy of a communications vehicle, coupled with the extent to which the senses are stimulated by the medium, determines a type of medium "power": the ability to affect our perceptions and perhaps our behavior. From this standpoint, television, with its omnipresence, its continuous access, and its ability to provide pictures and sound, clearly has had the greatest power of any medium. Power to do what? Power to influence the way we perceive the world, our sense of right and wrong, our leisure activities, our lifestyles, what we consider luxuries and what we consider necessities, and ideas about who should lead our country from the White House in Washington. Yes, it's an awesome list, but when we talk about the influence of television on our society, we should be fully aware of the enormity of the subject both in the breadth and strength of its impact.

This power has become even greater in the age of the Internet and wireless communication, where instantaneous and ubiquitous reception prevails. In this first decade of the twenty-first century, we are seeing the merger of television and computers and the advent of technologies that eliminate the need for fixed connections of plugs and wire. Our computer monitors double as TV screens, and we don't even need monitors for we can receive news and programming on our cell phones, PDAs, and MP3 players. We can watch TV while we walk down the street or on a path far from any town or city. Now we can even be creators of our own content. However great the influence of television was in the second half of the last century, it is sure to become even greater in the years ahead—in whatever form it takes.

To examine the force of television on our world, it would be useful to consider what that world was like in the period preceding TV's advent. Someone born in the mid-1930s entered a world in which the means of mass communication included periodicals, radio, and talking pictures (movies). In their childhood days, they might join their entire family around the radio set on Sunday night to listen to Jack Benny and Fred Allen. But broadcasting designed for their age group was limited to several fifteen-minute series before dinner time, to programs such as *Hop Harrigan* or *Jack Armstrong*, and to Saturday mornings. Most of their free time was spent in play.

Their parents and other adults devoted a much larger part of their lives to listening to radio. According to Gerd Horton in *History Today*, by 1940 all but 10 percent of American homes owned radios, and people listened three or four hours a day. A popular show could attract an audience of close to thirty million. Clearly, radio served as America's most significant source of information and entertainment at the time the country entered World War II.

As early as 1931 the BBC broadcast the coronation procession of King George VI, and the National Broadcasting Company gave the first public demonstration of television in the United States in 1939 at the New York World's Fair. Several TV stations quickly developed, but World War II essentially ended commercial TV activity. Immediately after the war, however, development accelerated to where there were one million receivers in use by 1949 and fifty million only ten years later. Today there are over 100 million TV households in the United States, with more than 75 percent of those households owning more than one set. Television is like a tidal wave that has engulfed us with its presence and is a force to be reckoned with in almost all aspects of our lives — from what we eat to the opinions we have on a host of domestic and world issues.

As popular as radio was for the average person, television has become even more dominant; sets can be found in almost every home and are turned on for almost twice as much time as the radio was. A 2005 survey by Nielsen Media Research indicated that TV is on for an average of eight hours and eleven minutes a day in the average U.S. home. That's up from seven hours and five minutes just fifteen years ago. People are watching more than ever. Clearly, TV has become an integral part of our daily life, occupying a time span equivalent to work and sleep and causing us to modify our activities so we can find time for so much viewing.

The reasons behind the growth of TV are relatively obvious. The medium combines sensory appeal with the gratification of many content choices at the push of a button. The broadcast alone provides sound and color, and most people find it difficult to be in a room with the TV on without being drawn to the movement on the screen. Something is always happening in contrast to the usually static surroundings of furniture and decorations. But beyond that, TV offers instant content and information. Because of its immediacy, it has a strong draw for us to tune in to see the latest headlines, the latest twist in our favorite soap opera, the hottest stars being interviewed on morning talk shows, or the current top videos on MTV. There is also a form of continuity to TV watching because each show offers promotions that urge us to watch the shows that follow. Thus, TV has become not just a place to which we go to pick up some information or some limited dose of entertainment. Rather, it is a phenomenon we have woven into the fabric of our daily activities, dominating both our time and our attention.

Journalist Ignacio Ramonet, writing for UNESCO, explains TV's dominance:

> One central medium—television—produces such a strong impact in the mind of the public that the other media feel obliged to move with this impact, to sustain and prolong it. How has television achieved this supremacy? Not only because it offers pictures and a spectacle, but because it became a means of propagating information faster than the other media, and since the end of the eighties and the digital revolution, it has been technologically capable of transmitting pictures instantaneously, at the speed of light, by means of satellite relays.

The chapters that follow investigate—whenever possible, citing facts and figures—television's impact on American news media, politics, and education; on our attitudes toward law, crime, medicine, and sports; on our attitudes toward social norms, other people, and even ourselves; and on the way we literally perceive the world around us. But facts and figures don't tell the whole story. The analysis inevitably and necessarily leads to some interpretation and speculation.

Given the enormous access this medium has had to our lives, it is critically important for us to recognize the many ways it has changed us and our society. If we are to be effective parents, consumers, voters, and citizens, we must understand how we are being influenced by the most powerful medium of our time. This book attempts to provide that understanding and help develop more sophisticated television viewers.

Part I

Our Personal Lives

Chapter One

Pictures in Our Heads: "Watching" Radio

For several decades before the advent of television, radio dominated as a source of entertainment. For the first time in our history, Americans enjoyed an ongoing source of music, news, sports, comedy, and drama in their homes with the turn of a knob.

The console receiver was a prized living room possession. With a dial and large speaker on the front and the vacuum tubes hidden within, it served as a central piece of furniture; solid and imposing, the wood polished, it was an object of pride.

Families settled back on sofas and easy chairs while sound filled the room. The millions born into the age of TV may wonder, where did they look? What did they do with their eyes? At times people looked toward the speakers, but even then what they saw barely registered. More often, they gazed out into space, focused on the images inside their heads, visions of scenes suggested by the disembodied voices. And so when Jack Benny went down into his subterranean vault, his listeners could clearly picture the crocodile-infested moat and the enormous iron door that opened and closed with painful creaks.

In this sense, books and radio had something in common: both stimulated imaginations to create the people and actions described by words. Children of the time "saw" the Batmobile and the Green Hornet as— most likely, more—vividly than they were later portrayed in the movies and on TV.

For some radio devotees, fan magazines offered photographs of the performers, often standing in a cluster around microphones on tall metal stands. Some were familiar figures to most listeners, usually because of their appearances in movies and less so because of theater and vaudeville. The standard sobriquet for a radio celebrity was "star of stage, screen, and radio." For the most part, however, the listeners populated their imaginations with individual versions of the person behind the voice, much as readers of fiction still do.

Gaps in the Telling

Different as they were as media, radio shared an important feature with silent films: both developed a stylized method of storytelling. Silent film actors exaggerated their physical gestures and facial expressions. Radio actors addressed the microphone with distinct vocal mannerisms and relied heavily on exaggerated sound effects. Both media conveyed stories with many gaps in the telling, relying on their audiences' adjustment to the methods of the medium to fill in what was missing. Because silent movies preceded radio by several decades, it is likely that radio presentations were influenced by the devices of film storytelling, transmuting them from the visual to the aural, but maintaining an equivalent rhythm.

For generations brought up on TV, an old radio drama probably sounds archaic and corny, almost a parody of itself in the obviousness of dialogue, the sketchy plot, the simplified motives, and the jerky continuity. Yet radio could be very effective. One often-cited classic is an episode of the weekly horror show *Light's Out*, which featured a soliloquy by the lone occupant of an isolated lighthouse. First, he sees a ship drifting toward his island. Then he realizes that the ship has no crew, but is overrun with rats. Those rats rush onto the island and, in stages of heightening drama, into the lighthouse and up the stairs from level to level. The narrator's voice becomes more and more urgent, more and more terrified. The story ends with him trapped in the upper level of the lighthouse, with nowhere to escape and a swarm of rats gnawing at the wooden door. Listeners were equally terrified; they are likely to be now if they should hear the program on tape or disk.

In the years since, horror movies have used rats and equally repellent creatures to scare viewers. Yet the *Light's Out* episode is just as compelling, if not more so, than any horror movie. When telling a horror tale, one standard piece of advice is to delay entry of the source of the horror so as to escalate audience anxiety. Often the actual appearance of the thing of horror is disappointing because it does not measure up to what people have imagined, which inevitably is a variation of their own nightmares, their greatest fears. The *Light's Out* broadcast, being on radio, cannot show the rats; it only can suggest their presence through the sounds of their invasion. Listeners identify with the speaker's fear, each envisioning his or her version of the creatures' attack.

Radio's Flexibility

Radio comedy also benefited from people providing their own internal pictures. That feature gave radio a flexibility that was lost when some of the same programs—such as those of Jack Benny, Fred Allen, and Burns and Allen—made the transition to TV. Each week on radio, as a climactic highlight of their show, Fibber McGee, despite Molly's warnings, would open his famous overstuffed closet accompanied by great crashing sound effects and a roar of audience laughter. Literally seeing the objects come tumbling out of a closet might be funny once, but it would quickly pale, whereas McGee's radio closet was an illusion suited to every listener's fantasy. For the listener, the noises and the timing were the point, not a specific picture.

Examples from Jack Benny programs further illustrate certain advantages of radio. For years, one standing joke was his ancient Maxwell automobile, another example of Benny's legendary stinginess in refusing to buy a new model. The nonexistent Maxwell on radio was nothing but spits and sputters and a motor that eventually groaned into silence. On television, in contrast, viewers saw a classic car, a museum piece, an object of value.

For an example of a radio scene that could not translate well to TV, consider one particular moment in an episode of the Benny show. Benny and Mary Livingston are at a New Year's Eve party when Jack asks about his bandleader, Phil Harris, whose persona as a lush was as well established as Benny's as a miser. "Have you seen Phil?" Benny asks, and Mary answers, "You're standing on him." On radio it was funny because it was not "really" happening. Television would have to have shown one human being actually standing on another, and it would have come across as cruel.

To reveal the strengths of radio is not to diminish TV. Each possesses capabilities that the other lacks. The classics of TV comedy—Lucy and Ethel trying to wrap candy, for example—are just as funny, achieving their results from different effects. Little was said during the "Lucy" scene. It didn't have to be, because the comedy was purely visual. TV drama can also be quite powerful through its visual presentation. What clearly differs is the nature of radio's demands on the concentration and imaginations of its listeners.

5

Divided Attention

A TV screen in a room serves as a magnetic presence, drawing eyes to the movements of images, especially since the advent of color. Something bright and vibrant is taking place in the midst of all the familiar static objects we live with. It is hard not to look. Even babies a few months old stare, as do some cats and dogs.

Yet because TV inundates us with so much information, it does not demand the degree of intense and deliberate engagement that radio did. With radio, listeners had to rely on a single sense, their hearing. If they missed an item of dialogue, it was gone forever. The medium of radio accommodated by adjusting its pace to the limitations of aural processing, but it also trained its audiences in the ability to listen and watch in the imagination. Similarly, television has conditioned its audiences to see just what they are shown and to rely on the reinforcement of sound to apprehend what is taking place.

In the early days of television, viewers were much more likely to be mesmerized by the action taking place before their eyes. For people accustomed to radio, just being able to see a program in their living room seemed miraculous, the fulfillment of the impossible. But half a century later, TV is a given, a utility as universal and as familiar as the refrigerator; it is something to be grasped with just part of our attention. And just as we take TV for granted, we also take for granted how, within that half-century, it has changed the way we perceive what is on the screen and what is in the world around us.

Radio in the days of drama and comedy programs was a medium suited to a population living at a different pace, with fewer distractions. (Radio today often functions as background sound, listeners not really focused on the beat of music or the chatter of talk shows.) TV is a medium suited to busy people pulled by a range of demands, easily distracted and eager for something new.

TV facilitates what is now called multitasking, involvement in several tasks simultaneously. The term comes from computers, on which users can open several programs at the same time, switching from one to the other at the click of a mouse. The cable news channels have already adapted to viewers' ability to multitask by broadcasting text and graphics on the same screen—weather, time, sports scores, stock prices, and news headlines—that have nothing to do with the visuals or the words being spoken. Although the majority of programming does not feature such a busy screen, the remote control offers a variation of multiple viewing through channel surfing, especially the button that permits split-second shifting back and forth between two channels. Some sets with the capability for a picture within a picture make it possible to view two programs at the same time. In these cases, evolving technologies have produced a phenomenon that redefines the notion of watching TV. Such an audience is not really concentrating on a program but rather deriving its pleasure from a different kind of experience, the stimulation of constantly changing visual sensations.[1]

TV's combination of picture and sound results in many redundancies. Viewers can grasp what is going on through either their eyes or their ears, and thus they can let their minds wander without losing the thread of the program. For the most part, it isn't difficult to watch TV. Often, TV watching elicits a passive involvement with peaks and gaps in focus, which is higher when the actors' voices are raised, the background music louder, and the image more frantic. Viewers can skim the newspaper or hold a phone conversation and still be "watching." Often viewers can tune into the middle of an hour-long show and quickly grasp the essence of the story; no doubt, TV shows are designed to facilitate such drop-in watching to increase audience ratings and sponsor satisfaction. A 2003 study by BIGresearch verifies the extent of this fragmented focus. According to the findings, nearly 24 percent of men and 30 percent of women in the U.S. regularly go online while they are watching TV, while 8.2 percent of men and 10.1 percent of women read a newspaper while watching TV.[2]

Exact Time

Although radio today primarily serves limited functions of providing a steady output of music, talk, and news, most of what it broadcasts is not time-bound. That is, listeners can tune into the middle of a performance or conversation or ongoing cycle of headlines, weather, and traffic reports without the fear of missing the essence of the drama or comedy as they did when radio told stories. Yet radio established the rigid time expectations we now bring to TV viewing.

The spread of clocks and pocket watches in the eighteenth century and the shift of employment to factories during the Industrial Revolution made the Western world operate according to fixed hours. When people began to work together on power-driven machines, everyone had to be there at the same time. The invention of the time clock documented their daily appearance at the factory to the minute. The lunch whistle gave them a synchronized break. But it was radio in the early twentieth century that spread the exactitude of the clock to people's leisure. The audience had to tune in at the right time or miss part of the show.

There was no room for individual preference nor even a few minutes leeway if you wanted to hear the whole program. Television echoed that time imperative.

For contemporary Americans, it seems natural for the day to be segmented into units that begin exactly on the hour or half-hour, occasionally extended for movies or specials. That's TV time, just as it appears on the grid schedules of the program listings. But we don't have to refer to them to know how to plan the start and stop of our viewing. The TV clock is ingrained in our consciousnesses. With one or two odd exceptions on cable, we know that networks and local stations will begin and end their programming exactly at the hour or half-hour so that shows on different channels will not overlap. Sports, of course, can't be contained so neatly, what with time-outs, overtimes, and the vicissitudes of innings. Even then, stations fill the space until the next half-hour, when normal time returns. Every evening, millions plan their viewing around the schedule, timing trips to the refrigerator and bathroom according to the time boundaries of their favorite shows.

That's all changing. VCRs first put scheduling in the hands of viewers, though many never mastered the technicalities of recording shows. But devices like TiVo and cable companies' video on-demand services have greatly simplified the process. Though the great majority of viewers still adhere to rigid schedules, forming a collective audience in separate homes, the future may not be nearly as time-bound.

Inseparable from the World

One significant difference between radio in its heyday of drama and comedy shows and TV as a medium is that radio, for the most part, presented a self-contained and artificial world. Much of radio comedy was about putting on a radio show, and radio personalities appeared on each other's shows, perpetuating the mock quarrels of Jack Benny and Fred Allen, Bing Crosby and Bob Hope, and Charlie McCarthy and W. C. Fields. The patterns were formulaic and the regular characters obvious exaggerations. Even the dramas were artificial, gripping as they might have been.

Television overall, however, seems inseparable from the world around us. That's probably because we see as well as hear. Characters, no matter what their idiosyncrasies, are inevitably like real people, as noted in the Phil Harris example. Settings are concrete and actual. Dramatic topics are often "ripped from the headlines," like those of *Law & Order*. People, both celebrities and "ordinary," reveal their innermost secrets. The line between business, politics, and TV is vanishing, with California Governor Arnold Schwarzenegger announcing his candidacy on the Jay Leno show, others running for high office feeling the necessity of appearing with Oprah, Bob Dole making commercials, many politicians playing themselves on comedy and drama shows, and Donald Trump hosting a "reality" show. So many major events have played out live before our eyes—the McCarthy hearings, the Kennedy assassination, the disaster of 9/11.

When we listened to radio, we knew it was—except for limited news programming—artificial. With television it's difficult to separate the real from the contrived. In effect, the medium has changed our relationship with the reality around us and, in many ways, helped create that reality.

Even though it locked us into time patterns, radio was just entertainment, fodder for our mind's eye, a variation from the world we lived in. But television, despite the possible casualness with which we can watch it, produces a profound effect on our inner lives, our beliefs, our behavior, and what we perceive when the set is turned off. It becomes difficult to distinguish the pictures in our heads from what we see all around us.

Notes

1. For more information, see CAMagazine.com, "TV Viewers Like Multitasking."
2. See eMarketer, "Net Most Popular Media [*sic*] to Use While Watching TV."

Chapter 2

Learning to Watch: TV and Perception

Never in human history has a single communication medium so quickly influenced the way an entire population perceived the world as television did for Americans in the second half of the twentieth century. Certainly, print brought about a revolution, but that change took hundreds of years to penetrate so thoroughly. The impact of movies in the first half of the last century presaged the visual impact of TV, but not to the same far-reaching extent.

Movies were seen only a few hours a week, and their viewing was a special occasion—a group audience was relocated to a dark auditorium, surrounded by dozens of strangers, while images flashed on a huge screen. For most people the closest parallel experience may have been participating in religious services in a house of worship. Perhaps that is why movie stars became the deities of popular culture.

More significantly, movies brought a new level of reality to their audiences. Several decades before the invention of moving pictures, still photography for the first time permitted people to see images that duplicated and permanently fixed scenes and faces from the physical world. (Painters, of course, could depict a version of the world, but they did not have the same verisimilitude.) In movies, however, people saw ongoing action, active replications of life's activities in full scenic context, unlike in stage plays. And, also unlike plays, movies provided a new sensation of time passing and of the relationship of events. Movies could convey the passage of years with a device as simple as the flipping of calendar pages.

They could shift back and forth from one event to another. They could focus in and zoom out. Audiences had to learn a new way of seeing.

In the first part of the twentieth century, even though movies were typed as mass entertainment, serious novelists adapted cinematic techniques of juxtaposing time, people, and images. Even James Joyce, combining a fascination with film and an ongoing economic need, made an ill-fated attempt to operate a movie theater. More significantly, as an artist, he transposed this new way of seeing to his art, especially in *Ulysses*, where he cuts back and forth among scenes and people with a shifting focus. He even animated inert objects in the famous Ulysses in Nighttown section. Many writers who followed went even further in incorporating a cinematic approach to scenes, dialogue, and transitions. But it wasn't just writers. The population at large was infused with the cinematic imagination.

Listeners Become Viewers

Television eventually developed as a stepchild of movies, compressing on the small screen what people were used to on the large one. At first, however, TV served as another form of radio: it was radio with pictures, fulfilling the fantasies of radio listeners eager to actually see what they had only been able to imagine. Most of the performers and many of the programs came from radio. Listeners became viewers. They still sat in their living rooms, but stared instead at a small gray screen that replaced the speaker grill. The experience, remarkable as it was for those initial audiences, was merely a variation of a familiar pattern—a series of programs entering their homes on the hour and half-hour.

Because TV in its early years was live, it lacked much of the flexibility in depicting time and place that movies enjoyed. Stage sets were rudimentary, and performance was sequential, happening in what is now called real time. The image itself was merely blurred and grainy gray tones. For the most part, early TV either imitated the live stage (for example, *The Kraft Playhouse*), burlesque (for example, Milton Berle's show), or a radio news program with the addition of still photos or occasional newsreels.

In those initial years, television thus made a less dramatic impact on the way people perceived the world than film had. Other than bringing the miracle of moving pictures to the living room, TV at first did not change the way we literally apprehended the world. The power of the visual was not fulfilled in those first gray-toned years. That changed when color, imaginative editing, transportable cameras, and satellites came to TV. After those developments, what we saw, how we saw it, and what we registered were transformed.

In Bill Moyers' 1989 video *The Public Mind: Illusions of News*, Leslie Stahl of *60 Minutes* demonstrated how a report she did on a speech by President Ronald Reagan revealed the impact of TV's visual images. Before an enthusiastic crowd, Reagan was comely, smiling, and seemingly an all-around nice guy. But Stahl's voiceover presented facts that proved his actions in office were the complete opposite of his words. The piece was meant to be a negative evaluation of his performance. Yet when viewers were questioned about the report, their reactions toward the politician were positive. A White House official explained to Stahl that people didn't hear what she said; "They only saw those pictures." Surprised by what they had learned, the producers held focus groups in which people viewed other material with conflicting visual and auditory messages, and they found that the visual information was much more influential than the auditory.[1]

Ubiquity of TV

TV's transformation of the way people perceive the world around them has been more fundamental than that brought about by movies because of its ubiquitous presence. Because people had to go to a theater to see a movie, movie watching was an occasion, a limited immersion into an experience that was supposed to be different from everyday life. In contrast, TV now surrounds us; it is found not only in the living room and the den but also in the kitchen, the bedroom, and for some even in the bathroom, and beyond the home in offices, waiting rooms, restaurants, airports, and other public spaces. TV is now even on cell phones. TV is the norm, watched for hours each day; it permeates our consciousness without our awareness because of its omnipresence.

Perhaps the best way to illustrate the nature of one change in perception is to consider how commercials have metamorphosed from the first days of live TV to the elaborate productions of the present.

Commercials in the early days tended to flow into the shows they sponsored in pace and style; in fact, they were often presented by the performers themselves in a manner that simulated the basic style of the entertainment. Typical would be Arthur Godfrey doing an ad for Lipton tea, sitting at a table with cup, hot water, and tea bag, dipping the bag and speaking slowly in the low-keyed manner with which he hosted his weekly variety shows. For a full minute, he prepared his cup, stirred, noted the virtues of Lipton's, sipped now and then, and sighed with pleasure at the refreshment. For the millions of Godfrey fans, viewers who trusted him and felt at ease with his presence, just watching this simple action and hearing him tell about it served as part of their evening's entertainment. Some even went out and bought the tea. But there was no pressure, no urgency. Calmness prevailed. The commercial itself barely interrupted the show. Far from assaulting the viewer, it soothed and amused.

Production costs for such commercials were relatively low and probably were folded in with those for the show as a whole because they were, in fact, part of the show. The TV programs, like those of radio, tended to be under the aegis of a single sponsor, whose name was often integrated into its title—for example, *The Texaco Star Theater*, *The Colgate Comedy Hour*, and *The Kraft Playhouse*. But then costs escalated beyond the capacity of any one sponsor's advertising budget. Sole sponsorship became an impossible luxury; eventually even the sixty-second commercial became an excessive cost.

Constrained within fifteen or thirty seconds, commercials then had to make their point fast and make it vividly. An Arthur Godfrey could barely dip a tea bag or smack his lips in such a small segment, much less sustain the effect of a leisurely pace. Commercials had to rivet attention and deliver an impact before the viewer could even blink.

Unlike the commercial interludes of the early days, such ads are not part of the show, but instead are self-contained; they are totally different from the show in style and mood and are jarring both within themselves and within their context. Given the extreme pressure to make a memorable statement in just seconds, it's no surprise that a commercial can cost more to produce and that its creation receives more time and attention than an entire show.

The challenge of making an impact in such a short time led to a creative strategy that transformed not only the delivery of commercial messages but also TV itself—and as a result audience perception of information of all sorts.

Flash, Color, and Pulsating Sound

Now most TV ads rely on flash, color, and pulsating sound. They juxtapose dozens of split-second shots to assemble a dynamic message, jumping from image to image, person to person, and color to color. Usually, with music and choreographed movement, they animate an active, percussive high-energy world that functions at a peak of excitement. For instance, soft drink commercials often fill the screen with singers and dancers, even scores of extras grouped across the landscape, thereby associating drinking the beverage with fun and excitement.

Many commercials tell a mini-story. One Acura car ad shows a man and his wife rushing up a twisting mountain road, his hand on the shift as the vehicle slaloms into hairpin curves. A quick cut shows a woman real estate agent outside a for-sale house tapping her toes and checking her watch. The couple arrives in the driveway, the husband gazing back down at the corkscrew roads he has just climbed in his Acura. Not even looking at the house, he calls, "We'll take it." It's the thrill of the ride he wants. Granted, stories like this are simple. They use a considerable number of shorthand devices and rely on viewers to fill in details and do an interpretative analysis, making rapid mental connections and grasping nuances. The message is transmitted through implication rather than direct statement.

In the early days of TV, such commercials would have seemed a confusing jumble because the audience was not prepared to apprehend them; it was untrained in perceiving the presentational techniques. Over the years, as its technology and methodologies have evolved, television has brought viewers along with the medium. When they reach a new stage in the ability to understand, TV pushes them further ahead yet again.

Although TV commercials began to be transformed because of time and cost constraints that existed long before MTV debuted in August 1981, in its two-and-a-half decades that cable channel has had a significant impact on viewer perception. Even though its audience is primarily teenagers, those teens have grown up, and the makers of music videos have gone on to make films and TV shows. A frenetic urgency marks the majority of music videos, with split-second image changes, hallucinogenic action, and driving sound. The techniques have influenced both commercials and TV programming, as well as movies.

Ken Dancyger in *The Technique of Film and Video Editing* explains the MTV style:

> We must view the MTV style as a new form of visual storytelling. Part narrative, part atmosphere, sound intensive, and image rich, the form has a remarkable appeal to the new generation of film and video makers whose media viewing experience is preponderantly television. Although the MTV style has not made a broad entry into the feature film, it has characterized much of the style of those directors who began in commercials.[2]

Certainly a synergy exists between movies and TV because the techniques of commercials and MTV have become ubiquitous. Since

Dancyger wrote his analysis in 2002, the MTV style has become much more pervasive. Many movies, and some TV shows, go at the pace of a thirty-second commercial. They demand active watching, with the action often more important than its context.

Words cannot keep up with such rapid movement. Unlike radio-influenced, dialogue-heavy early TV, many contemporary shows communicate much more information through images and sounds than through expository talk. That's especially true of crime shows and other dramas.

In addition to being fast-paced, both dramatic shows and situation comedies now juggle multiple plot lines, usually within a single show but occasionally linking several episodes. At times the shifts from one line to another can be just momentary. Here too the viewer, to grasp what is going on, must keep track of and aggregate the fragments.

Confirmation of the enormous change in audience perception in five decades is the fact that the great majority of people take these rapid dislocations as a matter of course. They have become the norm, and viewers have no difficulty staying with them. They can follow all the action and events, no matter how bizarre, and can shift attention back and forth from program to commercial without a hitch.

Certainly the younger members of the baby boom and subsequent generations who watched these fast-moving scenes from early childhood on have no problems following these fast-paced shifts in action, no matter how extreme or frequent. But for the older boomers, watching *Howdy Doody* was not the same as watching MTV. Obviously, current senior citizens, who had no TV exposure as children, also were not conditioned to follow the rapid shifts in scene, action, and sound that are so common today. Few of them can tolerate watching a music video for more than a few seconds. Even the faster shifting of action in many of today's comedies and dramas may make them uncomfortable.

However, the younger generations have learned to perceive in a different manner from their predecessors, and for them the results of being raised on TV are not limited to the way they watch television. Changes in perception extend to other forms of entertainment as well—movies, computers, video games, and pop music—and unlike the generation of Arthur Godfrey viewers, the younger generations can sort out the constant and disparate information bombardment. They even expect it and are hard pressed to function at a leisurely pace. They want their tea fast and instant, bottled for quick delivery so that they can gulp it down and move on to the next taste, the next sensation. This style of living and perceiving would most probably not exist without TV.

Learning to Watch: TV and Perception

TV and Attention Span

In a more speculative vein, it is possible that the constant bombardment of colors, scene changes, and staccato noises has had some very serious and unintended side effects upon children raised within this context. In his book *Attention Deficit Disorder—A Different Perception*, Thom Hartmann presents a theory that attention deficit disorder (ADD) is really a form of behavior that was important to the survival of our ancient ancestors when they were hunter/gatherers before farming became the more reliable mode of survival. In brief, the theory posits that the characteristics of the ADD "sufferer" are those that made for the most successful hunter/gatherers among our distant ancestors. These characteristics include being highly observant, quick to act, eager for excitement, and possessed of a tendency to constantly scan the environment, searching for any changes that might signal opportunity or danger. These characteristics are contrasted to those of farmers, who emerged later as humans developed the ability to control their food supply. Given our success in the farmer mode, genetically most of us are farmers. According to Hartmann, the minority of hunters, who do not focus on single things for very long, are viewed as problems in the school environment and labeled as suffering from ADD. The author's point is that these children are suffering from being in the wrong culture and would probably excel in an entrepreneurial world if encouraged in their early schooling, instead of being forced to follow a farmer-like learning program and generally losing a sense of self-worth very early in life.

What does this have to do with television? A correlation exists between the TV viewing time of very young children and attention problems. Those were the conclusions of a study by Christakis and his associates reported in *Pediatrics* in May of 2004.[3] The team studied 1,278 children at age one and 1,345 children at age three, ages at which the brain develops rapidly but at which attention problems have not yet surfaced. The team found that each hour of TV viewing per day increased the chances of displaying ADHD (attention disorder with hyperactivity) symptoms at age seven by 10 percent, and those who watched most in childhood ended up in the highest 10 percent for concentration problems, impulsiveness, and restlessness (see BBC News, "Watching TV 'is bad for children'").[4] An editorial in the April 2004 issue of *Pediatrics*, in which the study appeared, called for pediatricians to caution parents about the potential role of TV in the nation's growing "epidemic" of ADHD.[5]

In the context of Hartmann's analysis, television, by constantly reinforcing the tendency to scan rather than focus, could be enhancing the hunter potential, which is then seen as a problem in the school system. If so, from this point of view television is creating an enormous problem for the school systems, enormous profits for the drug companies, and millions of children whose potential is systematically drained from them in early childhood. From another viewpoint, however, television may be helping produce just the type of people our society needs the most, those who if encouraged will constantly scan their environment for opportunities, for new ways to utilize technologies that others may not think of, or for ways to seize opportunities regardless of the fact that they represent risks to their security. Such a conclusion may be a huge leap, but others are making such an argument.

Author Steven Johnson, in his 2005 book *Everything Bad Is Good for You*, contends that the complexity of TV viewing, along with that of video games, enhances mental flexibility and therefore intelligence. Programs with multiple plots and visual complexity train viewers to find "order and meaning in the world." His critics attack him for ignoring the banality and offensiveness of TV content. But content may not be the issue. Even if the TV audience's ways of perceiving have not been skewed to a form of "abnormality" for the world they live in, these ways have undergone significant changes. Such changes have little to do with the content of television and everything to do with its methods of presentation. The implications are not just limited to TV watching. The effects can be seen in movies, literature, music, art, and in many of the ways in which people communicate. For many people, especially the young, multitasking is a way of life—that is, the simultaneous perception of seemingly disparate information with the ability to keep it all straight and even integrated. Many young people can talk on the phone, listen to music, send instant messages, and do homework while they also watch television. TV has played a fundamental role in bringing about this new way of functioning.

All in all, the decades of television viewing have had a significant impact on the way we perceive the world, how we focus our attention, and what other people expect of us in personal relationships.

Notes

1. Moyers, *The Public Mind: Illusions of News*.
2. Dancyger, *The Technique of Film and Video Editing*.
3. See Christakis et al., "Early Television Exposure."
4. See BBC News, "Watching TV 'is bad for children.'"
5. Healy, "Early Television Exposure."

Chapter 3

Watching Together or Alone: Uniting and Dividing

In addition to television's most overt function of supplying information and entertainment, as well as unintentionally affecting the ways we perceive, the medium has had unplanned social consequences: television can either bring people together or separate them in the "watching" experience. For the most part, whether we congregate or disperse has depended on technology and pricing; that is, the expansion of TV broadcasting stations, the production economies that eventually made TV sets an inexpensive commodity, and, more recently, the developments that have allowed portability all foster separate viewing experiences. Occasionally, actual events such as a national tragedy cause us to gather together to receive the emotional support of a shared experience, but they are rare.

Historically, as fireplaces relinquished their status as the main source of indoor heating, first radio and then television emerged as the household object that brings the family or circle of friends together physically. In the 1950s and 1960s, when most homes had only one TV set, if they had one at all, that set served as the focal point of the evening activity for the entire family. As sets in the home and the choice of channels started to proliferate, however, the television set began to physically separate the family, rather than bring it together. In its sixty-plus years of broadcasting to the public, television has gone from a mechanism that served to unite the family to one that has, in most cases, played a significant role in separating it physically and psychologically.

In TV's early days the sharing experience went beyond the family and friends who gathered in the same room to include a large percentage of the American public. Coincident with the limited number of sets available was the limited number of TV stations. In the early years of commercial television, some areas of the country enjoyed only one or two stations. Even large cities had only a few more, and programming was dominated by the offerings of three networks—ABC, CBS, and NBC. Such limited choices led to very large audiences for the most popular shows. For example, Milton Berle's *Texaco Star Theater* had a Hooper rating (predecessor of Nielsen) of 80.7—28.9 more points than its nearest competition. On January 19, 1953, when Lucille Ball as Lucy Ricardo gave birth to Little Ricky, the viewing audience was estimated at forty-four million. In that year, the U.S. population was 160 million, with only half of the nation's homes having TV sets, which means that half of those sets were tuned to Lucy that night. A decade later, when the Beatles first appeared on *The Ed Sullivan Show* on February 9, 1964, Nielsen estimated there were seventy-three million viewers out of a U.S. population of 191 million (see Lucyfan.com).[1]

Although these particular shows marked peaks in viewership, in general people could assume that on most mornings a good number of their friends and co-workers had seen many of the same television programs the night before, whether they were comedy, variety, drama, or sports. Though watching from their own homes, they had shared a mutual experience, something they could talk about. Considering how much of their lives were spent with TV, people could rely on a common set of entertainment and cultural references.

TV Sports and Socializing

Although audience share for all but a very few shows is greatly diminished today, one form of programming continues to bring people together—sports broadcasts. Going to a ball game has always been primarily a social event, with most people attending with either friends or family, rather than by themselves. Before TV, only a small proportion of the population at any given time could go to each ball game. Not only did television multiply exponentially the number of people who could watch athletic events, but it also became a means for people to join the crowd and simulate the dynamic of sitting in the stadium or arena. When television started to broadcast games in the late 1940s and early 1950s, it became a boon to local bars whose owners took advantage of this tendency for people to watch as a group. Because most people then did not own television sets, it was the rare bar that did not make the capital investment in offering television to its patrons, and the primary offerings were ball games. This created a mood of bonhomie because the bar had a single focus instead of many private conversations, and when the home team was playing, the viewers all shared a common passion that further brought them together.

Because today the penetration of television in American households is almost universal, one might think that the place of television in bars might have receded in importance, but the opposite is true. Sports bars now appeal specifically to those who wish to make their sports watching a social rather than an individual activity. A myriad of sets, many with large vivid screens, display different sporting events, and drinks are often sold at special discounts for key games. Of course, the sports bar is also a place for men and women to meet, which makes the televised sports event as much of an excuse for linking people of the opposite sex as it is a reason for people to get together to cheer on their team. Finally, because sports bars usually have the ability to broadcast games that have no connection to the area in which they are located, alumni of an out-of-town college or even fans of an out-of-state professional team will often congregate to socialize and to root their team to victory. In this case, they may not be able to get these games on their home sets without buying expensive additions to their cable or satellite systems, but more important, they are congregating for a social event.

The ultimate influence of television on group-oriented entertainment is manifested in the annual Super Bowl. Being part of a Super Bowl party is as important as having somewhere to go on New Year's Eve. Rituals involving what foods and drinks must be served and a myriad of betting pools involving such outcomes as scores by quarter or yards gained have evolved and become traditions of these parties. The catering industry, including food stores and restaurants, does a land-office business providing prodigious amounts of food to be eaten at these parties. It is interesting that just as television has made the Super Bowl into a major national sporting event each year, in a like manner, the Super Bowl has created a major national social event centered on the television set.

Bonding in Times of Crisis

Sports, for all the passionate emotions it stimulates in fans, is still a form of entertainment, and these emotions serve as a primary incentive to be part of a group when watching TV. But another set of much graver emotions lead us to seek the presence of others in times of crisis. When terrible events occur, we don't want to be alone. Television tells us what is happening, and the screen that shows the disturbing pictures serves as a magnet that makes a mutual experience possible, satisfying our need for comfort in human closeness.

Before the advent of television it was clear that radio had the ability to gather the family together for an evening's programming, and even more so to listen to important news. For the great majority of listeners, radio as a medium possessed an authority that led to listeners' deep trust in the validity of its reports. A rather unusual but real example of audience trust occurred on October 30, 1938, with the Orson Welles broadcast of *The War of the Worlds*, a drama about an alien invasion of New Jersey. The drama was so realistic and the listeners' trust in the medium so complete that many families reacted to what they were hearing by fleeing or going after the aliens with rifles.

Before Welles' broadcast, President Franklin D. Roosevelt (FDR) recognized the potential of radio to influence listeners. In his "fireside chats" broadcast nationally over radio, FDR communicated directly with the American people. The use of the word "fireside" to describe these talks clearly evoked the image of the family gathered around the hearth, but in this instance the hearth was replaced by the radio. The family would typically gather around the radio for evening programs, and FDR chose to deliver his chats on Sunday evening, when most people would be at home, to communicate his message as widely as possible. Having taken office during the Great Depression, he needed a way to calm fears and give people hope for the future. The first chat, on Sunday, March 12, 1933, concerned the banking crisis and is credited with helping avoid a collapse of the banking system.

Since then there have been many instances in which presidents have used television to talk directly with the American public about some national problem or opportunity. But today few occasions make hearing the president an imperative. Indeed, unless all TV networks cover a presidential address, it usually gets a smaller audience than some of the competing programs. This indifference lies behind network decisions not to broadcast the talk. Perhaps presidents use the television time to talk about subjects that many people do not consider significant. Or perhaps the people who are interested are confident that they will be able to watch the highlights at some later time and see no reason to miss their favorite programs. Either way, television rarely brings the family together to hear the president discuss some national issue.

There have, however, been times of crisis when the television set served as a focus for a large part of the population, and during those periods it has definitely facilitated the bonding of family and friends.

Watching Together or Alone: Uniting and Dividing

Perhaps the most dramatic example occurred when President John F. Kennedy was assassinated in Dallas on November 22, 1963. The nation was stunned and grief-stricken over the violent death of a president who had captured the imagination of America's youth with the establishment of the Peace Corps and had captivated the world with his youth, vitality, and good humor. In addition to a shared feeling of tragic loss, no one knew whether the attack had been perpetrated by a crazed individual or was part of a broad conspiracy. Was the assassination the end of something or the beginning? And unlike any previous tragedy of this magnitude, television cameras immediately showed scenes at the hospital where President Kennedy received medical attention, as well as the book depository where the fatal shots were fired.

For three days after the shooting, the three existing networks cancelled regularly scheduled programs and devoted all their time to nonstop coverage of the assassination.

Americans spent that entire weekend in the house with the television on. TV became the center of our universe and kept us together, sharing each other's pain. It was not that we sat and stared at the TV; rather we talked about how we felt about JFK, what would happen now, what the world had come to, and the myriad of other topics that one thinks of at a time like that. We sat in the living room with the set on, just to be sure that we didn't miss any new development. Nielsen estimated that during periods of peak viewing, such as when the news of Oswald's murder was broadcast, 93 percent of the TVs in America were on and tuned to the news. TV kept us in contact with the outside, but also provided the context for the extended family to come together to support one another.[2]

Those three days marked a transformation in the nature of TV coverage of an event and, as argued in a PBS documentary called *JFK: Breaking the News*, the turning point in which television surpassed newspapers as the source of breaking news. A ranking of television's top 100 moments by *Entertainment Weekly* placed the Kennedy assassination coverage as number one.[3] The assassination occurred shortly after FCC Chairman Newton Minnow's "vast wasteland" speech, and there was growing political sentiment to put restrictions on commercial broadcasting. In describing the impact of TV coverage of the Kennedy assassination on TV's status, the article in *Entertainment Weekly* notes, "Television on the morning of Nov. 22 was at best an immature medium that produced a disposable product. By nightfall that was no longer true.... By the time the murder of Lee Harvey Oswald was broadcast live on Nov. 24, TV had not only become legitimate, but necessary."

Many other unforgettable events have occurred since President Kennedy's assassination, including the assassinations of Robert Kennedy and

Martin Luther King, the landing of a man on the moon, the tearing down of the Berlin Wall, the invasion of Grenada, the conflict over the Panama Canal, and the two Gulf wars. But none had the equivalent effect of assembling the family around the television for an extended period of time. It was not until the 9/11 terrorist attacks almost forty years later that the experience of uninterrupted, extended coverage was repeated.

The 9/11 attacks on the World Trade Center and the Pentagon again demonstrated television's ability to bring the family together. The nature of the attacks caused people to want to be with their families, partly out of fear and partly to have the comfort of loved ones in facing an unknown future. Everyone was again glued to the TV set, eager for any snippets of news that would help them understand the present and the immediate future. But even in this situation, although interest in real news (as opposed to repetition of previously seen footage or human interest stories) remained high, the audience for the continuous news coverage waned after the first two days. Some days later, President Bush addressed a joint session of Congress announcing a war on terrorism. Eighty-two million people tuned in to this speech, which represented a large proportion of the adult population and a larger audience than for any previous State of the Union address.[4] Undoubtedly, with this many people tuned in, many were watching in the company of family or friends. In times of crisis people will gather together in front of their television sets to get a sense of what is happening to our country and how our leadership will react, as well as to gain support and comfort from those close to them.

Separating the Family

Although special events can bring people together around the TV set, the notion of a single set per household is obsolete. The drop in the price of TV sets has resulted in a proliferation of sets within homes. Also, although there are hundreds of channels to choose from, *The Economist* found that each individual usually chooses less than a dozen to watch with any frequency.[5] With so much choice and such diversity of tastes among individuals, individual family members tend to watch different programs on the numerous sets found in the typical home of today. Children frequently watch TV in their bedrooms or a recreation room while their parents watch it in the "main" viewing room. In the extreme, each child may be watching a different program, just as the mother may be viewing a different program from the father.

Watching Together or Alone: Uniting and Dividing

In the twenty-first century, therefore, TV for the most part tends to physically separate the family by generation and sex because their tastes tend to differ. Because they tend to watch different things, members of the family have less in common to form the basis for family discourse. It is only in times of crisis or on special occasions, like the Super Bowl, that television is once again able to bring family or friends together.

According to the U.S. Census Bureau,[6] Americans owned 248 million TV sets in 2001, almost one for every person in the country's population of 281 million. The average household owned 2.4 sets, up from 1.4 in 1970, and the average household contained 2.59 people, which also works out to almost one TV set for every person. When the proliferation of TV sets is combined with the greatly expanded variety of program choices and with new technologies that make possible television viewing over the Internet on computer screens or even on mobile devices, what we watch becomes more and more a private and personal choice.

We can only speculate on the causal role that television has played in fragmenting the family. We can make comparisons between the 1950s and the 2000s of such statistics as divorce rates or the number of families in which the children are living with both natural parents and find that there is much less family cohesion now than there was then. But this does not tell us whether or not separate TV watching by family members has been part of the cause of that erosion of the nuclear family. In fact, the fragmentation of the family in its TV watching is coexistent with other types of family fragmentation, such as families no longer eating together because of conflicting work schedules of the parents, conflicting activity schedules for the children, or the desire to give more freedom for the children to "hang out" with their friends and eat at a fast-food restaurant. What we can say is that television, by tending to separate the family at times when the whole family is at home, contributes to reduced family cohesion in terms of shared experiences and attitudes.

But fragmentation shows up not only in families but also in other arenas, such as the tendency for the electorate to be more polarized into two camps than to be distributed around a moderate middle. In this area TV's contributory role is more verifiable insofar as it has made it easily possible for us to listen only to those news sources that tend to tell us what we want to hear. What is clear is that we live in a more heterogeneous society at the beginning of the twenty-first century than we did in the mid-twentieth century. This significant change is coincident with the fragmentation of TV viewing, which ends up giving us much less to connect to and to share.

Notes

1. See Lucyfan.com, "In Loving Memory."
2. Doherty, "Assassination and Funeral."
3. Entertainment Weekly, "The Assassination."
4. Smith, "Presidential Ultimatum"
5. "Power in Your Hand."
6. U.S. Census Bureau, "50th Anniversary."

Chapter 4

Mainstreaming: How TV Creates Norms

Television may not be the only source of change in American society, but it plays a central role as an accelerator of shifting attitudes that create new norms. What the public sees day after day, for many hundreds of hours each year, becomes natural, a presentation of the way things are, even when those things were initially shocking to a majority and remain so for a minority of viewers. What had been forbidden or even unknown becomes transformed into familiar features of the American mainstream.

More than any medium before or since, TV gives us our impressions of what the world is really like—how people live their lives, the landscape and the buildings they inhabit, the ways they interact, and what they value. Even viewers who know on a rational level that TV is both artificial and selective cannot resist developing visceral assumptions about standards. As much as we think we are in charge, TV overwhelms us with sounds and pictures so vivid, tangible, and dominant that we can't resist.

For one thing, the screen, by drawing the eye to it, becomes the focal point in the room, one animated by moving figures and changing colors. Something is going on that is livelier than the pattern in the wallpaper or the flutter of leaves outside the window. There's a universe behind the glass screen. Though humans are not like the pet cat that peers behind the box for the creatures inside, we know that the screen gives us access to an unending range of people, places, events, and actions. At no other time in history have we been able to travel so far and see so much without moving from our easy chairs. We take this access for granted. Awash in so many images, so much seeming information, its no wonder that we believe so much of what we see, even when we say we don't. TV panders to our innate inquisitiveness and fills in the gaps in our experiences, the little we know firsthand.

How Others Live

Curiosity about the lives of others did not begin with TV, of course. Being nosy is a human attribute. But until recently the vast majority of people had only a limited range of people to be nosy about—neighbors in the village or perhaps people on the next farm. Occasionally, rumors of doings in another country or another continent would filter through. With few exceptions, though, information about the lives of strangers, people who did not exist in three dimensions before our eyes, was only hearsay, occupying a minimal percentage of our attention. How could we know what we could not see?

Since its invention in 1440, the printing press has provided information to a growing number of people. During the age of exploration, carefully written travel journals revealed the existence of distant lands, exotic flora and fauna, and strange natives. Beginning in the early 1700s, with the rise of literacy and the middle class in Europe, the art form called the novel merged travel and imagination in such works as *Robinson Crusoe*. But the majority of eighteenth-century works of fiction depicted local lives, scenes populated by people more colorful than the ones who read about them.

Before TV and movies, hardly anyone had access to more than just a little area, their own small space. With doors closed and curtains drawn, people could only imagine what went on inside their neighbors' houses, much less the homes of those in another social class or in another society on the other side of a mountain or across the ocean.

TV, of course, has moved beyond words to show us the residential nooks and crannies of the famous. The first show of this type was *Person to Person*, hosted by Edward R. Murrow, which ran from 1953 to 1961; its episodes included visits to such celebrities as John Steinbeck, Marilyn Monroe, and Margaret Mead. In 1984 a show actually named *Lifestyles of the Rich and Famous*, hosted by Robin Leach, used much the same format, calling on celebrities in their homes. However, it had a much flashier tone, oriented toward showing off the ornate surroundings and "things" that the stars accumulated at great expense. More recent news luminaries, such as Diane Sawyer and Barbara Walters, have carried on in some form the tradition of Murrow on occasional news specials in which they meet with celebrities in their homes; however, they give more attention to prying open their interviewee's psyches than their closets.

Yet, is what we are viewing on such shows any closer to a real picture than the make-believe of *Robinson Crusoe*? Does the mere presence of the TV camera inevitably falsify? Can anyone in front of a camera not be a self-conscious performer, especially when it is difficult to determine who is more of a celebrity, the interviewer or the interviewee?

And yet we believe. We believe we have gained insight into the existential authenticity of the star who wipes away a tear after a heartfelt Barbara Walters probe or the antic performer who plugs the latest movie or CD in conversation with David Letterman. Some viewers, albeit a minority, even confuse those acting in dramas or sitcoms with the characters they play, despite those celebrities' attempts to be themselves on talk shows and in *People* magazine spreads. The illusions of TV are difficult to correct or even to resist, mainly because we want to believe. That is, if what we are getting isn't accurate, then what are we left with? Any knowledge, even pseudo-knowledge, is better than ignorance. We accept TV as real because the world it provides us fills a vacuum.

Lessons in How We Should Live

TV came onto the scene just at the end of World War II, as Americans entered the postwar era of new affluence and new opportunities. Through the GI Bill, many men were receiving college degrees and joining the ranks of those with white-collar desk jobs. Also through the GI Bill, they and their families were becoming homeowners, acquiring cars and appliances, living at a level far beyond their parents. The shift affected millions, and they had to learn how to cope with new circumstances. The visual immediacy of TV satisfied that need; it was a centerpiece in the living room, a reward of the new affluence. The screen, even in the gray tones before color, provided examples of how people lived—how they furnished their homes, what they wore, what they said, how their families interacted, how they dealt with life's tribulations, and what they valued.

Radio, Movies, and TV

TV, of course, was not the first mass entertainment medium of the twentieth century. But its ability to create assumptions about our reality was more powerful than any other media. Going to the movies was an event, something people did occasionally, at most once a week and with an air of ceremony. They got dressed, went downtown, paid for a ticket, and sat in a large dark auditorium in anticipation, waiting for the screen to illuminate. And that screen was larger than life, both literally and figuratively, with the performers towering over mere mortals in size and reputation.

Certainly, many young people got lessons in kissing from steamy screen clinches that seemed to go on and on. And, famously, men's undershirt sales plunged when, in *It Happened One Night*, Clark Gable took off his shirt and revealed himself as bare chested. But these were incidental happenings; they were graspings to emulate that which was far beyond us, not unlike wearing a Michael Jordan sweatshirt as a form of hero worship, knowing we do not possess a fraction of his talent.

Radio, in contrast, was available all day at the flick of a switch, but it merely provided disembodied voices and stylized scripts, caricatures instead of characters. The role of the listener's own imagination was nearly impossible to deny. None but the most credulous believed Jack Benny was really a miser, that Fibber McGee's overstuffed closet would come crashing down week after week, that the Lone Ranger could hide his actual identity behind a flimsy mask, or that the Shadow could cloud men's minds so they could not see him. Radio gave us a world of obvious exaggeration, of comic and dramatic personas playing out make-believe.

TV started out as radio with pictures, with the same stars and the same programs shifting their familiarity to the new medium. Yet something happened to change that programming. Seeing and hearing were not the same as just hearing. The TV characters were fleshed out and became real presences in our living rooms. Consider *I Love Lucy*, which did not have a prior radio existence, but which had much in common with radio comedy. Lucy was certainly an eccentric, each week trapping herself in one bizarre scrape after another, like a dramatic equivalent of the McGee closet. Yet the world around her offered a normal contrast, peopled by the exasperated, compliant Mertzes and the long-suffering, always forgiving Ricky. Outlandish as Lucy was, the program revealed the essence of friendship and a standard for marriage—no matter what eventually happened to Lucy and Desi's real marriage off-screen. Viewers, at some level, thought, "This is how I should live; this is what is expected of me."

Less frenetic situation comedies projected more of an idealized version of the American family in such shows as *Father Knows Best*, *Leave It to Beaver*, and *Ozzie and Harriet*. The families were all white with two or three children (the actual average being 2.3 children per household in the 1950s) and lived in suburbia. The plots involved minor problems and mischief, never touching on subjects that dealt with the seamier side of life, such as drugs, gang violence, or teenage pregnancy. However, the fact that television was not displaying society's ills did not mean they did not exist. Indeed, families endured versions of these problems in those days as they do today. Clearly, back then television was not representing our society as it was but imagining the one in which we wished to live.

This model of the family evolved, so that by the turn of the twenty-first century, the representation of the American family had changed dramatically. Instead of the character Jim Anderson in *Father Knows Best*, we have Homer Simpson (in cartoon form) of *The Simpsons*, whose intelligence, morals, and family feeling are a far cry from what we found worthy of imitating in the fifties. Even more extreme is *King of the Hill* (also in cartoon form), where the mother is degraded because she's a woman and the father is an ignorant redneck who dislikes his son because he is his son. Less outré, but still unlike the fifties ideals, are shows like *Malcolm in the Middle*, *The George Lopez Show*, or *King of Queens*, where the husband and wife clearly don't sit down and talk through problems or pursue rational and intelligent solutions like their older counterparts. Finally, we have *The Osbournes*, an MTV reality show about a family whose bouts with drugs and alcohol and constant foul language are clearly not meant to represent any type of ideal.

Although cop shows, lawyer shows, and doctor shows may stimulate our imaginations, we don't associate them with our own reality because we know that we are not policemen, lawyers, or doctors. (They do, however, condition our attitudes toward members of those professions and toward the society surrounding our personal lives.) But family shows suggest a mode of behavior that may be "normal" in some way, and we may well wonder from the lives we see each week whether TV reflects what is actually happening in our society.

Making the Forbidden the Norm

Initially, in its earliest years as a mass medium, TV served as a conservative force for several reasons. It emulated the programming of radio, a self-contained world of comedies, variety shows, soap operas, serials, and audience participation quiz shows, with an occasional drama. References to the larger world outside the medium were rare and almost always tame, certainly not social commentary or criticism. TV stations themselves had minimal competition in most cities, and they adhered to minor variations of several basic formulas. But, most significantly, American society itself seemed monolithic, at least on the surface, the tensions unacknowledged and usually unreported. In their endorsement of the status quo, people in their living rooms would rather not know about those tensions.

Yet, in a short time and even before the advent of 24/7 news channels, TV became the reporter of those tensions. In the 1950s, live broadcasts of the Army-McCarthy hearings forced viewers to face the prospect of the existence of either a vast communist conspiracy in the federal bureaucracy or the blatant and fraudulent abuse of power by a U.S. senator. Then came the assassination of John F. Kennedy, the physical abuse of civil rights protesters in Alabama and Mississippi, and scenes of bloody combat in Vietnam. The living room was no longer a place of safe denial. Pictures made the difference: the sweat on Senator McCarthy's face, the outrage on counsel Joseph Welsh's, Jack Ruby shooting Lee Harvey Oswald, a riderless horse, a burned-out church in Birmingham, dogs and hoses in Selma, and body bags lifted into helicopters. They became etched into our national consciousness, unforgettable parts of our national memory.

Minority Equality

Before the civil rights movement, TV ignored African-American life beyond the Amos and Andy stereotypes, relegating black performers to song and dance and comic relief, usually as servants like Jack Benny's Rochester. African-Americans were ancillary presences for the medium, without real occupations or real families. TV wasn't about them.

They certainly weren't represented as being equal to whites, with the rare exception of a Louis Armstrong singing duets with Bing Crosby. And that was variety, not drama. When Nat King Cole became host of his own show, stations in some states in the South protested and some refused to broadcast it. Cole crossed another line by singing duets with white women, though the singers did not touch or feign desire even as they performed love songs.

Now interracial love and lust are everyday occurrences on television. African-American men and women serve as role models to enormously broad audiences—for example, Bill Cosby as a father and Oprah Winfrey as a self-made woman. Cosby came along early in the changed portrayal of African-Americans, co-starring with the white Robert Culp in an adventure series called *I Spy*. He evolved into a national figure and became a respected spokesman for Jell-O commercials, assuming a position Jack Benny held several decades before.

Not only did African-Americans come to play comic and dramatic roles equal to those played by whites, even portraying their professional superiors, but they also filled entire casts of shows devoted to family life, sitcoms with their own take on the tribulations of the white American households that dominated early TV. A number of these shows reveled in hip-hop fashion and Black idiom, not as a form of mockery but as black assertion.

Perhaps even more significant for mainstream acceptance than this sort of programming are commercials that use African-American characters as representatives of middle-class life, living in upscale houses, dressed in fashionable clothes, driving expensive cars, and with the same needs for effective toothpastes, detergents, and financial planning as everyone else. Occasionally, African-American sitcom stars appear in commercials, emulating the personas of their regular shows. However, usually, African-Americans in commercials are just everyday Americans—attractive, affluent, lively, and the way we all want to be.

Other minorities—Latinos and Asians, for example—do not yet have the widespread TV presence of African-Americans, but that also is changing, and those who do perform usually are cast in roles that do not draw attention to their ethnicity. Aside from Columbian drug lords in crime shows, Latinos are doctors, lawyers, secretaries, mothers, and fathers, and so are Asians.

Where both groups, along with African-Americans, enjoy disproportionate representation is as newscasters, both national and local. The phenomenon has been noted as excessive by some comedians and commentators, but it does serve as a force of change. Recognizable names and faces delivering the day's events with poise and authority emphasize the fact that we live in a multicultural society. They enter homes on screens large and small, becoming as familiar as the furniture around them. We take them for granted as facts of our realities—the way it is, the way it was meant to be.

Although racial and ethnic diversity exists at a very different level after a half-century of social change reinforced by TV portrayals, those with Arabic names and Muslim garb still exist at the fringes of acceptance; however, voices of heightened consciousness—including national politicians—call for tolerance in a way they were hesitant to do before the civil rights movement.

Sex

If racial equality was a forbidden topic at the dawn of the TV era, sexuality was avoided even more. Relegated to twin beds, husbands and wives were primarily asexual beings coping with the antics of children who appeared to have been conceived through osmosis. It was difficult, if not impossible, to imagine Lucy and Desi or Ozzie and Harriet in a passionate embrace, much less conjugal relations. Society officially condemned sex before marriage, sex outside of marriage, illegitimacy, homosexuality, and sensuality in general.

When R-rated movies and pay cable networks like HBO raised the titillation bar, network television followed a pace or two behind. With soap operas, both in daytime and prime time, passionate sex on silk sheets, upholstered furniture, and even in swimming pools became commonplace, the more illicit the better. Everyone participated in heightened games of seductions, with siblings lusting after a brother or sister's spouse, stepchildren after stepparent, and best friends after each other's partners.

Vice President Dan Quayle was fighting a losing battle, appealing to only a small fraction of the voting population, when he attacked the character Murphy Brown for having an out-of-wedlock child. He argued that TV, via Murphy, was sending a morally destructive message. The nation yawned. It was already shrugging at illegitimacy, adultery, divorce, and the increasing number of single parents, and it flaunted sexuality in general. These were all the changes behind the drama of prime-time staples, impossible for a viewer to avoid.

Commercials became emboldened and began to use double entendres. When once women's undergarments could be shown only on mannequins, if at all, provocative Victoria's Secret models now sprawl across the screen. Gay and lesbian characters now began to populate evening shows. Same-sex couples kissed and embraced; multiracial couples, whether heterosexual or homosexual, did the same. Of course, some people were shocked and outraged, but no one with power—certainly not the writers and producers of TV shows—cared. Homosexuality has become sufficiently mainstream that in at least one hit network show, *Will and Grace*, and in such cable shows as *Queer Eye for the Straight Guy*, *The L Word*, and *Queer as Folk*, the fact of homosexuality dominates.

Using the motion picture rating scale, the sexuality depicted on TV, even *NYPD Blue*'s flashes of partial nudity, is R-rated at most. What went further in concept if not in depicted deeds were the subjects of what could be called audience revelation shows like those of Maury Povich and Jerry Springer. On these shows, before large national audiences people admit to ongoing behaviors that not long ago they would have been ashamed to confess to a psychiatrist. Actually, some of the behaviors exhibited on these shows could probably still land a person in jail in a number of localities in the United States. Yet these shows go on weekday after weekday, seeking to outdo each other with more and more outrageous behaviors, flashing 800-numbers on the screen as casting calls for people who have engaged in such activities as incest, group sex, and S&M practices. And they find volunteers willing to bare all verbally, perhaps finding their fifteen minutes of fame more than ample compensation for what most would consider humiliating exposure. Although these shows are not really mainstream, they provide the outer limit of what can be presented on television, with those representing the norm following just slightly behind.

Today the language of TV accepts the four- and five- and ten-letter words that men once restricted to the locker room. "Hell" and "damn" were dicey when TV began; now they are barely expletives. Non-cable TV, of course, does not go as far as the movies; but each year what can be said expands, the once-banned now becoming commonplace. In the world outside TV—say, a high-school corridor—words once considered too shocking for print are now neutral adjectives.

The Janet Jackson Super Bowl "wardrobe malfunction" did cause a backlash, first among some of the public and then in Congress. The immediate result was legislation that multiplied the financial penalties for decency violations on radio and television. A few broadcasters made abject apologies, and the creators of shows and writers of scripts find themselves uncertain about what is permissible to show and say on the airwaves. It's too early to tell whether this situation is a temporary dislocation or the first indication of a permanent retreat. Yet, even steps back to greater legislative or self-imposed censorship, if they happen, will probably be minimal, certainly not a return to the severe restrictions of TV's early years. Fundamentally, we exist with a radically different sense of norms, the range of what is permissible.

Social and Personal Issues

But it's not just the sexual, the seamy, and the salacious that television has helped make mainstream. Social and personal issues of all sorts are now discussed openly. The non-sensational talk shows like those of Mike Douglas and Oprah Winfrey have shined a light on such topics as child abuse, sexual harassment, elder abuse, mental disorders, and certain physical illnesses. Talking about what was once hidden and shameful has become an indication of openness and forthrightness. The tight, repressed, denying society that existed when TV began exists no longer. There is a new mainstream.

Did television create it or merely depict it? For many of the social changes of the past half-century, the answer may lie in between. Yet it is difficult to imagine a transformation as fundamental as the civil rights movement succeeding without the disturbing scenes of injustice and intolerance broadcast to our homes.

Certainly, much of TV programming is escapist, deliberately not confronting the audience with troubling social issues. But TV doesn't have to be so direct. Just the human interactions on these shows include behaviors and value assumptions once shocking to the majority. As a result, the pervasiveness of television has been instrumental in remaking the American mainstream.

Chapter 5

Amateurs Performing: "Reality" Television

From its beginnings so much broadcast television has aspired to an illusion of reality, that it depicts the actuality of our lives and the world around us. As a medium with an ongoing presence in our homes, TV engages us directly and frequently assumes a familiarity between those on the screen and those in the living room. In television's early days, the interaction of hosts, guests, and contestants included the viewer directly or by implication. Even on variety shows, performers chatted with the emcee after they did their acts—after all, they were real people, much like us. The settings of many dramas and situation comedies mirrored our homes and neighborhoods, even if the action was an exaggeration of life's confusions or, in crime shows, a heightening of life's dangers. Overall, television shows in the medium's first decades were geared to a suburban audience made up of families, and they offered an ultimately comforting depiction of American life.

But TV representations of reality are very different in the early twenty-first century. The shows seek extremes—contestants courting seeming danger, hostile to their competitors; strangers thrown together in situations sure to exacerbate their antagonisms; celebrities revealing their weaknesses; and actual families exposing their neuroses and addictions. Outrageous action has become the norm for what is called "Reality TV."

Now, instead of families, the demographic targets for most TV marketers are the young and young adults, the age group with disposable income and a propensity for consumption. A product of the media they

37

have grown up with, primarily television but also action movies and video games, this group expects constantly improving technologies—larger screens, more vivid color, and cameras adapted to remote locations. They have seen broadcasts of actual warfare, the technology of smart bombs, and the dangers of urban combat. In addition to watching TV, many played brutal and bloody video games, often on their TV screens, competing against immoral monsters and evil foes. They went to action movies filled with explosive violence and special effects. They saw many of these effects transposed to television programs that attempted to compete with those same movies. Weaned on *Sesame Street* and with their hormonal changes of puberty stimulated by MTV, their TV norm is rapid action, quick scenic juxtapositions, loud pulsating sound, and bizarreness. For such an audience, reality is not the dilemma of junior denting the car, of psychological tensions, or of long stretches of dramatic dialogue. It assumes extremes—dog-eat-dog aggression and emotional and physical danger.

Expecting Thrills

When a viewing audience has heightened expectations for new thrills, the creators of new reality shows strive to satisfy them. Although people may watch Reality TV with a certain suspension of disbelief, knowing they are enjoying a contrivance, they still see the world beyond TV—that of warring nations, danger on the streets, social and political quarrels, workplace tensions, and family clashes—as one filled with conflict, where personal survival is truly at stake.

New York Times TV critic Julie Salamon wrote, "It doesn't matter that many reality shows seem so contrived, because younger viewers have a more jaundiced view of authenticity." She quotes Jeffrey Scones of Northwestern University's communications school: "This generation is very conscious that one is constantly performing in real life—performing the roles of potential employee. Maybe we've always done that, and they're just more aware of it."

The term "reality television" emerged to designate a specific type of programming in which a group of strangers are thrust into new and difficult situations that test their abilities to cope and/or survive. The winner receives a handsome reward, usually monetary, after several weeks of enduring hostile forces, including cutthroat companions equally obsessed with winning the prize.

Salamon sees these rewards as the lure of a new existence, the chance to remake oneself. "While conniving and bickering, shame and humiliation often remain essential ingredients of these shows," she writes, "many of them also reflect a mutation of the basic American desire for transformation. But now transformation has become a byproduct of voyeurism and can seem easier than ever: to change your life, just go on television."

All this, of course, has very little to do with the reality of our lives beyond the fact that the shows do not take place on a stage set or studio and are only minimally scripted. The adventures and their handicaps are contrived and artificial, the participants handpicked for their potential to win viewer allegiance and fit into predetermined dramatic categories—the innocent, the egomaniac, the old guy, or the bitch. Although the escalating physical tests seem to be high points of these shows, what fascinates most of the audience is the tense interplay of personalities, which determines which person will be banished by a vote of the others; at times this interplay is heightened by titillating eroticism. The implied reality is Hobbesian, a view of life as short, nasty, and brutish; the results are no less stylized than car chases and action thrillers.

The first reality TV shows were fairly domestic, with handpicked young people living together in a house or apartment. MTV started the genre with a show called *Real World* that began in 1992 and followed the lives of several young housemates. Before long the reality TV settings moved to exotic landscapes and involved increasingly baroque entanglements as the networks escalated their competition to put a new slant on the genre. The concept took off in 1999 in the Dutch original series, *Big Brother*, which focused on a group of isolated contestants kept under twenty-four-hour surveillance. Its ratings success spread the concept to Britain and the United States, where reality shows enjoyed equally high ratings and news value. In the United States, some of the reality performers even capitalized on their exposure by appearing on talk shows, emerging—at least for a short time—as celebrities in their own right.

Ratings and Reduced Costs

What shows like *Big Brother*, *Survivor*, or *Temptation Island* actually did was provide the major networks with a new genre of programming that combined audience appeal with low production costs. They filled programming time, especially as substitutes for summer reruns, and often drew high ratings; in fact, several reality shows placed in the top ten. They helped stem the audience slippage to cable while functioning as programming fodder in the event of a writers' strike. Unlike the high-paid stars of the usual dramas and sitcoms, the amateurs on Reality TV were a bargain, willing to put themselves on display merely for a chance at fame and fortune.

Because of their attractiveness to the networks' bottom lines, the numbers of reality shows multiplied. Their prevalence can be seen in both numbers of viewers and numbers of shows. For example, for the 2002–2003 TV September-to-May season, they comprised five of the top ten shows in ratings. Even more telling is the number of shows in the reality category broadcast during this period, twenty-six in a single week. At one point a Web site called "Reality TV World" (http://www.realitytv-world.com) listed the current or past programs by network or cable channel, with the networks dominating by far. Fox had the most, twenty-four, with NBC's twenty-two not far behind. ABC had seventeen and CBS fifteen. On cable, MTV had nineteen shows, and all other cable channels combined had fifteen.

With so many shows, time slot competition became inevitable. Some flourished, some floundered. The competition and the brief life span of certain concepts led to attempts to contrive more and more outlandish situations. At one extreme, NBC devised *Fear Factor*, with contestants forced to confront trials like eating worms, being submerged into tanks of water snakes, or dangling from extreme heights. These situations were like scenes from nightmares, likely to make the audience squirm, yet watch with an anxious fascination.

More often, the new concepts revolved around matters of sexual attraction, with shows like *The Bachelor*. In these shows, sets of attractive young people, obviously selected for their looks, vied to win the affections of a particular man or woman in tests that were both titillating and belittling. That is, they provided a contrasting set of vicarious sensations to the audience, engaging the fantasy of having a host of sexually attractive ideal beings fighting over you and at the same time seeing such attractive people squelched and humiliated.

A Fundamental Fakery

The Bachelor built tension by actually culminating in a wedding of the winners, along with a cash award. The show made headlines that continued when the couple quickly split because they really weren't matched despite their on-air compatibility. However, rather than resulting in a scandal that undermined that show and, by implication, much of Reality TV, the news of the divorce just increased publicity and ratings in general. Perhaps viewers all along understood that it was all pretend and that what mattered was the spectacle.

In fact, later reality shows exploited the viewer's knowledge of a fundamental fakery at the heart of the contest, with every one but the contestants in on the deception. The women fighting for the heart of *Joe Millionaire* didn't know he actually was not a rich man, despite jetting to what the women thought was his French chateau. The network reported that the real person playing Joe was a laborer making $19,000 a year and neglected to add that he also was a part-time model.

A variation, *Boy Meets Boy*, joined trickery with gay sexuality. Gay men compete to win the affections of other men they believe are also homosexual. The contestant doesn't know that one of the apparently gay men is actually straight; if he can entice that man, he wins a cash prize.

The relation of the audience to such performances has much in common with the experience of viewing comedy. Much, perhaps most comedy, from Shakespeare to the latest sitcom, gains its effect from characters holding misleading or mistaken assumptions about their situations. The audience knows the truth and, therefore, can laugh at their actions, having the satisfaction of feeling superior, yet at the same time regarding the characters with a degree of affection. After all, they are only behaving foolishly, and the rest of us have been in similar situations ourselves.

Reality TV may also share a similar dynamic with professional wrestling, in which the viewers know they are watching a staged event rather than a true sport but do not care. They still cheer for their favorites and become emotionally involved.

The Lure of Celebrity

The people who appear on reality shows probably play along, willing to endure physical ordeals, psychic tension, and public putdown for the opportunities to win prizes, bathe in the spotlight, and perhaps find futures as professional entertainers. Shows like *Star Search*, *American Idol*, and *Fame* actually serve as auditioning platforms for "undiscovered" amateurs, resulting in recording contracts and concert appearances. *American Idol*, for example, markets what it calls collectibles as offshoots of the show—CDs by the performers, books, posters, and even concert glow sticks. Moving from the TV screen to live performance halls, *American Idol* participants go on national tours.

But those on other shows also are lured by the potential of fame, starting with a guest appearance on Letterman and Leno and leading who knows where. The dream of stardom serves as a vicarious outlet for the audience's fantasy. If television shares our homes as a familiar conversational presence, engaging us with people on screen whom we know better than our neighbors, with welcome visitors, why shouldn't our neighbors or we ourselves take the step from the sofa to the screen? After all, we are all good sports, willing to swallow a mouthful of worms if that's part of the game.

Candid Cameras

It's not that Reality TV isn't without precedence. The shows, in fact, can be seen as supercharged updates of several early programs—*Candid Camera*, *Ted Mack's Amateur Hour*, and *The $64,000 Question*—as well as others that emulated these approaches.

From its beginnings, television has offered some form of programming that belongs under the generic category of Reality TV. A basic definition of this genre might be real people being themselves, or apparently so. One example from the early days of TV, which first aired in 1948, is the show *Candid Camera*, in which ordinary people filmed by hidden cameras found themselves in trick circumstances that made them behave in comic ways. The basic setup, explained in advance to the audience, placed a normal person in what should have been a familiar situation, but in which things didn't function normally. For example, a man turning a doorknob finds the knob frozen and the door sealed. He twists, knocks, and yells, but no one comes to his rescue, while the audience watches via a hidden camera.

The victim provides "true" reactions to the dilemma that are often funnier than anything a writer could contrive, although stunts that flopped were no doubt discarded. Although *Candid Camera* still exists in syndication, its legacy can be seen in such successful programs as *America's Funniest Home Videos*, in which viewers submit their own videos of spontaneous slapstick performed by their children and pets. Shows like *Joe Millionaire* can be considered an elaborate extension of the trick played on unsuspecting participants.

The premise of *Ted Mack's Amateur Hour*, as well as a similar show hosted by Arthur Godfrey, can be found in its title. On each show a group of amateurs sang, danced, did magic tricks, and played instruments, all in hopes of gaining the loudest audience applause and being declared the winner. *American Idol* and the like are staged with more glitz and glitter, but, at their essence, differ little from those shows. The early nadir of this genre was *The Gong Show*, in which any judge could stop the performance by sounding a gong. It signaled a significant shift from sympathizing with the would-be performers to mocking and humiliating them, a characteristic essential to many current reality shows.

Game Shows and Quizzes

Although *Candid Camera* and the *Amateur Hour* occupied a fraction of total TV programming time, quiz shows and game shows like *The $64,000 Question* filled many hours day and evening. Their status as prime-time entertainment may rise and fall, but they are ongoing staples of the medium, with contestants plucked from the ranks of ordinary people—salespeople, schoolteachers, truck drivers, dental hygienists—given the chance to win money or prizes. The audience plays along, trying to answer the questions or solve the brainteasers, rooting for favorites, and coveting the prizes. These shows, however, have a fundamental difference from Reality TV. Those contestants seemed content to take their prizes and return to their ordinary lives, rather than coveting ongoing fame and careers in the realm of stardom.

One early example of an attempt to turn a contestant into a star involved the 1959 scandal of Charles van Doren and the quiz show *Twenty-One*. Van Doren, who had a Ph.D., taught in the Columbia University English Department, and was the son of a professor and nephew of an important American poet, endeared himself to audiences with his attractive presence and his calm ability to answer tough posers. Then it turned out that he had been fed answers in advance and that the entire contest between van Doren and his rival, Marty Stempel, was staged, with van Doren in the white hat and Stempel in the black. In 1994, the story was dramatized in the film *Quiz Show*. Back in the 1950s, before the public had become more cynical about performances, the betrayal of a seeming hero shook millions.

Interestingly, in 2004, the show *Jeopardy!* produced a "celebrity" contestant of its own after its producers changed the rules so that a contestant could continue playing indefinitely instead of being limited to five days. In the fall of 2004, Ken Jennings had won more than $2 million and the show's ratings rose significantly. This mega-winner was featured on the first page of *USA Today*, appeared on both the Jay Leno and David Letterman shows, and has made commercials, so he has definitely achieved instant celebrity status.

Today, the viewing audience would probably yawn if told a reality show was rigged, perhaps expecting no less and not caring about the contrivance if they were amused. Now, competition is encouraged, and the conflict of personalities is in the forefront. The audience understands that the contestants were selected just because they exemplified certain types. That's part of the fun. Contestants are expected to play dirty. Cheating can become a source of admiration. Clearly, the audience is much more cynical, expecting a form of personal Realpolitik in human behavior.

Celebrity Visits

If a definition of reality television is real people being themselves, then the variations of that approach to the medium must be expanded far beyond what is commonly called Reality TV. We can delineate at least four additional categories: interviews of well-known people, documentaries, actual events—both live or recorded, and people living their daily lives in front of cameras.

A prototype of the celebrity interview was Edward R. Murrow's *Person to Person*, which began broadcasting in 1953. Actors, musicians, politicians, and other well-known personalities would allow Murrow and his cameras into their homes for a room-by-room tour and the sharing of seeming insights into their domestic lives. Viewers had a unique opportunity to get to know Mr. X's wife, to see him as a loving father, or to get a glimpse of him lounging at the pool or displaying his collection of Toby jugs.

This all took place in black and white, assuring the audience that no matter how prominent the person, he or she was accessible and essentially like the rest of us. With the advent of color TV and the audience's increasing affluence, viewers often craved something more; they wanted opulence and conspicuous consumption. The result was *Lifestyles of the Rich and Famous,* hosted by Robin Leach. Rather than the comfort derived from knowing that celebrities were as down to earth as the rest of us, people now wanted to aspire to the excesses of those who had "made it."

Perhaps more direct examples of Murrow's legacy are the in-depth interviews conducted by hosts like Barbara Walters and Diane Sawyer. At times they are as chatty and innocuous as Murrow's visits, but often they probe—to a degree—the impact of a trauma or a scandal on the person. In some cases, as with Monica Lewinsky, it is the scandal that has made the person famous. In contrast, when a celebrity is engulfed in a scandal, he or she gets an opportunity to mount a defense or make an apology for the wrongdoing, all to the accompaniment of extensive promotional fanfare, even with snippets on the news. For instance, after movie actor Hugh Grant was arrested with a prostitute, *Tonight* show host Jay Leno's first question to him was, "What the hell were you thinking?"

Documentaries

Documentaries have much less audience appeal, even though they often deal with issues of greater significance than the tribulations and sufferings of a specific person, famous or amateur. Yet because they lack the human touch, their viewership is limited, with the networks offering them as a form of medicine, something that is good for the viewers. Presenting documentaries fulfills the networks' obligation to be serious and educational. Weeks can pass without the airing of a network documentary, though they are shown frequently on public television. Their subjects tend toward matters like toxic waste, Third World poverty, and endangered species. Despite the limitations inevitably resulting from slant and editing, they are certainly about real events and circumstances. Ratings prove that the great majority of TV watchers, however, prefer "reality."

Courts and Cops

If people are going to view a show that offers direct reporting of unstaged happenings, they often choose to watch the real-life drama seen by cameras in a courtroom or scenes of real police chasing real suspects. In these shows people can be sent to prison or suffer significant fines. They are a staple of the cable channel Court TV, and the networks occasionally use the format in a summer replacement like NBC's *Crime and Punishment.*

Cops is the best-known chase show; each week, the police pursue probable criminals to their homes, usually rundown houses or apartments in bad neighborhoods. Doors are battered down, unshaven men in undershirts forced against a wall and handcuffed, and women and children become hysterical.

A variation on this type of reality programming is the car chase. Such scenes are extremely popular and almost obligatory in action movies. With local stations often flying helicopters for morning and evening traffic reports, the live following of a pursuit becomes relatively simple. In fact, several Los Angeles stations interrupt regular programming whenever they have the opportunity to broadcast a chase, often to the dismay of law enforcement officials concerned that the chases encourage lawbreakers.

Living in Front of Cameras

The first extended intrusion of TV cameras into an ordinary home came with the 1972 PBS series *An American Family* about a family living in

Santa Barbara, California: Bill and Pat Loud and their five children— Michele, Delilah, Grant, Kevin, and Lance. Wife, husband, sons, and daughters allowed their lives to be filmed *cinema verité* style for many hours, with the results edited into a multishow series. Midway into the filming the parents decided to divorce and other family tensions emerged. The most obvious question that viewers asked was, would these lives have been affected so severely if they had been lived in normal privacy? Then the next question was, what kind of people would allow their lives to be recorded so fully, to be exposed before millions of eyes? Ultimately, it is impossible to find "innocent" participants in such an experiment. The very fact that someone is willing to submit daily existence to camera scrutiny skews the circumstances.

In the decades since *An American Family*, a number of variations have evolved, primarily in recent times. Probably the most successful offshoot has been *The Osbournes*, revealing the dynamics of a fading rock star's family life. Although the Osbournes were a nuclear family, comprising an actual father, mother, son, and daughter, they could not be considered representative of the population with their diseases and addictions and particular dysfunctions.

Yet the majority of family-like situations tend to be even more contrived, in which unrelated people are selected to live together in a long-term experience. For example MTV's *Real World* shows a group of Generation X representatives uprooted from their regular lives who move into the same living quarters. This show can be considered a predecessor to *Big Brother* and its many iterations. The primary difference is that *Real World* does not force competition by staging a contest in which participants vie for prizes. The tensions among people seem spontaneous and may actually be so when they are not scripted. PBS has taken a more benign approach to the formula, picking real families for *Colonial House* or *Frontier House*, series in which people accustomed to modern conveniences attempt to exist under the day-to-day conditions of a century or two ago and grumble about their frustrations.

Artificiality

At one point in television history, westerns dominated both in the time allotted to them and their popularity; then they vanished from the programming schedules. The future of Reality TV could be as dire, especially with such a glut of offerings and their increasing contrivances and artificialities. So far, the audience doesn't mind. As long as I'm entertained, they seem to be saying, I'll play along and ignore the issue of authenticity.

After five decades of TV, the public seems to have realized that very little that they see on their screen is not artificial to some degree. The very presence of a camera on the scene changes the ingredients—the mix of participants, physical objects, and even the issues at stake. Someone is watching, and even if those being filmed or taped are not self-conscious, even if they are fully relaxed before the camera, they are still aware that something is at stake. If not, why else would someone have bothered to bring a camera?

Cameras are everywhere, and those operating them are similar to the wedding photographer who directs the ceremony for the sake of the pictures. In a 2005 *New York Times* op-ed piece called "Was It Real for You, Too?" writer Bob Greene tells of his experience on a Southwest Airlines flight that had to turn back because of engine problems. The moment the plane landed a TV crew entered and focused cameras on the traumatized passengers, seeking material for an A&E reality show called *Airline*. Yet this footage may never be broadcast because, as the field producer explained, their reactions lacked the drama of "someone having a panic attack."

Self-Seeking

The many changes evident in the comparison of TV's pretense of reality in the 1950s to today's Reality TV illustrate our changing sense of and relation to the world around us. People watch to be entertained, of course, but these shows expose frenetic and often unfeeling self-seeking. Their message is, look out for number one and win any way you can. Does that translate to viewers' behavior when they are the actors in their own lives?

A 2001 *Psychology Today* study of reality program viewers conducted by Steven Reiss and James Wiltz of Ohio State University suggests that the message does affect their lives:

> But the attitude that best separated the regular viewers of reality television from everyone else is the desire for status. Fans of the shows are much more likely to agree with statements such as, "Prestige is important to me" and "I am impressed with designer clothes" than are other people. We have studied similar phenomena before and found that the desire for status is just a means to get attention. And more attention increases one's sense of importance: We think we are important if others pay attention to us and unimportant if ignored.

Programming Our Lives

Reality TV allows Americans to fantasize about gaining status through automatic fame. Ordinary people can watch the shows, see people like themselves, and imagine that they too could become celebrities by being on television. It does not matter as much that the contestants often are shown in an unfavorable light; the fact that millions of Americans are paying attention means that the contestants are important.

Viewers crave status and recognition. There's no conclusive evidence that we will act out on these fantasies in our daily lives, but there's no doubt we have accepted a much broader range of what is normal and permissible in the non-TV world.

Chapter 6

Airing Our Lives: Broadcast Revelations

It's an emblematic scene on one of the daytime talk shows—a sullen teenage girl still pudgy with baby fat and dressed in a miniskirt and tank top, pierced and tattooed, sits on a chair next to her distraught mother, avoiding eye contact and pouting because the mother won't let her boyfriend move into her bedroom. The mother throws up her hands, saying, "She won't listen to me." The host asks provocative questions, makes moralistic generalizations, evokes boos and cheers from the audience, and then produces the boyfriend, who shuffles out from backstage staring at the floor. A version of this interaction goes on five days a week, with each program announcing an 800-number seeking volunteers with equally titillating problems: Does your teenage son sleep with your best friend? Does your husband sit up all night with computer porn? Does your husband know the baby is not his?

Although such shows may be at the extreme end of a continuum, they exemplify the willingness of people to disclose the most intimate details of personal lives on TV. Many of these admissions reveal behaviors most of us once would have been reluctant to confess to trained therapists. And those therapists sat behind closed doors bound by professional ethics of confidentiality. Yet now, in front of cameras and live audiences, many people make their addictions, fetishes, traumas, and dysfunctions public knowledge, encouraged by hosts and, ultimately, sponsors. Even if seemingly ashamed of their circumstances, those confessing are essentially flaunting them.

Such shows should be distinguished from Reality TV programs that create highly artificial situations that are essentially fictional. In those programs, participants are cast as carefully as the actors in a Hollywood movie, chosen for their appearance and personality. In contrast, in shows where ordinary people actually reveal themselves, producers are concerned with participants' lives before the actual broadcast, rather than tests they must pass on camera.

The most extreme of these shows to date is that of the notorious Jerry Springer, which brings together violence-prone participants bearing grudges against each other. Physical assaults are routine, the audience roaring like spectators at a pro wrestling match. Bleeped obscenities fill the air, and people on stage and in the audience expose graphically censored body parts. The Springer show, despite wide condemnation, still finds outlets and viewers. DVD versions are sold with scenes "too hot for TV." Springer even has played himself in movies, exploiting his notoriety and being rewarded for it with fame as a household word, not to mention money.

Occasionally, these shows do cross a boundary, even though the standard of what is forbidden becomes more and more extreme. Lawsuits result, and not only from the censored moments relegated to DVDs. Probably the most serious violation occurred when Jenny Jones tricked a young man, Jonathan Schmitz, into appearing on her show with the lure that he would meet a romantic admirer. That person, Scott Amedure, turned out to be a gay male. Outraged and homophobic, Schmitz killed Amedure and was sentenced to twenty-five to fifty years in prison for second-degree murder. For all the condemning editorials and public outrage, these shows continue to flourish, perhaps with a lure like the anticipation of a fiery crash that attracts crowds to auto races.

A more structured variation of these talk shows can be found in the competing court shows in which antagonists bring petty claims before a variety of TV judges, with and without actual bench experience. The issues are penny ante; for example, estranged lovers contesting the payment of $500 for car repairs. Was it a gift or a loan? The "crime" itself serves as a catalyst for the opportunity to watch two people call each other liars before an often scornful arbitrator. Every case ends with a decision and a lecture by the judge in which he or she berates the loser and sometimes the winner as well.

Why Confess?

Why do so many people do it—reveal their failed relationships, their most intimate secrets to a nationwide audience? Such shows can be found throughout the day and even compete in the same time slots, seeking more and more outré subjects to expose. Each year, in total, thousands of people are willing to bare their lives while millions watch.

Does being on TV give people permission to reveal intimate secrets, as if they are in a performance detached from the reality of their lives, like actors in one of the hundreds of dramas they have watched? Do they think the exposure will allow them to distance themselves from the sources of their distress? Or is being on TV an ultimate reward, worth any price, including their privacy?

A significant change in audience expectation and engagement has occurred in the six decades of television viewing. Shows in the early years of TV tended to be low-key and a bit bland, suitable to existence in the conformist fifties, and viewers sought to emulate what appeared on the screen. TV programs functioned as a template in the service of daily life in the kitchen and living room. But over the years, a reversal seems to have taken place. TV for many has become the end, rather than the means. That is to say, their goal is getting on TV, as if the years off screen are preparation for the performance on screen. Perhaps a TV appearance validates their humanity and assures the rest of the population that they are one of us. This validation is sought not only by those who confess. Political candidates for the highest offices play an instrument, perform cameo roles on sitcoms, and trade quips with Leno or Letterman. Once out of office they make commercials.

In the twenty-first century the question is not so much how or whether TV reflects some objective reality but rather if there is a reality beyond TV and, if so, how we will ever be able to apprehend it. French social theorist Jean Baudrillard believes we no longer can, arguing that the images we receive through the media have a diminishing relationship with an external, non-media reality. Media images, he says, are simulations that refer only to themselves, and we, bombarded by them, assume they represent a "real" world that we are no longer experiencing. Baudrillard, of course, is controversial, but his theories do resonate in an age in which we are overwhelmed by on-screen images.

Why Watch?

What motivates the viewers? Those of us who watch may do so with a sense of superiority or relief. No matter how dysfunctional our lives may be, they are not nearly as bad as those of the people they watch. In many ways, the talk shows are real versions of daytime soap opera, and their extreme subject matter leads the soap operas to adopt more and more bizarre plot lines that incorporate murder, kidnapping, rape, and terrorism;

in the process, the soaps move far from their origins as domestic dramas. As the soaps strain credibility, the talk shows present new permutations to the dilemmas of "ordinary" people. Yet the relationship of viewer and revealer may go beyond escape and relief to a closer connection.

Not all talk shows, of course, seek the extremes of family malfunction. Some aim to be uplifting by uniting long-separated siblings or presenting people who have overcome severe illness and personal tragedy; they show examples of both ordinary people and celebrities who have turned tragedy into triumph. Oprah, as compassionate host, exemplifies this uplifting type of show. Not only does she encourage people to read books with hopeful messages but she also appeals to our better natures, almost as an antidote to the hours of public humiliation. By featuring people who have defeated their demons, she provides lessons for the rest of us and lets us know that we too can take charge of our lives. It is noteworthy, however, that such positive shows are in the minority. Is it that audiences prefer to watch people at their low points or that those who have triumphed are harder to find?

Occasionally, talk shows rely on appearances by celebrities, who in addition to the requisite plugging of new movies, TV series, books, or plays, talk openly about their own life traumas—overcoming a broken marriage, substance abuse, sexual indiscretion, eating disorders, or childhood molestation. In some cases, these celebrities have written books about their ordeals, which in any event are usually public knowledge. They alternate between smiles and tears, occasionally embracing the host interviewer or just squeezing hands. Celebrities with all their performance experience carry it off with flair and style, charming the audience and making themselves more sympathetic and likable.

The more prestigious prime-time news magazine programs like *60 Minutes* and *Dateline* engage in intense competition to go beyond the headlines by persuading those central to the news event to submit to an interview. Politicians and celebrities, through their press agents, are usually eager volunteers. Ordinary people may require more convincing, especially if the news is bad: for instance, the parents whose child stole the family rifle to gun down schoolmates, the parents accused of murdering their daughter, or the man whose brother mailed letter bombs. It may be even more difficult for the parents of a murdered child to appear on these programs. But reluctant as they may be, they usually consent to appear. Are their motives the same as those who appear on the Springer show, or has some skilled TV producer convinced them that they will feel better if they are able to tell their side of the story? Or given our present-day norm of bearing one's soul publicly, are they made to feel that they really don't have a right not to appear? In fact, anyone who doesn't agree to appear on these programs is treated as a spoilsport, cheating the curiosity of the nation.

Celebrities of any stripe are particularly condemned for not baring their souls. If someone high and mighty won't come down and walk among the crowd, that person—performer, athlete, or politician—will be humbled by the exposés of magazine journalism and tabloid TV. Actors who use drugs, ballplayers who abuse their partners, elected officials who dally with interns—all are fair game. Their scandals dominate the headlines; their associates and victims are interviewed on show after show, now and then turning this instant fame into a career by exploiting their moments in the spotlight as household names.

TV and Intimacy

Both the willingness of people to air their lives and the availability of television as an outlet for outrageous revelations raise several questions about changes in our cultural standards and the relationship of TV to those changes. As with so many other transformations of the past half-century, we have to ask whether television served as a central cause or just reflects the changes brought about by other societal forces.

The restrictions of early TV are well known: the "rule" that even married couples like Lucy and Desi sleep in twin beds, the prohibition of profanity or even suggestive language, the inability to address many controversial subjects, and the forbidding of physical contact between people of different races. These limitations reflected the sexual mores and the reticence prevalent in the larger culture at the time. That which was painful or disturbing was not addressed. For example, many people would not admit that a loved one or a friend had cancer, as if the disease itself were shameful. At most, they might say, "She has C," with the "C" not vocalized but just mimed with an exaggerated mouth movement. Now AIDS victims can appear on TV to discuss their illness openly, news broadcasts report studies on the frequency of married sex, and commercials tout cures for sexual dysfunction.

Perhaps the key between the relationship of television as a medium and the topics it broaches can be seen in the concept of intimacy. The TV screen puts people in our living rooms, kitchens, and bedrooms where they share our personal space. From the beginning, those who conceived TV shows either consciously or intuitively understood this feature of television and took steps to give those we saw human dimensions; they became part of a homespun interaction that included the viewer by implication.

We become part of the process, identifying with those on the screen rather than being awed by them. Such a connection unites the watcher and the watched, those in the room and those on the screen, in a way that produces a kind of intimacy. The specific behavior being discussed is less important than the drama of seeing other people confess to behavior that violates what is normally acceptable. Viewers sympathize with the emotional trauma of confronting the forbidden.

Boundaries Stretched

And yet the boundaries are continually stretched: what constitutes the forbidden becomes increasingly extreme as specific transgressions become old hat and stale because we have heard about them so often. With that familiarity, the particular act becomes part of the cultural norm, acceptable for most audiences without the frisson of shock value. For example, having erectile dysfunction would no longer be sufficient to get a man a spot on a daytime talk show. How could it when star athletes and a former leader of the U.S. Senate and presidential candidate are advertising Viagra on TV?

Many examples exist to show that this expanding norm affects the behavior of people in their non-TV-watching lives. For most of us, the stigma has been removed from pregnancy before marriage, unwed mothers, homosexuality, living together, casual drug use, and other once widely condemned activities. If we as viewers participate in the medium in a way that makes us relate to the people we are watching, we may become less judgmental. We may become more tolerant and accepting of what was once considered aberrant behavior.

How far this trend will go and what behavior will become normative in the future are open questions. Many in American society are urging a retreat to more traditional values. We've already seen this trend in Congress multiplying the fines for obscenities on radio broadcasts. But is that a harbinger or a one-time headline grabber? Is the momentum of TV too powerful to turn back? Is it something that needs turning back?

The Question of Authenticity

But beyond the effect of TV on social norms, another issue emerges—the very authenticity of airing one's life before a camera. With the prevalence of TV cameras in our society, it's nothing special to see ourselves on screen. Yet does a form of self-consciousness emerge when we know a camera is focused on us? That is, do we have a tendency to satisfy the demands of the medium and perform?

Those chosen from all the applicants to appear on talk and court shows, both ordinary and famous, must pass some sort of test to ensure that they will make a good presentation. They must be sufficiently animated and articulate, even at a basic level, and willing to spill their emotions. In short, they have to engage the viewer's interest and overcome his or her impulse to change the channel. Perhaps most of the ordinary people selected are natural performers. In any event, they are watchers of the show and are aware how their predecessors behaved, so they are likely to emulate that behavior.

A prerequisite for a successful television performer—whether actor, news anchor, talk show host, or celebrity guest—is the ability to appear natural and spontaneous before the camera. How often is that naturalness, to some degree, a pose or itself a type of performance? Are the people airing the secrets of their lives aware that they are putting on a show?

In addition, are people in their daily lives affected by what they have watched, not only in what they consider acceptable behavior but also in how they present themselves to others? How much do we all act as if we are on camera? It may be that TV, in informing us about what we can do, also gives us a template for how to do it.

Chapter 7

The Price of Admission: Commercials

Although we take commercials for granted when watching TV, our passivity may be the result of conditioning that overrides a basic element of our usual interaction with the external world—that is, our ability to control the focus of our attention, what we see and what we hear. Certainly, advertising existed before mid-twentieth-century media entered our homes—in print, on signs, and on displays. But these ads were essentially background phenomena, optional in the sense that we could go about our business and ignore them. For the radio listener and then television viewer, however, ads became inescapable intrusions in the sequence. Although attention could drift, eyes could wander, and messages could presumably be ignored, commercials were still interruptions to the subjects of our interest.

Decades of market research and the development of ever more sophisticated visual techniques have made it increasingly difficult to ignore the commercial messages that bombard us. As a result, they have become the norm. Now for us it seems perfectly natural to have the mood and visual world of a TV program suddenly replaced by a radically different reality with new sounds, new rhythms, and new images and for that reality to be quickly followed by a series of other new realities before we can return to the "real" program.

It's often said that television programs exist to sell products and services and that the content of the show is incidental to the goal of advertisers as long as it attracts an audience of the right demographic group. Viewers, of course, don't see it that way. They want to be amused and so accept commercials as the price of admission, the trade-off for what is seemingly free entertainment.

Commercials and the Landscapes of Our Lives

But it's not that simple. Commercials are not just like a dose of castor oil, a quick swallow of an unpleasant taste that is quickly forgotten. After years of viewing commercials for many thousands of hours, we take them and all that they represent directly and indirectly as integral to the landscape of our lives, as much a part of the order of things as the water that flows from our taps. Commercials are part of the rhythms of our lives. The products they feature also have become comfortably familiar, icons and objects that help ground our sense of identity at a particular time and in a particular place. We are at home with them, and the commercials that urge them upon us may seem essential for our daily lives.

For many TV viewers, therefore, commercials are not bitter medicine. Many become mini-treats, lively and clever sources of pleasure in their inventiveness. We even look forward to our favorites—the duck that quacks "AFLAC," the boy who goes "Zoom, zoom." Advertisers would like us to talk about them as much—or even more—than we do about the programs. The per second production cost of many commercials far outpaces that of programs, in part because commercials have only a very short time to get their message across; therefore, they must be concise, even compelling, in their appeal. Every word, every sound, and every image counts, so production values are high. Their directors occasionally go on to achieve fame in the movies. The most striking and successful commercials have become cultural markers, remembered and even revered long after the programs they sponsored have disappeared. Their slogans become cultural catchphrases: for example, Nike's "Just do it." Their melodies stick in our heads. Two-year-olds delight their parents by mouthing their lyrics.

In a pop culture society, commercials are among the most important artifacts. Boundaries between high and low, art and commerce, this reality and that one blur and even vanish. Hit songs of one decade become the background music of commercials in the next, even when the messages are radically different. Janis Joplin's satirical paean to a Mercedes Benz becomes a tune to pump up sales of that car. Political leaders quote commercial tags: "Where's the beef?" Sports teams flaunt logos on the shoes they wear and receive an endorsement fee. Public schools give exclusive deals to a specific soft drink brand in exchange for funds for band uniforms. Novelists and filmmakers define their characters by the watches on their wrists or the vodka they drink. Almost everyone wears hats, T-shirts, jackets, or tote bags emblazoned with brand names. Products have become engrained in our daily lives, inseparable from the way we live now.

Visual Impact

Before television, of course, people knew many brand names from radio and print advertising. They recognized products on store shelves. But TV has made brands ubiquitous because of the visual impact of the constant repetition of commercials.

TV, the first intimate visual communicator in our homes, obviously has enormous power to influence us with visual images, and the industry has learned more and more how to do that effectively. Advertisers understood the power of television from the first days of TV, probably more than those responsible for creative program content. They quickly learned that the new medium was not merely radio with pictures, but a visual outlet that could be exploited by graphic images.

Today's commercials clearly reflect the lessons learned by their producers of the power of visual impact. Many ads now display just a concept, and the viewer does not know who the advertiser is until a brief visual or auditory mention at the end. For example, the Gap developed a series of commercials in which bands play or dancers dance to a short musical piece, and the name GAP is only displayed in the final seconds. The message is totally visual—youthful performers dressed in attractive clothing from the Gap—with no lyrics or script "selling" the product. Other commercials, especially for firms in the "new economy," deliberately omit references to or displays of the product or services and only indicate the name of the company. Often the visuals create an aura of making sense out of complexity, through energized graphics; for example, fragmented pieces come together to form a picture. The eye can't resist.

TV and the Consumer Economy

Have television and its commercials been instrumental in this all-consuming product identification, or are they only another crest in the tidal wave of consumerism? Did they help cause the storm or were they just caught up in the swell? An argument can be made that they were more cause than effect.

The explosion of product names and icons coincided with the flourishing of the consumer economy after World War II. The standard of living was rising, as were consumer expectations. More people had more money and became driven by a desire to buy, to possess. As millions of people achieved their goal of entering the middle class, new products, new brands, and new needs burgeoned in the final decades of the twentieth century. There was so much more to consume, so many things we believed we couldn't live without.

But would this burgeoning consumerism have occurred without TV commercials or at least to the overwhelming extent that it did? Many of the brands and products that prevailed did not advertise on television. Yet television may have played an essential role in changing expectations by authenticating consumption and by making it exciting to consume. In fact, TV sent a message that you were depriving yourself, were missing out, if you didn't consume. The very fact of their being sold on television gave products a certain cachet, as revealed by the claim on signs and print ads: "As advertised on TV."

The commercials themselves played a part in this transformation. Unlike radio and print ads, those on TV conveyed movement and action. With the advent of color, TV commercials increased in vividness and energy. Sound, image, pacing, and graphic appeal were all intensified with new rhythms and new urgencies. Alka-Seltzer's rudimentary "Plop plop fizz fizz" evolved to fully choreographed musical dance numbers like those of the Gap commercials. Products shown in pulsating action became enlivening; they are seen as the means to satisfy new enthusiasms, to achieve personal transformations. Drive this car, drink that beverage, and you will realize your dreams, perhaps even beyond the limits of your imagination.

The programs themselves—the packaging for the commercials—augmented this transformation by depicting enviable lifestyles, even in the crime dramas and soap operas whose characters were disturbed or corrupt. They were only fictions, but their homes, their pools, their panoramic vistas, and their possessions became objects of envy. We developed our own expectations, desiring products that had moved from luxury status to necessities. Why not flaunt the brand names that surrounded you, which you owned? It wasn't conspicuous consumption in competition with their neighbors as much as it was people's pride in what they were able to own.

It's not just Americans who have become avid consumers. Now that television is increasingly a global phenomenon, the drive for consumption has become ubiquitous, led by American marketing techniques and American products. Chip Walker, discussing the 1996 New World Teen Study in *American Demographics*, writes:

The Price of Admission: Commercials

The New World Teen study reveals that global teens are a generation with startling commonalities as consumers. Despite differing cultures, middle-class youth all over the world seem to live their lives as if in a parallel universe. They get up in the morning, put on their Levi's and Nikes, grab their caps, backpacks, and Sony personal CD players, and head for school.

More Ads, Less Programming

As much as consumers have embraced the products promoted on TV and the creativity of certain ads, we may be approaching a turning point where the amount of advertising will turn viewers away from the medium. Economics, of course, lies at the heart of the dilemma. The networks find themselves in a bind. The cost of commercial time has to strike a balance between ensuring a profit and not chasing sponsors away with the per-second cost. "So," according to J. Max Robins in *TV Guide*, "the networks up the number of ads, though they then risk alienating viewers."

Robins cites a 2004 study by PhaseOne Communications that found an average of fifty-three minutes of commercials for every three hours of broadcasting, almost one-third of the total. That's 8 percent higher than the results of a 2000 study. Over a twenty-year period, commercial time has doubled, with the average break lasting three minutes.

One avoidance tactic used by viewers, in addition to the occasional snack and bathroom break, is channel surfing with the remote, sampling one or more other programs and then clicking back when they guess the original program has resumed. For many, that tactic may lead to frustration and a desire for an alternative method of avoiding commercials.

Commercial-Free Viewing

Even though some of us find that certain commercials offer aesthetic pleasures, a growing number consider them a nuisance that interrupts the intensity of drama and the pace of comedy, especially as they increasingly eat into programming time. These viewers would prefer television without commercials. And technology is now permitting that option—for a price. We are now able to own devices that make our viewing commercial-free. But where do we learn of their existence? In an ironic, perhaps self-defeating, paradox, advertising touts the virtues of products that permit the avoidance of ads.

VCRs were the first such devices; until the recent surge in the sale of DVD players, there was at least one in almost every American home. They probably are still there, but unused and replaced by a later technology. Despite the protests and legal efforts of the TV networks when VCRs were first sold, their owners gained the right to record programs for viewing at their own convenience. One issue arose from this ability to time-shift. If advertising rates were based on the Nielsen rating of program audience, what would happen to the accuracy and validity of that figure if people had an alternative that overrode the measuring devices? What would happen to time-slot comparisons if people could watch one network show at, say, 9 P.M. and record its competitor for watching at a different hour? Another issue was the fast-forward capability, enabling the VCR user to push a button to speed past the commercials. Some later VCR models even do that forwarding automatically. The catch is that most VCR owners use them for movie rentals, never mastering the steps needed to actually record a show.

Now that DVD player/recorders have become affordable and more movies and TV show compilations are available on disk than on tape, VCRs are almost obsolete. Will consumers really use DVD devices to record, or will they turn to devices called digital video recorders (DVRs)? Digital video recorders—with names like TiVo and Replay TV—function on the principle of a computer hard drive to simplify the recording effort and store many times the program content of a VCR tape or DVD disk. One way or another, they zap commercials, though broadcasters have launched a legal battle against that capability when it is an automatic function of the DVR. The costs of DVRs have come down significantly, and alternatives to the monthly fee for the recording services are available. Cable and satellite companies are developing or licensing their own versions to be built right into their delivery systems.

For several decades, cable and satellite providers—for fees beyond that of basic service—have provided access to commercial-free films and television shows, such as those on HBO and Showtime. But because of these channels' frequently repeated programming and limited new productions, people still must devote the majority of their viewing time to "free" network, local, and cable channels replete with commercials.

Digital cable and satellite transmission might change that situation. Among the hundreds of available channels—the exact number depends on the level of service purchased—many are commercial free, especially the thirty to fifty movie channels that play film after film at no extra cost twenty-four hours a day. These movies can be recorded as well. For a small fee, several pay-TV services offer on-demand programming. For example, for about five dollars a month, HBO makes available approximately 150 broadcasts from its own series and Hollywood films that can be played like rental tapes; that is, they can be started at any time, paused, rewound, and fast-forwarded. In addition, some cable operators offer long lists of movies that can be rented at a cost similar to that charged by the local video store. Conceivably, viewers willing to spend the money can go through the week never seeing a commercial other than ones promoting another commercial-free program or movie.

New Strategies for Advertisers

Aware of this threat, regular broadcasters and advertising have been seeking alternatives to traditional commercials. Some believe that audience skepticism has diminished their effectiveness anyway. As a result, they have devised a number of strategies to increase product awareness

Advertisers realize that the visual power of television goes well beyond commercials. Product placement, which has been around for a number of years, is the practice of paying for having a product placed in a scene of a movie or television program. Characters on TV shows and films drive certain cars, fly certain airlines, eat at certain fast-food restaurants, and consume certain soft drinks, all for a consideration paid to the producers. For instance, if the scene is of a family having breakfast, a package of Rice Krispies may be sitting on the table. The show's producers did not pick a cereal randomly, but were paid by Kellogg's to use their product in the scene. We will see more product placement in the coming years.

A *Time* magazine article in June 2001 pointed out that the process of product placement has evolved to product integration in TV, in which the products become an integral part of the story. For example, Mountain Dew and Doritos are used on the reality show *Survivor* as "not just prizes but icons of civilization," noting that the "goodies are to the Survivor's cast as apple pie and baseball were to GIs." Product integration may herald the future of TV advertising, replacing the distinct commercial message that interrupts the show and can be zapped by new technology.

More extensive product integration into the flow of the show using digital technology will also increase. Digital technology now allows electronic billboards to be inserted into ball games, for example, on the barrier behind baseball's home plate. These signs don't exist for spectators in the park, only for those watching on TV. Similar signage and product icons can be integrated into any program. Ads for future programs on a channel are superimposed onto a corner of the picture during a show's broadcast similar to pop-ups on the Internet, and they cannot be zapped or avoided by fast-forwarding. In a recent ploy, celebrities have been paid to tout the virtues of products when they appear on talk shows, though some broadcasters say they will expose the presence of such endorsements. Still, we can only expect new strategies to outpace the audience's attempts to avoid the familiar forms of commercials. Perhaps we will see the realization of the urban legend that subliminal messages are being flashed on screen below the level of our conscious awareness.

In addition to the technological threats to traditional commercials, viewer sophistication is reducing their effectiveness. Even when people watch commercials, they are aware that they are being manipulated by clever advertisers and therefore are more skeptical about the messages. The many headline exposés of corporate deceptions in financial reporting and product defects feed viewer suspiciousness. Even more so, the emphasis on behind-the-scenes reporting that focuses on deception and fraud has conditioned viewers to expect such dishonesty.

Television feeds into the cynicism that undermines the effectiveness of its financial base. Magazine shows, such as *20/20* and *48 Hours*, dramatize case after case of consumer fraud and malfeasance. Local news programs focus on fraudulent merchants who rip off customers. Going beyond these specific examples, people now live in a culture where doubt is much more pervasive than during the early years of TV. Those dancing Old Gold cigarette packs from the fifties have been revealed as cancer sticks and the cigarette company executives as blatant liars. Who can we trust?

In June 2004, *The Economist* printed a special report on the future of advertising called "The Harder Hard Sell: The Future of Advertising" (subtitled "More people are rejecting traditional sales messages, presenting the ad industry with big challenges"). The study noted the difficulties of measuring the effectiveness of print and media advertising and the fact that many makers of consumer products have been seeking advertising alternatives to TV. Part of the problem might be characterized as audience burnout, with 65 percent feeling "constantly bombarded" by ads, 59 percent claiming that ad messages have little meaning for them, and 70 percent favoring products that gave relief from ads. The report cites studies that found fewer than half of media ads result in a positive return on investment. As alternatives many companies are turning to what *The Economist* calls "below-the-line" advertising: "They range from public relations to direct mail, consumer promotions (such as coupons), in-store displays, business-to-business promotions (like paying for shelf space), telemarketing, exhibitions, sponsoring events, product placements and more."

The Price of Admission: Commercials

Television, of course, is trying to stem this erosion with new strategies to individualize their messages that are borrowed from Internet marketers. One such strategy reported in June 2004 by the *New York Times* would be more regionalized than personalized at this point. The Weather Channel plans to launch ads tailored to the forecast or to the weather conditions in a particular part of the country. The cable company Comcast is giving advertisers an opportunity in the countries' ten largest markets to base spots on "geographic, demographic and other factors."

With the advent of digital cable and two-way interaction between viewers and their cable companies, the technology exists for ads to be as personalized as those on the Internet. As noted above, customers can order on-demand movies and programming for their own homes. What cable lacks is the broad knowledge of consumer interests that Internet search engines compile from the range and variety of their Web searches. But cable companies probably can come up with ways to ferret out this information or may just buy the data.

How can our consumer culture, in which new products are being introduced at a faster and faster pace, continue to exist if the buying audience doesn't know what's out there to want? Even if TV commercials as we have known them become memories in a broadcasting museum, there still will be some form of advertising on TV. Whatever the devices we have for storing and viewing and whatever apparent commercial-free options we may have, sellers will find a way to transmit their messages. Our way of life depends on it.

The question of cause and effect may be more problematic than it was in the early, innocent TV era. Viewer choices, attitudes, and preferences now put pressure on advertisers to find ways around growing resistance to commercials. Still, in a consumer culture, people—despite their claimed dislike of advertising—are curious about the latest products that can add convenience to their lives or glory to their egos. Television with its multiple sense modalities has probably been history's most powerful force in stimulating our consumer economy. Marketers no doubt will find a way for the TV screen to continue its role as a major stimulus to consumerism.

Part II

Our Democracy

Chapter 8

Staggering Costs: TV and Elections

Surely, TV has had a very significant impact on the process by which we choose our government representatives, from the local councilperson to the president of the United States. Because of its reach and its ability to tailor a quick message to either a broad or relatively homogeneous audience, TV has become the medium of choice in all sorts of elections. According to Lynda Lee Kaid, professor of telecommunications at Southern Illinois University, TV spots alone consume 50 to 75 percent of campaign budgets in races at the state and local levels. Because of the cost of TV advertising, television has upped the ante significantly for anyone who wishes to run for public office, thereby increasing the influence of those who are able to come up with significant amounts of cash. This is especially true for the presidential election. The fact that TV is a major player is not arguable, for TV has changed the game in many ways.

In 1948 television was in its commercial infancy, with only about 350,000 sets in the public's hands. To get his message across to as many people as possible, President Harry Truman traveled over 30,000 miles on his train, the "Truman Special." His opponent, Thomas E. Dewey, governor of New York, was widely expected to win the election, but Truman's down-to-earth, shoot-from-the-hip style, which he was able to communicate in these local speeches, carried the day. Most important, however, this was probably the last election in which television did not play a significant role. By the 1952 election, Dwight D. Eisenhower's campaign had engaged Rosser Reeves, a successful advertising executive, to produce a series of spot advertisements that would appear during commercial breaks. These were the first political advertisements on television. Today, the candidates themselves, as well as many issue-group proxies, spend hundreds of millions of dollars in television advertisements, sometimes presenting the candidate and his views, but much more often attacking the opposition candidate with half-truths, innuendos, and outright lies.

TV Influence on Campaign Financing

Because of its high cost, TV has certainly had a strong influence on the amount of money needed for a credible campaign. Because TV is able to reach into so many homes, candidates, especially those running for governor, senator, and president, must now raise significant amounts of money for their campaigns. TV advertising is even more important for individuals who are new to politics and do not have names that are recognizable to the electorate. However, money does not guarantee success, as was demonstrated when Ross Perot spent $62 million of his own money in a losing presidential campaign in 1992 or when Michael Huffington spent nearly $30 million of his own money in his unsuccessful campaign for California senator in 1994. On the other hand, two senators from New Jersey, Senators Frank Lautenberg and now-governor John Corzine, are multimillionaire businessmen who originally won their seats without having served in any previous publicly elected positions. Both spent large amounts of their own money on their campaigns, Lautenberg $6 million in 1982 and Corzine $60 million in 2000. A large proportion of all that money was spent on TV commercials as the quickest and surest way to gain name recognition. This has made it likely that our Senate will become more of a rich person's preserve with each passing election.

Campaigns at a more local level have also been self-financed. In 1989, Ronald Lauder, chairman of Estée Lauder Cosmetics, spent a then-record $8 million in an unsuccessful bid to become mayor of New York City. Perhaps that failure prompted Michael Bloomberg, another multimillionaire businessman, to demolish that record in 2002 to gain that office. Mr. Bloomberg spent a total of $69 million dollars of his own money first to achieve name recognition and then to bury his opponents in an avalanche of TV advertisements in the most expensive media market in America. That mayoral election may foreshadow the extension of the power of TV to draw multimillionaire political newcomers to vie for more local positions than the senate and presidential races that drew them previously. Fortunately for Arnold Schwarzenegger, his campaign for governor of California was so short that he did not have to match the amount spent by the mayor of New York City. But the fact that he already had name recognition and could immediately fund whatever was needed for a campaign from his own resources were two crucial factors that enabled him to win the race for governor.

At the presidential level, the money spent on television is staggering. A one-time insertion of a thirty-second spot on a prime-time network show costs approximately $150,000. Although commercials in smaller markets and less desirable time slots are proportionately less expensive, the amount of money needed to keep the candidate's name and message in front of the target audience very quickly adds up. The Media Literacy Clearinghouse "reported that $1.6 billion was spent on television ads in the nation's 100 largest media markets this year [2004]...a total of 1,950,737 political spots aired this year on 615 stations... At 30 seconds each, that would be the same as 677 solid days of advertising."

The increased cost of campaigning has clearly increased the role of special interests in the election process, especially on a national basis. Because of the amount of money the major parties have to raise and spend in the presidential election years ($1.2 billion in 2004, by one estimate), it is inconceivable that, under our present system, the sums needed could be raised in small increments from individual voters, even considering the amounts given the major candidates from public funds.

Given candidates' needs for these high levels of funding, businesses, unions, trade groups, and other organizations like the AARP or the NRA have become major donors at all levels of government. Clearly these organizations don't give the money because they believe in supporting the democratic process. They do so at the very least to buy access to the individuals who will have a role in proposing or passing laws that will affect them and, at worst, to buy the needed votes.

Recently, the campaign financing rules have changed. The McCain-Feingold Act of 2003 prohibited direct hard money donations to national parties and congressional committees from labor and corporate contributors. However, so-called 527 organizations are allowed to produce "issue ads" that do not include language that clearly supports or urges a vote for one candidate or the other. Extremely wealthy individuals on both sides have created such organizations and, in the 2004 Presidential campaign, spent heavily on TV ads that attacked one or the other candidates.

The one recent exception to the trend to seek money from large donors was Howard Dean's use of the Internet to raise millions of dollars from small donors as well as an army of volunteers during the 2003–2004 Democratic primary race. This may presage a shift in the power of big donors to influence elections, but such a shift is not highly likely, and it does not change the fact that a great deal of the money, wherever obtained, will be spent on television advertising.

Money's influence in politics is not new and existed long before the advent of television. But the cost and power of the medium have considerably raised the ante and continue to raise it higher with each passing election. Clearly, the higher the stakes, the greater the influence of the bigger players, and the less the small and moderate donors count. Although there is almost constant pressure for reforming campaign financing, every law that has been passed has contained large loopholes, and businesses, individuals, and interest groups with large funds at their disposal have found ways around the intent of the laws. The lure of TV is too great for candidates, parties, and their supporters to ignore. As long as we have television, campaign financing will continue to be a big business.

Candidates as Television Personalities

It's not only campaign costs that TV has escalated; the medium also has caused fundamental changes in the way candidates campaign. Television has made the candidates "TV personalities" with all the scrutiny given such people for their looks and their delivery, rather than what they say. Consider these comments: "Doesn't Oprah look great since she took off the weight" or "no wonder everybody loves Raymond, he's so cute." In a similar vein, during the Bush/Gore campaign we were subjected to endless discussions of how many sighs Gore emitted and how many times Bush used the phrase "fuzzy math" in their first debate. We were even treated to an analysis of the number of times each candidate blinked his eyes and the portent that had for the ultimate vote count, which predicted a Bush victory on the basis that he blinked less often. Indeed, why even hold the elections? For better or for worse, it is clear that the existence of TV has, like it or not, made our politicians part of the television "scene."

Although the medium has given us much more personal exposure to presidential candidates, it may actually have resulted in us knowing less about what these candidates think than we knew before. In an interesting analysis between the appearances of two "JFK's" on the *Tonight Show*, Frank Rich compared the first appearance of a presidential candidate on a late night talk show to a recent one. When Senator John F. Kennedy appeared on Jack Paar's show in June 1960, he was asked questions by Paar, guest Peggy Cass, and the studio audience. These questions covered the "U–2 incident, the failed Soviet summit, Cuba, and 'the Catholic question.'" Rich contrasts this with Senator John F. Kerry's appearance on Jay Leno's show in November 2003. Instead of appearing in a suit and tie, Kerry arrived on his Harley-Davidson motorcycle dressed in typical motorcycle garb of a leather jacket and jeans and boots and armed with a number of quips to project more of a hip image than a "Boston Brahmin." Although the comparison does indicate the degree to which today's candidates will go to manipulate their images on TV, Rich makes the point that such manipulation even occurred in the 1960 interview. Although Paar thought he was conducting a relaxed, apolitical interview with Kennedy, what he actually got were responses carefully crafted from Kennedy's stump speeches and designed to tone down his natural wit and youthfulness and project a mature and serious persona. So even in the first example of a presidential candidate appearing on an entertainment show, there is good reason to believe that the audience got to see little of the "real person" and much more the image that the candidate was trying to portray in the campaign.[1]

But TV is a close-up medium and brings a new dimension to how physical appearances affect the voter. Perspiring under hot lights, blinking, tapping one's fingers, or other such physical habits are part of normal living, and their presence or absence is in no way indications of a person's qualifications for high office. However, in the glare of the TV camera, these common everyday characteristics can become a death knell for a candidate.

This was dramatically evidenced in the first Nixon/Kennedy debate in the 1960 presidential election. Nixon had recently suffered a serious illness and had just completed a vigorous campaign trek around the country the day of the first debate. Kennedy, on the other hand, had taken three days off the campaign trail to prepare for the debate and was well rested. Kennedy refused to wear makeup, leaving Nixon little choice but to follow suit lest that become a news story in itself. Nixon came across on TV with a pasty complexion and he perspired a good deal, whereas Kennedy presented a youthful, hale appearance. Most press reports had Kennedy winning that debate, but numerous sources indicate that, among those hearing the debate on radio, Nixon was judged the winner. The debates, especially the first, were viewed by a tremendous number of people, and according to the Library of Congress,[2] pollsters estimated that 3.4 million voters made their choice on the basis of them alone. Given the razor-thin difference in votes for the two candidates, the influence of TV in this instance may well have been commanding.

Kennedy's appearance on the Paar show may have been the first for a candidate on an entertainment show, but it was by no means the last. An appearance on each of the late night shows (Dave Letterman and Jay Leno) as well as the top talk shows (Oprah Winfrey and Regis Philbin) is now a must for the major candidates. In these forums, the questions tend to be more personal with less follow-up than in a news conference, in an effort to show the candidate as a person. But given the horde of media advisors a candidate would have, the chances of any unintended look "inside" are nil. There is a great deal of preparation for "putting on a show," and no candidate leaves a late-night show without having gotten off a few good gag lines and probably a sight gag as well.

But the medium again wields its special type of influence as the candidate interacts with the camera. For instance journalist Jonathan Alter of *Newsweek* notes that "Bush did well with Oprah; it helped that he leaned forcefully into the camera (Gore leaned back, a bit haughtily)." Because a person comes across differently on film (or pixels) than in person, Hollywood would not dare cast someone without a screen test. It appears that the voting public now submits its presidential (and other) candidates to the equivalent test, even though the test rewards somewhat stereotypical personas. In a sense, we have become a society of voyeurs peeking in on the private lives of our heroes, but what we end up getting, and making our voting choices on, is far from what we think it is.

Sound Bites Über Alles

The fact that television has changed the way in which we perceive, teaching us to receive our information in short, quick bites, has had an enormous impact in increasing the importance of the candidate's personality, rather than his or her positions on issues. Indeed, television has given the electoral process some of the qualities of the Miss America contest. Most news coverage of a candidate is in the form of a thirty-second news story that either shows a still shot in back of a reporter's spiel or shows the candidate delivering one or two lines of a speech. By the 1980s, the average sound bite projecting the candidate's actual words was down to about nine seconds. A candidate has considerably less time to present ideas and positions than a Miss America candidate has to present herself in any single category.

Because of the time constraints of television stories and the desire of candidates to appear in the nightly news, it is not in their interest to produce complex policy statements, because doing so leaves it up to the TV reporters and editors to choose the idea(s) best communicated in thirty seconds. Such ideas may or may not be the real core of the policy, but rather the idea that will make for most interest. For instance, rather than give an explanation of the shortcomings of the inheritance tax and of alternative ways to raise the funds necessary to balance the budget, it is far more effective to say, "I am firmly against the death tax," a statement that carries a clear message and has a high probability of being shown on the six o'clock news.

Thus, it is in the best interest of the politician to make a short speech that includes an obvious sound bite that can be reported. Doing so is the best way for a candidate to ensure that a key idea he or she wishes to communicate will be left in the mind of the voter. Regrettably, ways to cope with our problems as a major nation are not usually reducible to sound bites, and only slogans that often mask the real intentions of the policies or the difficulties are communicated easily. TV has changed the nature of what we attend to from our candidates and in turn has changed what our candidates are willing to tell us.

Although slogans have always been a large part of any political campaign, it is only in the last fifty or so years of our nation's more than 200-year existence that any more than a small minority of voters have actually been able to both see and hear the candidates at the same time. Prior to television, whistle stop tours reached only a small part of the electorate; radio provided only their voice, and newspapers only static pictures. Television allows candidates to be seen and heard by many millions of voters on any given day. However, as we've indicated above, the medium does not allow them to *say* much more than might be gotten across in a news anchor's review of the day's activities.

Constant Coverage

Presidential primary campaigning was usually a very lonely process, with the candidate often greeting people one-on-one on their way to work or shopping. Today it is extremely rare for any serious candidate to be in public without having TV cameras aimed at him or her. Even at the beginning of the primary season the major contenders are followed by an army of TV cameras, recording not only their major speeches but also their every little stop in a local luncheonette or factory. No action is taken without a consideration of how it will play on television. The camera is no longer merely an observer of the action, but a force whose very presence defines the nature of the action.

The candidate's objective is to provide the right sound bite that will be broadcast on the evening news, which may be quite different from the news crew's objective. The goal of reporters is to get a brief piece of interesting film, whether in the form of parts of an interview, a speech, or the interaction between the candidate and an "ordinary" citizen that will have entertainment value for that evening's news program. It is entertainment that gets the ratings and sponsors. Thus, the coverage that is broadcast is rarely an explanation of a candidate's position on an issue, but most often a human-interest story, such as John Kerry windsurfing in Cape Cod or George Bush trimming underbrush on his ranch. Even more likely to hit the evening news program is any gaffe the candidate makes. Thus television news may not have told us anything about George Bush's thoughts on the extent to which the "no child left behind" initiative would be funded, but we were treated to numerous repetitions of his statement during a bill signing—"Our enemies are innovative and resourceful, and so are we. They never stop thinking about new ways to harm our country and our people, and neither do we." Nor are we likely to forget that Theresa Heinz Kerry told a reporter to "shove it" as he continued to press her to agree that she said something that he had taken out of context. These things may be minor gaffes, but they receive greater coverage by far than do actual statements of policy.

Thus, television has tended to narrow campaign coverage not only by limiting its stories to a matter of a few minutes but also by choosing inherently entertaining items to fill those minutes rather than those that will increase the public's understanding of the candidates' positions. Indeed, in the *Chicago Tribune* Tim Jones reported that a University of Southern California study of seventy-four stations in fifty-eight media markets during the 2000 elections found that "on a given night, local stations devoted an average of forty-five seconds to candidate discourse— defined as federal, state and local candidates actually talking about the issues." We may be getting campaign coverage on television, but it is not coverage of the candidates' issues.

Election Night

Television's final influence on the election process comes on election night in the race to call the winner, whether at the presidential or more local level. The story of election night coverage really begins in 1848 with the establishment of the Associated Press (AP) by a number of New York papers. This represented a pooling of resources to collect news (originally from dispatches carried by ships making port in Nova Scotia on their way to Canada or the United States), summarize the facts, and wire it to the subscribers. Eventually, on election nights the AP would station reporters at key election districts to wire in results to a central location as soon as they were tabulated. In this way, the newspapers were able to print the winners for the early edition even though all the votes had not yet been counted. Of course, some newspapers would jump the gun as when the *Chicago Daily Tribune* printed the 1948 headline, "DEWEY BEATS TRUMAN," before Truman emerged as the actual winner.

When TV came upon the scene, the desire to be first with the results was very strong, because viewers would be drawn to any station that consistently reported who the winners were before the other stations. On a presidential election night, from about eight o'clock on, all three networks run nonstop election coverage, and it would get pretty dull if all they could report was the numbers of votes, rather than who were the winners and losers. The TV stations use AP reports as well as their own resources in an attempt to predict each winner as soon as possible. In 1964 AP, UPI, CBS, NBC, and ABC set up the News Election Service (NES) to collect vote tabulations from key districts all over the country and supply them on an equal basis to the participating networks.

In a further effort to obtain earlier predictions, the networks began the process of systematic exit polling in 1967. Here, people are interviewed after they vote and are asked why they voted for that candidate and their opinions on the issues in the campaign; the interviewers also try to obtain information about the voter's demographic characteristics. This information is coupled with sophisticated statistical models to produce a prediction of the winner, usually well before actual voting tabulations could. The techniques became good enough that in 1980, the networks announced Reagan as the winner before the polls closed on the West Coast, causing a major furor and leading to an agreement among the networks that they would not call winners in elections in which polls were still open.

This technique became so important to TV that in 1990 the broadcast networks combined their exit polling operations into the Voter Research Service (VRS) and in 1993 merged it with NES to form the Voter News Service (VNS). Its mandate was to conduct exit polling and collect vote returns to provide projections of winners to their owners as early as possible. The owners of VNS were CBS, ABC, NBC, CNN, Fox, and AP. In effect this was an organization set up primarily by television companies for the same reason that newspapers established the AP: to enable the pooling of financial resources and talent to get the facts as quickly as possible.

VNS had been relatively effective. Throughout the 1900s, except for very close races, most election winners were announced on TV shortly after the polls close. This success took a nosedive, however, in the 2000 presidential election as networks first announced Gore as the winner around 7:00 P.M., then characterized the election as too close to call, and finally called Bush the winner a little after 2:00 in the morning, a fact that was actually to take many more days, and the Supreme Court, to establish. These foul-ups arose from problems with VNS's computer program as well as mistakes by voting officials in localities in Florida. In 2002 the vendor installing VNS's new computer system failed to deliver it in time for the elections, which caused the networks to close the company.

Regardless of the 2000 election, TV has made election night a very different experience than it once was. Before the era of mass communications, the election winner might not have been known in some areas of the country for weeks after the election. Even in the days of radio, communication of the results was not the focus of the entire night of broadcasting. Results were reported as they became available, and winners announced when they had clearly won. With TV, election nights, like many other aspects of life, have become sources of entertainment, and in doing so, television has become as much of a "player" as a reporter.

A Dollar Is Worth a Thousand Words

To recapitulate, one of the major influences of TV on the political process has been to raise the bar on how much it costs to run for office. Because TV is unparalleled in its ability to get the candidate in front of potential voters, it is almost imperative for individuals without high name recognition to advertise heavily on TV. This is especially true in the presidential, senatorial, and gubernatorial races, and somewhat less so in congressional races, where the TV market is often much larger than the constituency. The high cost of campaigning has led to the phenomenon of newcomers with very deep pockets being able to win various political offices including senator. It also raises the question of whether in the future individuals without high name recognition will be able to achieve high public office in large television markets unless they are able to put tens of millions of their own money into the effort. Raising the bar has also placed more of a premium on large donors, increasing the relative influence of the haves over the have-nots and the ability of well-financed interest groups to influence (or even control portions of) our political agenda.

Our candidates as well as our elected officials have now become TV "personalities" who must *look* like the office they seek or hold and must be entertaining as well. Possibly most important of all, they must be able to communicate a simple idea in a few seconds to get their desired coverage on the evening news. This combination of physical and oratorical requirements may call for *ubermenchen* within our government, but in reality it produces individuals who are dressed and preened by professionals and rarely say anything publicly that has not been scripted by a staff of professional speech writers and political handlers. Finally, election night has turned into a race for ratings that has left truth and integrity running a poor second. Indeed, television has had a very powerful influence on elections and politics in the United States, and it is difficult to find any positive aspects of that influence in the sea of negative effects.

Notes

1. For more information, see Rich, "Paar to Leno, J.F.K. to J.F.K."
2. Library of Congress, "The Great Debates of Nixon and Kennedy."

Chapter 9

Pressure through Pictures: Governing and TV

To a large extent, the process of governing for a national leader revolves around deciding what actions are "right" for the country to take and then persuading others, politicians and the public at large, to support those decisions. In this regard, TV has assumed an important, and in many ways unanticipated, role in the way in which this country is governed. One very direct and powerful effect is on the range of choices open to our leaders in establishing and pursuing national policy. This range of choices is widened or narrowed depending on the believability and stature of our leaders, the techniques by which they try to mobilize the national will, and the effect on public opinion of viewing events on TV. Although this analysis focuses on the presidency, it is to be expected that many similar influences are at work in governing at the state and local level.

Anyone who heard President Roosevelt tell the nation that December 7, 1941, "is a day that will go down in infamy" or Prime Minister Churchill characterize the efforts of the outnumbered and exhausted RAF pilots fighting the Battle of Britain as "this was their finest hour" will not forget the drama and sheer power of those historic moments. Radio, which brought those words to many millions of people simultaneously, was certainly an important asset in enabling national leaders to rally the populace toward an urgent national goal. The force of their words broadcast live to a large portion of their constituents has been a major tool of leaders, both good and bad (Hitler comes to mind), to mold public opinion and steer the country's resources in the directions they believed to be best. Whether it was Roosevelt in a wheelchair, a short obese Churchill, or an almost comical looking Hitler, people could be swayed by the power of what these leaders had to say, rather than how they looked saying it. Indeed, historically, gaining control of the national radio system (and now the television system) has been well recognized as one of the first and primary objectives of any group initiating a coup d'état.

The Television Persona

Television brought another dimension into play: the ability to see as well as hear the speaker. Even before the advent of television it was common knowledge in the motion picture business that the camera "loved" some individuals and "hated" others. This love/hate relationship has carried over to the TV camera as well. Richard Nixon was well aware of how his appearance on camera in his first debate with John Kennedy may have cost him a large number of votes in the 1960 election. Eight years later, when Nixon ran against Hubert Humphrey, wasn't his appearance on *Laugh In* to deliver the famous "sock it to me" line an attempt to change his image? Some political pundits even believe that his brief appearance on the variety show made Nixon sufficiently down to earth so as to tip the scales in the public's mind and make him the winner in another very close election.

When Nixon did become president, he continued to have problems with his TV persona. Comedians universally portrayed President Nixon as shifty-eyed and sneaky, certainly not someone in whom you could put your faith and trust. It did not matter how accurate these characterizations were; the essence of comedy is to capture a subject's distinctive features and overplay them to the point where they are funny. In effect, the comedians lampooned what the TV camera actually showed, and that visage certainly did not make it any easier for President Nixon to govern.

The president's power is influenced by yet another aspect of TV, the tendency for the late-night talk shows to lampoon that day's presidential comments or actions. Since the Nixon presidency, it has become almost a nightly occurrence for the opening monologues of these late-night shows to include a series of jokes on the current president. *Saturday Night Live* has institutionalized impersonations of the president, none of which show the officeholder in a positive light. For many people, Dana Carvey imitating George H.W. Bush is more of a reality than the real former president. Such a constant barrage of lampooning cannot but lower the stature of the president and the office in the eyes of a segment of the public. It raises the question of what effects, if any, that lowered stature has on the ability of our leaders to govern.

Of course, lampooning a leader, whether he or she is prime minister or president, is not new. Political cartooning has a long history, certainly dating from before the United States gained its independence from England. Probably the most well-known political cartoons in America were those done by Thomas Nast in the 1870s attacking Boss Tweed and his Tammany Hall organization that controlled New York City politics. The power of the picture over the word is suggested by Jim Zwick, who quotes Tweed as saying: "Stop them damned pictures. I don't care what the papers write about me. My constituents can't read. But, damn it, they can see pictures." Thus, long before TV was developed, Tweed recognized that the picture was much more powerful than words. The frequent repetitions of caricatures on TV and the larger audience seeing those caricatures make TV's version of a political cartoon that much more powerful.

Lampooning is one of the characteristics of TV that political leaders must learn to handle. One of the ways to use television to project the "right" persona rather than that portrayed by the lampooners is to place the leader in the types of situations and saying the type of things that one wishes to have identified with him or her. Thus, President George W. Bush lands a military aircraft on a carrier with the TV cameras present not for the sake of expedient transportation, but to draw a clear demarcation between his "manly" heroic type and the anti-military Democrats, a theme that he later reinforced in various speeches. Of course the "Mission Accomplished" banner ultimately came back to haunt Bush as the Iraq War dragged on, but the initial impact of the scene was very positive. Contrast this effective use of media with President Clinton telling an interviewer that he "did not have sex with that girl"; this news clip was played literally thousands of times after the truth of his affair with Monica Lewinsky came out.

Finally, there is the issue of how well the president or any other elected official can communicate on TV. Al Gore's senior thesis at Harvard dealt with "The Impact of Television on the Conduct of the Presidency, 1947–1969." According to Peter Marks of the *New York Times*, the thesis examined, among other issues, the impact of TV on the presidential news conference. Gore wrote:

> Before the advent of television, the president was much less guarded in his statements. He had the prerogative of giving background and going off the record completely. If he made a mistake, he could correct it before it got into print... Because there is no longer a margin for error, the president is forced to view the conference much more

seriously, and...prepare for 10 times as many questions as are asked.... The result of this for the president is that he is able to get away with pre-polished answers lacking any depth.

In addition, the many news programs that will cover the press conference later that evening and the next morning will show no more than a few seconds of what is actually said. Thus, the president is strongly motivated to speak in slogans that can readily be picked up as sound bites on these programs, rather than in more accurate and more complex answers that cannot be boiled down to fifteen seconds in length. In his analysis, Gore clearly presaged what has happened not only to presidential news conferences but also to the presidential debates, in which canned speeches are substituted for responses to questions.

Live History on TV

Another major effect on the ability of our leaders to govern has been TV's evolving sophistication in visually portraying live events, history in the making. One of the most significant pieces of on-the-scene reportage occurred in the early 1960s when the U.S. Ambassador to the United Nations, Adlai Stevenson, confronted Ambassador Zorin of Russia with film footage of nuclear launching sites being prepared in Cuba. The drama of the pictures themselves and this exchange before an audience of many millions could not have been staged to provide any greater impact if it were done on a Hollywood sound stage with all the techniques available to the professional illusionists:

> Do you, Ambassador Zorin, deny that the U.S.S.R. has placed, and is placing, medium- and intermediate-range missiles and sites in Cuba? Yes or no—don't wait for the translation—yes or no.

This event, coupled with President Kennedy's appearance on television to announce that we were facing a grave threat, allowed him to pursue a blockade of Cuba with total public support, even though it was arguably an act of war and certainly an act of nuclear brinkmanship. Whether Kennedy would have gotten such strong support to risk a nuclear war with Russia without the dramatic demonstration of the evidence on TV can well be questioned.

Indeed, as the last attempt to gain international support for the invasion of Iraq, President George W. Bush had Secretary of State Colin Powell address the UN and, through television, the American public, displaying pictorial evidence of Iraq's weapons of mass destruction (WMDs). Of course, we later learned that, in fact, the "evidence" was not valid and the case for WMDs was dubious at best. Despite this, Colin Powell's presentation carried the day, and the United States invaded Iraq, with a large majority of the American population supporting President Bush's decision.

At the time of Powell's presentation many newspapers made comparisons between his speech and Stevenson's, assuming correctly that the segment of the population that was old enough to remember the Cuban missile crisis would clearly remember Stevenson's performance on TV. These articles in 2003 referring to an incident in 1962 are a tribute to the power of television to make an impression on its audience. In the case of Iraq, the power of the medium was sufficient to cause the majority of the population to accept a series of conclusions that were, in retrospect, basically unjustified.

Secretary of State James Baker, who served under the first George Bush, in his book *The Politics of Diplomacy*, points out numerous instances where TV either limited or expanded President Bush's options for conducting international diplomacy. Two examples demonstrate these possibilities. On the issue of how TV limits a president's options, Baker discusses the effect of the world watching the Chinese tanks attacking the demonstrators in Tiananmen Square in 1989. As he saw it, "The terrible tragedy of Tiananmen was a classic demonstration of a powerful new phenomenon: the ability of the global communications revolution to drive policy." Although the Cultural Revolution had been at least as bloody, it had occurred when China was generally closed to foreign TV cameras, and certainly to any filming of events that showed the governing regime in an unfavorable light. Baker states that even American diplomats were largely unaware of the extent of the repression during that era, but at Tiananmen Square it was there for all to see: "The brutality of the regime was undeniable. There was no question that a stern response was essential." Thus, in this case as in others, the fact and drama of the event, particularly when recorded and repeated endlessly on television, to a large extent dictated the nature of the response.

But is it always a positive influence to put the president into a position where a stern response is essential? Our relationships with the countries around the world are complex, and we do not always do things that large parts of our population think are "right." The more that such incidents as Tiananmen Square or the dragging of the bodies of U.S. servicemen through the streets of Somalia put pressure on the president for immediate, overt reaction, the less he has the option of using quiet diplomacy, which can often accomplish our desired ends, perhaps even more effectively.

In contrast, the widespread and frequent airing of key events can also give the president the ability to mobilize the resources of the country quickly and with little resistance. This was the case with the footage on 9/11 and its influence on George W. Bush's decision to attack Afghanistan, home to Osama bin Laden and many members of Al-Qaeda. Objectively, our country was in no more danger from Al-Qaeda on September 12th than it was on September 10th. Fundamentalist Islamic terrorists, most of whom had some loose relationship to the Al-Qaeda network, had clearly demonstrated that they were determined to do harm to the United States by attacking the World Trade Center in 1993, our embassies in Kenya and Tanzania in 1998, and the *U.S.S. Cole* in 2000. But President Bush might have faced very considerable opposition if he announced on September 10th that we were going to war with Afghanistan because Osama bin Laden was headquartered there. Yet, he faced almost no opposition to this decision after September 11th.

Would the country have been as outraged without seeing the television pictures over and over again for literally weeks on end? Or without that repetition, would there have been some sense of relief in other parts of the country that the attack didn't happen there, along with a diminution of active anger over time? Given our response to Pearl Harbor, one would assume that the mere fact of being attacked would strengthen our resolve to go to war, but in this case, we were invading a nation because we were attacked by a relatively small group of people who lived there. Most likely, President Bush would have been able to go to war with Congressional backing whether or not the horror of September 11th was reinforced by repetition on TV, but television made that step much easier.

The role of television continues to be an important one in what President George W. Bush has called the War on Terror. Osama bin Laden and the insurgents within Iraq have been successful in getting their messages out to the entire world by sending TV tapes to the Al Jazeera television station in Qatar. Once aired by Al Jazeera, portions of the broadcasts are repeated frequently by television stations in almost every country in the world. Very often, the insurgents' messages show one or more hostages, surrounded by their captors, pleading for their home country to do as the captors demand in order to save their lives. Although some countries or companies have made accommodations demanded by the terrorists, as far as we know, the U.S. government has not engaged in any type of negotiation based on such demands. Nevertheless, such messages represent the direct use of TV to put pressure on foreign governments to act in certain ways.

Another major impact on U.S. policy has resulted from the release of photographs of the mistreatment of detainees in Abu Ghraib prison in

Iraq. These photos were shown repeatedly on TV and raised an uproar about our treatment of prisoners, our command structure in military prisons, and whether we have violated the Geneva Convention. To date some of the prison guards have been tried and convicted, but as of this writing the issues of problems up the chain of command and the relationship of the CIA to the Army command structure have not been resolved. Given the existence of the photos, Abu Ghraib would eventually have become a scandal, but with the omnipresence of TV it became an immediate issue of national concern and forced the government to take quick action.

Finally, Osama bin Laden released a tape a few days before the 2004 U.S. presidential election. In the tape he spoke about how he would bring America down economically and how it was unable to effectively combat his form of terrorism. Some argue about which candidate the tape was designed to help or hurt, but there is no disagreement that its worldwide broadcast was a powerful recruiting tool for Al-Qaeda that would exacerbate the problems of the next president, whoever he would be.

In a very different arena, Howard Baker's book describes an incident where the existence of television gave a U.S. president an alternative option. This incident occurred in 1991 during the period in which Russia was moving from communism to democracy. While Gorbachev was on vacation, Russian Vice President Yanayev took over as president and instigated a move by a State Emergency Committee popularly referred to as the "Gang of Eight" to return Russia to a communist form of government. In a televised press conference President George H. W. Bush responded to this action by saying, "The unconstitutional seizure of power is an affront to the goals and aspirations that the Soviet peoples have been nurturing over the past years." Then he announced, as one columnist put it, "the electrifying news" that he had just spoken to Boris Yeltsin and had "assured Mr. Yeltsin of continued U.S. support for his goal of the restoration of Mr. Gorbachev as the constitutionally chosen leader." The president had used the fastest source available for getting a message to Moscow: CNN. Thus, although we hear much about back-channel communications between diplomats, this case illustrates that TV has provided a new and very rapid front channel for the conduct of national policy and international relations.

Metamorphosis of TV Coverage

Though war coverage and the events leading up to war are the most dramatic examples of the evolution of TV's role, there are other events whose depictions on television have either spurred presidents to act or narrowed their choices for action. The civil rights movement received widespread public support when TV news aired footage of Birmingham Chief of Police Bull Connor ordering his men to break up a peaceful freedom march with fire hoses or of children entering Little Rock High School under protection of the National Guard. Public airing of film showing how the policy of apartheid was being carried out in South Africa made it almost impossible for the United States to keep doing business with that government. However, despite these examples, the most dramatic impact of television upon governmental decisions was first seen with the war in Vietnam and still tends to be related to war.

In the early days of television, people schooled in radio ran the new medium, and the structure of programs was much like it had been for radio. This was true not only for sitcoms and variety shows but also for news programs. Take, for example, an edition of the *Camel News Caravan* with John Cameron Swayze, broadcast in 1950. This was a fifteen-minute program aired in the early evening and was the only news broadcast on that network in that time period. The Korean War was in progress at that time, and it was the lead story. Most significantly, a map was shown but no films from the battlefield were aired. The closest the show came to depicting battle conditions were interviews with wounded soldiers back in Philadelphia. A segment of equal length was devoted to films of a kilted Scottish unit—the "Ladies from Hell"—marching off the boat into service in Korea, to the background of stirring martial music. These interviews and parades had a minimal visual impact.

By the time we were involved in Vietnam in a major way, TV news coverage had advanced well beyond what we had seen in 1950. Although there was usually a few day's lag between the filming and its presentation on network television, the footage was often taken directly from the war zones. Sometimes it showed interviews with soldiers who had been in combat, photos of wounded and dead soldiers, and even firefights. The desire to air action footage had its own cost, with nine network employees killed and many others wounded in covering the war. Many of these latter stories also became part of the evening new coverage.

The fact that the reportage was more timely and realistic during the Vietnam War not only marked an advanced use of the TV medium but also had direct effects upon our leadership. As the public saw footage of futile sorties and wounded soldiers displayed side by side with demonstrations against the war, it became increasingly more difficult to maintain public support for our presence in Vietnam. The options for pursuing the war narrowed so much that two presidents lied to the public in order to pursue the course they felt was correct—Lyndon Johnson when he said that our ship had been fired upon in the Gulf of Tonkin and Richard Nixon when he said we had not sent troops into Laos. Would these lies have been necessary, and would still more aggressive actions have been taken, if the public had not been barraged with a daily dose of pictures from the front and demonstrations at home? Possibly yes, but TV clearly brought a new dimension to the complex process of governing and proscribed the range of actions the Commander-in-Chief had open to him.

Possibly the most direct effect of television on a president occurred when news anchor Walter Cronkite, in a special report on the 1968 Tet Offensive, reported that in his opinion the war was unwinnable and that the government would have to find a way out. Daniel Hallin, a professor at the University of California, reports in "Viet Nam on Television" that

> Some of Lyndon Johnson's aides have recalled that the president watched the broadcast and declared that he knew at that moment he would have to change course. A month later Johnson declined to run for reelection, and announced that he was seeking a way out of the war; David Halberstam has written that "it was the first time in American history a war had been declared over by an anchorman."

This interaction between TV coverage and national policy did not end with the ending of the Vietnam War. But our leadership, aware of television's influence, began to manage TV coverage by limiting the opportunities for TV stations to obtain the type of direct action pictures they did in Vietnam. President Ronald Reagan, who as an actor had understood well the power of the motion picture camera, did not allow reporters and cameras into the battle zone when we invaded Grenada until the fighting was completed. Stephen Zunes of the University of San Francisco wrote a history of that war that builds a detailed case that the government lied to the American people about many of the facts advanced for going to war; thus it presents a strong motive for Reagan's decision to prohibit reporters and TV cameras from getting too close to the students we were there to protect (90 percent of whom did not wish to leave) or to the administrators of the medical school those students were attending. The change in strategy may have had more to do with hiding facts than it did with the safety of the reporters. Because the war was over in a few days and the interviews with the smiling students on their return made for good photo opportunities, there was little in-depth investigation into the validity of the war.

The TV coverage of the first Gulf War in 1991 illustrates well its management by the military and the government. Initially, while missiles were being fired on Baghdad, the American public had direct and immediate access to the story. CNN's reporters gave us vivid descriptions of what was happening in Baghdad, and we could see for ourselves the tracer bullets attempting to bring down the missiles and the explosions as each one reached its target. However, the lessons of how powerfully TV coverage could limit leaders' freedom of action had, by this time, been sufficiently ingrained. Therefore, when it came time for a land battle, military officials, citing the possibility of large numbers of friendly casualties, no longer allowed the news cameras free rein to record the battle from the front lines as they had in Vietnam. For the most part, a small pool of reporters was chosen to represent the entire press corps, and even the selected pool had limited exposure to battlefront conditions. Most of the film shown on TV was from the gun cameras of warplanes, which were chosen and supplied by the armed services, and invariably showed direct hits on the targets involved.

Interestingly, by the time of the second war with Iraq, the government reversed its position significantly and "embedded" reporters and cameras with front-line units from which they were free to broadcast via satellite what they saw and heard. This approach gave the world a front row seat on just what was happening in many sectors of the fighting day by day, even including a behind-the-lines rescue of PFC Jessica Lynch from an Iraqi hospital that rivaled the best action scene produced by the Hollywood studios.

However, while embedding newsmen with front-line units to record actual battle scenes, authorities allowed no footage to be taken of the hundreds of coffins containing the bodies of our soldiers and marines who had made the supreme sacrifice. In fact, when one government contractor took such photos, he was fired. Thus, the government's sophistication in the use of the visual media continues to develop, and but for a free press willing to be persistent in its pursuit of the truth, television might well be a major step toward achieving the type of mind control depicted in *Animal Farm* or *1984*.

TV as Impetus to Government Action

Although the military may be able to restrict the access of TV cameras under battlefield conditions, it is much more difficult for it to implement such restrictions in situations that may, at some time in the future, involve us in military actions. Thus, as night after night, every national news program showed pictures of children starving in Somalia because of the actions of a distant and unfamiliar warlord, President Clinton and his advisors felt a tremendous sense of pressure to do something about the situation, and this resulted in our use of troops in an area that had little strategic value. Of course our involvement was initially only a mission to bring food to the hungry until next we saw our dead soldiers being dragged through the streets after an unsuccessful raid to capture that warlord. At that point the pressure on our leaders became just the opposite, and our troops were quickly brought home. In this entire affair, it seemed clear that national policy being made in the White House was not based on some coherent sense of what the role of the United States was in the post-cold war world, but indirectly by the news directors of the networks, all-news channels, and local TV stations throughout the country in their choice of what pictures to air and how often to air them.

The influence of continual TV coverage on encouraging action by our government is probably just as valid for our involvement in Kosovo as it was for our entry into Somalia. The nightly pictures of rape and murder overrode the administration's desire to stay out of the situation as the previous administration had. However, it was clear that going into Kosovo and fighting a land war would result in heavy casualties. It was just as clear that viewing these casualties as a steady TV diet would quickly change "the story" and would exert great pressure on President Clinton to pull our military out of the fray. Therefore, we took a middle course of using air attacks only, which many military leaders believed would prove to be futile. Fortunately for the administration, they were wrong, and our objectives were accomplished with almost no casualties. But the point is not what actions the United States took, but *why it took them*: the TV story was the reality to which our government was forced to react. This scenario is almost frightening when one considers that the reality that TV creates is dependent on directors and producers who choose the two or three minutes of today's war that we will see and hear largely on the basis of what will earn the highest ratings. This control has ominous implications for the future as TV outlets are constantly being consolidated in fewer and more powerful hands. We may be coming to the point where the chairman of a major media company like Fox or Time Warner may have more to say about our participation in yet another trouble spot in the world than our president, cabinet, and national security advisors. This is not a new phenomenon, insofar as William Randolph

Hearst, with his newspaper empire, put a great deal of pressure on President McKinley to go to war in 1898 with Spain over Cuba. With the power of television, however, the pressure is magnified many times over.

The politically liberating effect of television also became very obvious after the terrorist attacks on the World Trade Center in New York and on the Pentagon in Virginia. These were events of such overwhelming impact and importance that the networks had no choice but to give them 24/7 coverage. It was also an event that combined the power of CNN's early coverage of the Gulf War from Baghdad and the day-to-day coverage from the rice fields of Vietnam. Will anyone ever forget the picture of the second plane making a turn to crash into the second tower on live TV or the pictures of the rescue workers picking their way into a pile of rubble ten stories high? These are images that will live in our memories until our dying days, and it is these images that enabled the president to gain immediate bipartisan support for almost any response to these horrific acts. Forgotten was any argument of budget shortfalls or limitations on the powers of the president to declare war. With the horror of the terrorist actions for us to see, the president's options were greatly expanded.

What Hath TV Wrought

The influence of television has been a two-edged sword with which our elected leaders must cope. On the one hand television makes it easier for a leader, particularly a president, to communicate directly with the people, and convey an idea around which he wishes to mobilize them. When President George W. Bush appeared on television and announced a war on terrorism, he received overwhelming support resulting in approval ratings far higher than enjoyed by most presidents. This, in turn, resulted in his ability to easily push many programs quickly through Congress, including a Homeland Defense Agency, which might otherwise have met strong opposition.

On the other hand, television's ability to display scenes of American soldiers being killed on foreign soil strongly limits the president's ability to commit our forces to battle. Although our military and governmental leaders have been skilled at adapting to TV by either limiting (Grenada) or facilitating (Iraq) access to the battlefield, that is not always possible (Somalia). Therefore, at the very least, TV must be reckoned with as a force in military strategy and tactics as well as in national policy itself.

Pressure through Pictures: Governing and TV

It is clear from even this brief review of issues and incidents that the ability of television to record what is happening while it is happening has had a very significant impact on how our leaders govern. From how they are elected and how they are able to mobilize the citizenry toward certain national objectives to what constraints are placed on their freedom to act, the presence of television has had an important and occasionally decisive influence on what actions our leaders take or don't take.

Chapter 10

Bleeding Leads: News Dissemination

For most of humankind's time on earth, news, the reporting of current events and ideas, was passed on by word of mouth. Travelers were the source of news from outside the immediate area, and this method of news dissemination was improved on modestly by the introduction of town criers who would "broadcast" the news on relatively regular schedules. The invention of the printing press had an enormous effect upon the ability to pass on the news, as materials could be written and distributed widely either free or for profit. In the United States, both newspapers and political pamphlets had been well-developed sources of news by the time of the American Revolution. Indeed, such writings as Thomas Paine's pamphlet *Rights of Man* are still studied in some elementary and secondary schools. As the political process heated up before and then after the Revolutionary War, the newspapers, which were mainly party organs, took strong and opposing positions on the issues of how our country was to evolve; sometimes they played fast and loose with the truth. Since then, U.S. newspapers have evolved in two ways. Their editorial pages are often strongly partisan and politically oriented, but for the actual news presentation there has grown a tradition of seeking objectivity and "getting the story right."

The Evolution of News Delivery

Since colonial times the United States has had a thriving newspaper industry; until recently residents in most cities and even many small

95

towns had two or more papers from which to choose. These papers were independently owned, and undoubtedly their owners' opinions on local issues were reflected in their pages. For instance, if the local publisher also owned the town's mill, the paper was not likely to push a story about overcharging for milling grain. However, as the number of newspapers grew, it became more important to get the story right, for a paper that often printed actual falsehoods or failed to report pressing news would not be able to survive very long with the facts readily available in other local or regional papers.

Yet, a subtle form of bias always exists in the selection and organization of stories to be printed; that is, what the newspaper chooses to print is, by definition, news. Anthony Marro in the *Columbia Journalism Review* deals with this issue when he writes,

> It's a given that most news stories are incomplete, that many lack proper context, and that much misinformation gets passed along to the public. But the theory of a free press isn't that any one story will ever get to the real truth of an issue, no matter at what length it's written or how well it is done. Rather, it's that if enough people examine something from enough different perspectives over a long enough period of time, something approaching truth will emerge.... People get enough information over time that they can make up their minds whether they'd prefer to see dams built or snail darters live.

This argument presupposes that the "story" will be given considerable exposure and be examined in detail from a number of perspectives. It also assumes that people will actually read the newspapers that supply this type of in-depth analysis, a situation that, as we will see, has been changed considerably by the growth of television newscasting.

Radio did provide a source of competition for newspapers, but for the most part the two coexisted with relatively little influence upon one another. Papers came first thing in the morning, and that's where the news came from. During the day there might be short news spots on radio, and on the way home from work dad got the afternoon paper to read after dinner. During the evening, there were also a few radio news commentators who provided news and observations.

In contrast, there are now some radio news-only stations that repeat the news cycle about every half-hour; it changes only when new details about a story or an entirely new story emerges. Thus, for the most part these stations present the same news, including sports, weather, traffic, maybe farm prices (depending upon location), other business news, and headline stories, throughout the day. Add in commercials and it is obvious that the stories are not dealt with in any depth.

One additional news-related show that has become very popular on radio is the call-in talk show, which in many ways parallels the editorial section of a newspaper. The host usually has a clear political bias that is shared by most of his or her callers. The callers are most often laypeople who have very strong opinions about these subjects. These shows are very poor sources of information as their hosts routinely twist facts to justify their preconceived positions.

Changes in the Television Age

Either parallel with, or as a result of, the growth of television, the delivery of news has been modified extensively. For one, according to the Newspaper Association of America, the number of daily newspapers has decreased from 1,772 in 1950 to 1,480 in 2000, with daily readership declining from 80.8 percent of the adult population in 1964 to 58.3 percent in 1997. The decline of newspapers has been much more precipitous in the large cities, with the decrease in the number of papers being masked by the growth of local suburban papers. These latter papers, however, tend not to cover any national or international news. In a study reported by Scott Althaus on where people get their news in times of crisis, for the first time more people cited cable TV than newspapers in January 2002, after the events of 9/11.

More important, the readers of newspapers are significantly older than the general population. A recent study reported by Joe Strupp in *Editor & Publisher* indicated that 60 percent of regular readers are forty-five years or older as compared with their representation in the general population of 35 percent, and only 20 percent are between eighteen and thirty-four though they make up 30 percent of the population. In addition, younger readers may not necessarily read newspapers for their news content. A Gannett poll showed that 72 percent of those between eighteen and twenty-four said they read the classified ads at least once in the past week and as such may consider themselves regular newspaper readers when questioned by pollsters. Because individuals in the younger age groups also tend to be avid television watchers, it is likely that they now get their news primarily from television.

Concurrent with the shrinkage of newspapers and readership, there has also been a trend for the ownership of multiple newspapers and/or radio stations to be consolidated under a single individual or corporation.

As a result, there is less diversity of opinion in editorializing and in the choice of stories featured on both media.

Television has followed a somewhat different path. News presentation in the early days of television was limited to the three networks and local unaffiliated stations because there were no cable stations. Other than news-oriented specials, the nightly news programs like that of NBC's John Cameron Swayze were originally limited to fifteen minutes in the evening. This can be contrasted with today's menu of ninety minutes of evening news on network affiliates, at least the same amount of time devoted to news on local independent channels, Sunday morning network news shows (e.g., *Meet the Press* or *Face the Nation*), local news-only channels much like the news-only radio stations, and national news-only TV cable channels (CNN, Fox, MSNBC, CNBC, and C-SPAN). With such an array of programs, one would think that the amount of detail the average person gets about current stories is far beyond what he or she got in 1950. However, for a number of reasons, this is probably not the case.

For one, television is a visual medium, and all presentations, whether pure entertainment or factual news items, are presented visually if at all possible. This affects the choice of stories and how they are treated. A story of an arrest with a "perp walk" is likely to get more exposure than an arrest with no visual material. The mother of all visual stories was 9/11 in which the original footage was repeated endlessly for many days, even though almost everyone in the country had seen the films by the first evening. But because of the spectacular visual impact, the repetition continued until the scene had become so disturbing to so many people that their tendency to turn off the television led stations to stop the constant display. The importance of the visual component of a story has actually narrowed the range of stories that are shown. The guiding philosophy seems to be "If it bleeds, it leads."

Another influence on the depth of stories is the rhythm of TV time and the amount of airtime that can be devoted to any one story. Just as with radio, TV news programs deal with many routine subjects (i.e., sports, weather, stock market, traffic, etc.) in addition to pure newsworthy events. With commercials taking up close to ten minutes of every half-hour, this leaves relatively little time for each of the approximately fifteen stories touched upon in a typical local half-hour TV news program. Typically stories are given between thirty seconds and two-and-a-half minutes, and their average length is somewhere near one minute.

In contrast, a typical newspaper covers well more than fifteen stories. In some of the larger papers there might be that many stories in the sports section alone. For example, in the *New York Times* issue of

Bleeding Leads: News Dissemination

Monday, January 14, 2002, there were twenty-two stories in the sports section, as well as the standings in all the leagues. Many of these stories were of sufficient length that it would take most people at least two minutes to read them fully. This was just the sports section, which, on this day, represented less than one-fifth of the paper.

Clearly TV cannot cover news in this depth within its thirty-minute format. As a result, in TV news programs there is much more stringent selectivity in what stories are covered at all, and then there is even more selectivity in what is covered within the story, a state of affairs that has led to the art of the sound bite discussed earlier. With the steady increases in time allotted to commercials, even the sound bites for a political candidate have shrunk from a little under thirty seconds in the days of Walter Cronkite to under ten seconds in recent times. Given all this selectivity, TV news has become more of an editorial reflecting a reporter's or news editor's views of what is important than actual in-depth coverage of the news.

Even the cable news networks, which provide endless hours of "news," are as much geared toward entertainment as to in-depth reporting. For one, each story needs pictorial action to accompany it, and there is a tendency to repeat the same film clips, with the same reporter on location many, many times during the day, rather than to expand upon the story with relatively duller facts and analyses unaccompanied by visual imagery. Another technique is to pit "talking heads" against one another in a battle of who can paint the story most convincingly for the audience. However, the "facts" that each presents usually concern their own case and rarely answer the other's arguments, so that the viewer is often left to wonder whether the adversaries are talking about the same story. Rarely is the viewer exposed to the myriad of facts and follow-up analysis that good newspaper coverage of a story will provide. Perhaps C-SPAN and Court TV come closest to providing news in-depth, as these channels will cover an entire press conference or trial. But the total audience of these channels is minute, even smaller than that for the twenty-four-hour news channels. According to Journalism.org, in the months before 9/11 the combined audience of the CNN, Fox, and MSNBC news channels was less than 0.5 percent of adults in America. After 9/11, the audience spiked to more than 1 percent, but settled down to about 0.75 percent by January 2002.

Although television provides less in-depth coverage of stories, its twenty-four-hour presence does allow it to customarily scoop newspapers on any breaking story. Before the advent of television, when a really big story broke, newspapers might come out with a special edition to get the news in the hands of the reading public as quickly as possible. Now, with television on the story within minutes it would be futile for newspapers to try to compete on speed. Although a few big city papers do provide the in-depth coverage missing on television, there is a growing tendency for papers such as *USA Today* to attract readers with feature-type material and the generous use of color, thus, in a way, coming closer to what the audience gets from the TV medium. But regardless of how fully newspapers cover a story, if we combine the fact that fewer people read fewer newspapers with the fact that television provides superficial coverage, it appears that the population, especially the younger population, knows less about what is going on in the world around them than their predecessors. This, in an era during which the United States has a more central role in the world than it ever had before, does not bode well for participatory democracy.

News or Entertainment?

Former Secretary of State James Baker's book *The Politics of Diplomacy* describes an incident that as much as any other demonstrates the impact of television news coverage. Before the 1991 Gulf War, Baker and his staff visited Russia to ensure their cooperation. He describes an incident involving the Russian diplomats and members of his staff in the following way:

> Meanwhile, Tarasenko had picked up his American counterparts and chauffeured them to the Foreign Ministry for consultations. "Let's find out the latest information," he suggested. Ross assumed he would summon a subordinate for an intelligence briefing. Instead, he turned on CNN.

When powerful nations with all their resources for intelligence turn to television news for the best information, the industry can well be proud of what it has created. This incident, along with many others described in this book, demonstrates that TV has had numerous finest hours during which the people of the world watch TV as observers of history in the making.

But regrettably, most TV news coverage does not rise to these heights. We have already mentioned that much news is now presented with a sharp eye toward its entertainment value. Traditionally in television, there was a strong separation between those responsible for entertainment and those responsible for the news. News was thought of more as a service and public obligation than as a way to generate profits. After all, weren't the stations given licenses to broadcast as a way to serve the public interest? This is one reason why there was traditionally a "Chinese Wall" between the news department and marketing so that the interests of advertisers did not exert undue influence on the choice of stories or their presentation.

However, as we elaborate below, all the major TV networks have become part of larger companies. The primary purpose of these companies is to serve their stockholders by producing the consistently rising quarterly sales and profit targets demanded by Wall Street. Serving the public good may be found somewhere in their corporate credos, but it would normally be translated into such actions as avoiding unsafe products and would only be one of a number of business-oriented objectives. Given the ultimate objectives of the corporate officers who are senior to the network executives, it was inevitable that those whose fortunes (and we use that word literally) depended upon meeting the financial targets began to treat TV news the same as any other aspect of the business. Thus, executives looked toward the entertainment value of news as a way to bring in higher advertising revenues and higher profits.

In addition, the cable news channels and the numerous Internet sources that many people monitor daily almost always scoop the network evening news shows on any story that breaks during the day. This is another factor that causes network news producers to look for feature stories that have high entertainment value to draw an audience for the evening news programs.

As a result, the distinction between news and entertainment has become somewhat blurred over the years. Programs like *Entertainment Tonight* or *Inside Edition* cover entertainment subjects and are more like newspaper gossip columns than front pages. There are also news shows in prime time, such as *Dateline, 60 Minutes, 20/20,* or *48 Hours,* that, because their production costs are lower than dramas or sitcoms, are popular with network executives. Although these shows often follow a hard news story in depth, they also often give in-depth coverage to human-interest stories, rather than the top stories of the day. But even these shows, which are generally considered to be good journalism, are not always allowed to pursue stories that might produce some negative fallout for their owners. Finally, there is a tendency to look for the human-interest aspect of hard news stories in interviews with famous people conducted by TV personalities, such as Barbara Walters, Jane Pauley, or the network anchors.

Earlier, we described radio call-in shows that represent a type of editorializing on the news, which is a very dramatic departure from traditional middle-of-the-road news coverage. Rupert Murdoch, seeing the huge audiences attracted by Rush Limbaugh on radio, decided to capitalize on this type of editorial programming by establishing Fox News Network in 1996. Headed by a veteran of partisan political warfare, Roger Ailes, the station signed on a lineup of show hosts including Bill O'Reilly, Sean Hannity, and Newt Gingrich, all of whom frequently equated the words "Democrat" or "liberal" with traitorous, unpatriotic, and craven. Under the banners of "fair and balanced" and "we report, you decide," the main format of most shows is a type of attack journalism that blasts away at the mainstream press, which is accused of having a liberal bias, and at anyone in or associated with the Democratic party. Although the body of research on media bias tends to yield inconsistent results, the accusation trumpeted repeatedly by Fox News, like many others, has taken on a life of its own and is probably believed by a majority of Americans. As on radio, this attack format, which is more entertainment than true news reportage, has been highly successful in drawing a loyal audience, quickly propelling Fox News to the top spot among the three news channels. It has been so successful that MSNBC felt it necessary to follow suit by putting former Republican Congressman Joe Scarborough on the air in the same type of attack format to win back some market share.

Although a dedicated audience enjoys these shows, they are certainly not helping create a more informed America. As indicated in a poll by the Program on International Policy (PIPA) at the University of Maryland and Knowledge Networks, "the frequency of American's misperceptions varies significantly depending on their source of news." A total of 48% of those surveyed "incorrectly believed that evidence of links between Iraq and Al-Qaeda have been found, 22% that weapons of mass destruction have been found in Iraq, and 25% that world public opinion favored going to war with Iraq." However, the frequency of these misperceptions varied dramatically depending upon where people reported getting their news. Among those reporting Fox as their primary news source, 80% had one or more misperceptions, contrasted with 55% reporting NBC or CNN, 47% reporting print sources, and only 23% reporting NPR/PBS. The differences did not merely reflect whether respondents indicated a likelihood of voting for Bush or the Democratic nominee in the coming election, but more accurately suggested that the source of the news is more important to the individual's knowledge than his or her political attitudes. Clearly, where we get our news from has a very significant impact on our knowledge of the facts.

It has always been the objective of news reporting to make its audience more knowledgeable. In this case it appears that television news delivery has begun to do just the opposite. Worse, although rational decision-making requires obtaining all the facts and making a judgment on them, a Pew research study conducted in 2004[1] suggests that, more than ever before, people are choosing to watch only news channels that agree with their own political opinions and they distrust what they hear on the other channels.

When the trend toward attack journalism is coupled with the trend to present news from the standpoint of its entertainment value, it seems clear that most Americans are getting less in-depth hard news, free of the provider's own viewpoint, than they did before the advent of television.

TV Ownership

The consolidation of TV station ownership and control is also having an impact upon what and how news is delivered. According to the media watchdog organization, Fairness and Accuracy in Reporting, although the number of TV stations has increased substantially between 1975 and 2000 from 952 to 1,678, the number of station owners actually decreased from 543 to 360. Since the 1980s, there has also been an avalanche of consolidation of TV and other media outlets and the tying of TV networks to many other businesses through their acquisition by very large, diversified corporations. This tying of the interests of those responsible for news delivery to the very different interests of other businesses presents an obvious potential for conflict. This section traces some of the corporate relationships of the major networks to businesses within and outside TV. We deliberately write "some," because a complete listing of every subsidiary and business under a corporate umbrella would run quite a few tedious pages.

NBC is part of General Electric, a large conglomerate that manufactures a wide range of products including military and civilian aircraft engines, medical technologies, electrical and electronic equipment, train engines, consumer appliances, and turbines for nuclear plants. GE is also a major participant in the financial industry, with insurance, commercial finance, consumer finance, and other subsidiary businesses. In the spring of 2004, NBC accounted for only 5 percent of GE's total revenues, but 10 percent of its operating profits.

ABC's corporate owner is the Walt Disney Company through its acquisition by Capital Cities Communications (ABC's corporate parent at that time) in 1996. Before the acquisition, the Walt Disney Company encompassed film studios, record companies, printing companies, magazines, theme parks, and a National Hockey League franchise (Mighty Ducks). The Capital Cities acquisition added a host of ABC affiliates, as well as ten TV stations and twenty-one radio stations. Disney also owns the cable-TV Disney Channel, 80 percent of various ESPN channels, and 50 percent or less of various other cable channels including E!, Lifetime, and A&E.

CBS began as a radio network in 1927, merged with Westinghouse Electric Corporation in 1995, and in 2000 was acquired by Viacom, becoming the second largest media company in America behind AOL Time Warner. Under the Viacom umbrella are the CBS and UPN networks, as well as a number of cable stations, including MTV, TNN, TMC, BET, Nickelodeon, VH1, TV Land, Showtime, CMT, and National Network. Viacom also owns thirty-eight TV stations, 186 radio stations, Paramount Pictures and theme parks, music publishing, and Blockbuster video rental stores.

Fox Network was created by the News Corporation Limited (NWS), which got its start as an Australian newspaper publisher and has grown, mainly through acquisitions, to become the world's largest newspaper publisher. In addition to the Fox Network, NWS is the outright owner of thirty-five TV stations in the United States, as well as a number of cable channels, including Fox News. In various areas of the world NWS is a major participant in satellite TV, pay-TV, and book and magazine publishing, and it also owns Chris-Craft Industries, makers of classic leisure boats.

Time Warner Inc. does not own one of the major networks, but it is the biggest media company as measured by revenues. Its television holdings include many regular and premium cable channels, including the first cable news channel, CNN, as well as HBO, Cinemax, WB Network, TBS, TNT, Cartoon Network, and TCM. This company has over thirty-four million Internet access subscribers through AOL and Compuserve and runs a host of Internet services (for example, Mapquest and Moviefone). It supplies cable service to over eleven million customers and is a major feature film and TV series producer through its Warner Brothers unit. It also owns hundreds of magazines, including *People*, *Time*, *Fortune*, and *Money*, as well as record companies that have some of the major international performers under contract.

Clearly, television news is now part of big business, with all that implies for the delivery of news. This issue relates to how much control a single company should be allowed over the media in a market. It brings up frightening images of thought control, because in a tightly controlled market, the same biased message might be conveyed whether one reads the local newspaper, listens to a local radio station, or tunes in to a local TV broadcast.

Media consolidation is a major concern, and the FCC and at least the Senate, if not both houses of Congress, are currently at loggerheads over it. In 2003 the FCC announced that it would loosen the regulations on ownership of multiple media in a market. The Senate then passed a bill prohibiting the rule changes, and the issue is currently also in the courts.

An equally frightening issue relates to conflicts of interest. Can a network that is owned by a manufacturer of medical equipment be expected to run an expose of how that equipment was causing deaths? Or would an evening news reviewer give a terrible review to a major motion picture put out by a sister company? Although these are hypothetical questions, a Pew Research Center survey[2] of national broadcast journalists and news executives reported that 35 percent of the respondents commonly or sometimes avoided a story because it might be damaging to the financial interests of their news organization.

Diane Ainsworth reported an example of this phenomenon in an interview with Lowell Bergman, currently a professor at the University of California at Berkeley, but formerly a producer of the television show *60 Minutes*. While still a producer, Bergman had developed a relationship with a former executive of the Brown and Williamson tobacco company and got him to agree to go on the air with the story that the company was doing research to increase the known addictiveness of nicotine in cigarettes. This incident formed the basis of the movie *The Insider*. As a result of a threatened lawsuit by the tobacco industry, CBS decided to cancel the airing of what would have been a powerful program on the subject. The thinking was that the lawsuit would "jeopardize its then-pending sale to Westinghouse Electric Corporation." Later, CBS aired a "watered-down, edited version of the story, against Bergman's wishes."

Less Information, More Advocacy

With television becoming a major, if not the main source of news, and with so much consolidation in the media business resulting in less control of television news by journalists, certain conclusions can be drawn about news delivery in the television age. First, most people are getting less in-depth coverage of major stories and more repetition of visually oriented aspects of news stories. Second, there is a greater tendency for television stories to represent more of a portrayal of someone's point of view rather than following the traditional news ethic of presenting all facets of the story. The point of view portrayed is often the person being interviewed who provides a sound bite that's too good to resist. Worse yet are programs that are actually pure advocacy for certain points of view, but mask as even-handed news programs. In line with the tendency for advocacy to be presented as news, the American population is probably more politically polarized today than it has ever been before.

The embedding of the major television networks in large conglomerates with many complex business interests enhances the possibility that news stories will either be dropped or slanted to coincide with the interests of the corporate parent.

Although developments in television clearly raise questions about how much news we get and how much we can trust it, the advent of the Internet with its mountains of totally unreliable information coming from unknown sources has significantly elevated the problems of news delivery to the American public. The bottom line is that in an era of instant news availability and with a plethora of delivery vehicles, people are probably less informed and less aware today than ever before of the many aspects of major news stories affecting their lives.

Notes

1. Pew Research Center, "Self Censorship: How Often and Why."
2. Pew Research Center, "News Audiences Increasingly Politicized."

Part III

Our Society

Chapter 11

Learning from the Screen: Television and Education

From its inception, television has enjoyed tremendous educational potential, whether viewed in a classroom setting or in the home. In some ways the ubiquitous TV set has been detrimental to learning, but TV has also provided to people of all ages, especially schoolchildren, a myriad of opportunities to learn and to be informed. This chapter examines the impact of television on various types of formal educational programs, whether delivered through direct broadcasts or by videotape or DVDs and whether shown in classrooms, libraries, or in the home. Although television is currently being augmented or replaced by computers in the classroom, it has proved to be a major aid for teachers in bringing subjects alive and demonstrating to students that learning can be fun.

Of course, this would only be true if teachers adopted effective TV technology in their lessons. Some people argue that this has not been the case any more than the minimally effective use of film and radio in the classroom. However, a study by the Corporation for Public Broadcasting[1] conducted in the early 1990s suggests that, in the case of television, its usage as an educational tool has been more widespread. The average number of TV sets per school ranged from 9.5 in elementary schools to 20.1 in high schools. The percent of students experiencing any use of TV or video in academically oriented courses ranged from 21 to 73 percent in elementary school and 32 to 93 percent in secondary school, depending upon the subject being taught. Possibly most significant is that three-fourths or more of all secondary students were exposed to television presentations in each of the core courses of their curriculum except math.

Surprisingly, the study showed greater use of television in secondary schools, which might go against expectations, as we tend to associate TV with children's shows like *Sesame Street* and *Mister Rogers' Neighborhood*: these are among the most popular and longest-lasting shows on television. Many other broadcast shows are geared toward older children as well, but for teaching purposes there is also the widespread availability of more sophisticated learning experiences provided through tapes and shows produced either by single educational institutions, regional consortia (including educational agencies and institutions, nonprofits, or a combination), or profit-making companies. Whatever the delivery system or school level, TV has made significant inroads into the educational process, becoming a common adjunct to the teacher in the classroom. The question remains, however, to what extent, if any, has it improved learning.

Preschool Education

From broadcast television's early years, there was a realization that children in preschool and the early grades represented a major market, and programs were developed to serve that market, although not necessarily to fulfill an educational objective. Perhaps the most popular early children's show was NBC's *Howdy Doody*, which ran between 1947 and 1960. According to the Museum of Television and Radio Web site, the show's creators made a conscious effort to integrate educational material into the program's songs and stories.[2]

In October 1955 CBS began *Captain Kangaroo*, which ran for twenty-nine years until its final performance in December 1984. Host Bob Keeshan was like a grandfather to young children, and the slow pace and lightheartedness of the show provided a secure and happy context for its audience.

Perhaps the first nationally televised children's show that consciously addressed child development was *Mister Rogers' Neighborhood*. Although it had existed in various local formats since 1963, in 1968 National Educational Television (NET) made the show available for national distribution.

Host Fred Rogers and his show were laid-back and relatively slow moving, embodying a consistent theme of love for others, as well as for oneself. The stated intention of the show was to foster the healthy emotional and intellectual growth of his viewers. With his soothing voice and unhurried manner, Rogers introduced his audience to the "Neighborhood of Make-Believe" where they would meet his puppet characters as well as his live guests. The last new episode aired in August 2001, but reruns are still seen regularly on PBS stations around the country.

Learning from the Screen: Television and Education

In contrast to *Mister Rogers' Neighborhood, Sesame Street* was a preschool learning show with animated action. Funded by Head Start, from the very beginning its concepts of teaching and educational effectiveness were evaluated through research; before the first episode aired, these findings were substantiated and built into the design of the show's format.

1. Animation was superior to still images in getting children to pay attention.
2. Certain types of repetition were superior to others in fostering learning.
3. It was possible to get children to interact with the TV image to reinforce their learning.

Based on this research, the show was built more on a *Laugh-In* model with rapid stimuli and changes in action than the slow and soothing *Mister Rogers'* model. Of course, both shows had certain features in common, such as puppets, live guests, and live hosts. But *Sesame Street* was mainly aimed at specific intellectual development and *Mr. Rogers' Neighborhood* more at emotional development. Also, over its lifetime *Sesame Street* has been geared more to the changes in how children perceive, which were brought about by the existence of TV and its growing tendency to present fast-paced action with rapid changes of scene. The show has continued to adapt to the perceptual changes in its audience and is still a regular morning feature on PBS.

A body of literature indicates that watching *Mister Rogers' Neighborhood* and/or *Sesame Street* has positive effects on later school achievement. Huston and colleagues[3] found that watching these programs increased children's ability to learn letters, numbers, and other cognitive skills and improved their vocabulary. A Markle Foundation study[4] even found that this effect carried through to higher grade point averages in highschool English, science, and math (see Anderson, Huston, and Wright). A study by Wright and Huston concluded that watching *Sesame Street* as a preschooler led to better paragraph comprehension and overall school adjustment in first or second grade as judged by teachers. Zill and Davies reported that watching PBS children's programs resulted in higher levels of emergent literacy and less negative feedback from teachers to parents on either conduct or performance. The positive effect of early TV watching on later outcomes was especially strong among low-income families.

This is just a sampling of the positive outcomes that have been found to be related to preschool children watching educationally oriented TV. Many other studies show the same or similar results. However, these findings must be viewed in context. There are also many studies that show that, to develop the emotional maturity and cognitive abilities necessary to succeed in school, children need contact and interaction with their parents or other caregivers with whom they have close relationships. To the extent that interpersonal relationship time is replaced by television watching, the results could be quite damaging to the child's future educational success.

School-Aged Children

The positive outcomes above result from children watching educationally oriented TV. Regrettably, that is not the only type of programming watched either by preschool or older schoolchildren, especially when their TV watching is not supervised. As noted earlier, the average eighteen year old living in the United States will have watched 35,000 murders on TV during his or her lifetime. According to a summary article by Professor John Murray of Kansas State University, the more hours that children and adolescents watch violence on TV, the greater the probability that they will be more aggressive in their attitudes, values, and behaviors. This general finding has held true across a large number of correlational, experimental, and field studies and ratings and observations of aggressive behavior. There are competing theories as to the mechanisms that may link watching violence on TV to subsequent aggressive or violent behavior, but the weight of the evidence seems to indicate some causal relationship.

In 1955 cartoons first made their TV appearance on the *Mighty Mouse Playhouse*, but it was not until the 1960s that children's cartoons became a weekend morning staple. Yet, because cartoons themselves are often filled with violent behavior, children are exposed to hours of violence even if they watch mostly cartoon shows. Another negative effect of TV watching is indicated by a recent study released by the National Endowment for the Arts; it found that the reading of literature has decreased significantly in the population, especially among young adults, and that those who do not read literature watch significantly more television than those who do.

One step in the direction of making more educational TV programming available to children and parents is the issuance of the new Children's Television Act rules by the FCC in September 1997. To get their licenses renewed without review by the full commission, broadcast licensees, including network and local TV stations but not cable networks, must demonstrate that they have aired at least three hours per week of "core children's programming." "Core children's programming" is defined as serving the educational and informational needs of children ages sixteen and under. Although this definition is intentionally vague, it is designed to encourage the industry to try a variety of imaginative approaches to the problem, rather than have government define specific acceptable formats. Since this rule went into effect many new shows that were designed to meet the criteria have gone on the air, and some have gone off as well because they did not draw a significant audience. Some network executives complain that the quality programming cannot draw children away from more action-oriented non-educational shows. Others claim that some of their existing children's shows fit the definition of being educationally oriented, claims that many parents have a hard time accepting.

But despite problems in implementation, there is now a good deal more educationally oriented children's TV available than there was before 1997, and much of it is not only quality TV but is also commercially successful. An outstanding example is the cable channel Nickelodeon, which offers programs like *Blue's Clues* and *Rugrats* that fall within the educationally oriented category. Both are very popular with children and are very acceptable to parents.

Therefore, when used wisely by parents, broadcast television, especially that which is specifically oriented toward preschool education, has had a very positive effect upon children and their ability to thrive in a school environment. Even beyond preschool, there is enough quality, educationally oriented television available to interest older students and to have positive effects throughout the school grades.

However, when television is used as a babysitter or no parental guidance is given and programs are watched indiscriminately for hours on end, TV can have a very harmful effect ranging from retarding the development of interpersonal skills to decreasing the desire to read and instilling a propensity for violence. Perhaps more than in any other area of its impact, TV can have a profound effect on education for a large segment of the population, and it is vitally important for responsible adults to make sound judgments and exercise sufficient supervision to ensure that the outcomes of TV watching will be positive.

Television in the Classroom

The introduction of television into the classroom from first grade through graduate school has been nothing short of a revolution. Although movie projectors were used in the classroom for some time before television, their availability was limited, as was any programming produced for their educational use. The availability of TV programming either through direct broadcast or through reproduction has led to sufficient use by teachers so that it is no longer an oddity in the classroom. Today, as noted above, it is rare for a school not to have a TV and VCR or DVD player available for use in the classroom, and in many schools, each classroom is equipped with its own machines. For example, if one is teaching a section on African geography, why not show a tape of a trip down the Nile River, or to illustrate what a Shakespearean play looks like on the stage, why not put on a tape of *Hamlet*?

A large number of companies produce educational material that can be profitably used in these machines, and there are many educational channels that can be accessed directly in the classroom. CNN's "Cable in the Classroom" provides classroom material for all levels. Other quasi-educational channels like TLC, Discovery Channel, History Channel, Biography Channel, and others often produce individual shows that are clearly appropriate for use in specific classes, although in the competition for ratings their shows are often more entertaining than educational.

National and regional organizations have evolved to help teachers make use of classroom TV. For example the Regional Educational Technology Network (RETN) is a consortium developed to provide educational programming to twelve towns in Vermont through local cable television. RETN broadcasts twenty-four hours a day, seven days a week such programs as "The Duel of Hamilton and Burr: An American Experience" or a program of music composed by students throughout the state in grades two through twelve. This consortium is typical of many throughout the country.

Clearly, TV and TV recording technology have had an important positive effect on enabling our schools to meet their educational mission. Introducing TV into the classroom has not revolutionized what happens in the classroom, but it has made immediately available a countless store of rich and interesting content for classroom use. Of course, the extent to which the technology lives up to its promise is dependent on two factors. As with any other aspect of education, better-funded schools probably provide more access to television in the classroom with all its resultant benefits. But that is not a limitation of television; it is a limitation of how public education is funded. Most often it is up to the individual classroom teacher to decide how much use will be made of the technology. There is little doubt that its potential is far greater than its actual use.

Because children are now accustomed to getting information via a screen, the introduction of television may well have paved the way for the next revolution currently taking place in the classroom, the introduction of personal computers.

Telecourses

Television is not only a medium for providing educational content in a classroom but it has also taken on a life of its own as a replacement for the classroom. The early history of television courses (or "telecourses") has been described in some depth by Ken Freed in the Media Visions Web site, and the following description has been taken from it. In 1972 California funded a task force of the public colleges in that state led by Dr. Bernard Luskin, vice chancellor of Coast Community College, to determine the telecourses of the future. The task force defined a telecourse as an entire course in a given subject, not merely materials to support a course, complete with methods for answering student questions, giving and grading tests, and reporting student accomplishments to the school. The task force developed a plan by which the colleges using the telecourses would pay a fee to the distributor, who in turn paid the course producers. The plan was implemented by establishing the first "virtual college," Coastline Community College, which broadcast its courses over public television station KOCE. By 1976 Coastline was serving 18,500 students within a 150-square-mile area of southern California.

In the 1970s, Dallas Community College also entered the telecourse business but with a different approach. Instead of beaming the courses over cable television, Dallas packaged them on videotape and sold the tapes to colleges, providing more flexibility for students to take the courses at their convenience. This quickly became the preferred method of distribution, and since the 1970s many states and countries overseas have established their own virtual colleges. An article by Carnevale and Young reports that, although Internet courses receive a lot of press, it is estimated that more people take courses each year delivered by television, either direct or on videocassettes or disks, than from the Internet. Many of the closed-circuit live courses provide for two-way communication, so that the classroom is the same as a traditional one in all ways except that the teacher is at a remote location. In addition, preplanned supplementary text and graphics can be added to the screen by a technician.

Clearly, television has had a significant positive impact not only on K–12 education but at the college level as well. The formal education model has been extended from the classroom to anywhere a student has access to broadcast television and/or a TV set with a VCR or DVD player, whether at home, in a library, or perhaps even in the workplace.

Television as a Feedback Tool in Education

In addition to television's role as a source of content in the classroom, it has also been employed as a tool within the educational process. As we describe in the next chapter, closed-circuit television has been adapted to facilitate the observation of and the giving of feedback to medical interns performing examinations of patients. This is but one instance of television being used in professional training.

Some other applications use TV to film elements of student performance in courses on public speaking, public presentation, or even gymnastics. Students in these courses are taped making their presentations, and then the class discusses what they might have done right or wrong. The use of TV taping gives the instructor the ability to go back over specific aspects of the student's performance to point out particularly effective or ineffective aspects.

Even more pertinent to the subject of television's use as an educational tool is how it is being used to supervise student teachers through videoconferencing. A program at the Purdue University School of Education[5] allows faculty members to view real-time video of student teachers in classrooms around the state instead of making personal visits to those classrooms. The faculty involved cite not only the time and cost efficiency of the process, but they also feel that the teachers being observed are more relaxed, even though they know they are being observed. One professor commented that when an observer goes into the classroom, his or her very presence changes the nature of the student-teacher interactions, whereas the influence is much less so in video observation.

Finally, TV has been used very effectively in classes in English as a Second Language (ESL). Here closed-captioning presents written text of the conversation on the screen. Numerous studies have demonstrated that the use of two modes of simultaneous transmission through closed-captioning produces better learning and student sense of accomplishment in ESL classes than traditional methods. It has also been found that these results are obtained with both adults and children and with people who have varying initial levels of knowledge of English. Given the large number of non-English-speaking immigrants entering the United States each year, the use of closed-captioning has had a significant impact.

Successes and Failures

It is indisputable that television has had a significant positive impact on the formal educational process. From preschool to college, educational opportunities conveyed through direct broadcast or tape/disk are available and being used in a variety of ways both in and outside the classroom. Hundreds of entities, including government-sponsored organizations and consortia and other profit-making and non-profit organizations have been developed to produce and distribute the materials to be used in TV-assisted learning. The major limiting factor to how much of an impact TV has had in the classroom is the willingness of individual teachers to integrate the technology into their curricula. Research suggests that this has not been revolutionary, but that its adoption has been greater than previous technologies.

The most-studied effects have been those of public television on preschool children, and here the results have been quite encouraging. As noted above, *Sesame Street* clearly has a number of positive influences in preparing young children to succeed in the school environment. Combined with the Head Start program, there have been significant inroads made in reducing the early educational achievement gap between advantaged and disadvantaged children.

Finally, TV used as a tool rather than as a source of content in the classroom has extended the ability of teachers and supervisors to monitor and evaluate students in realistic situations more effectively and at less expense. It has also prepared the way to introduce much more powerful technology in the form of personal computers into these same situations as well as into the classroom. Finally, the use of closed-captioned TV has significantly enhanced the teaching of ESL to both children and adults.

Television, however, has not come without its costs. The most studied of these is the propensity for children to watch television to the detriment of other interpersonal activities. Such activities are an important part of a child's maturation process, providing a real-life laboratory for learning such necessary qualities or skills as sharing, negotiating, and caring for others. Furthermore, a good deal of what children see on TV is violent in nature and tends to suggest to young minds that violence is a way to deal with life's problems.

Programming Our Lives

Another possible societal cost of television is that the time spent in front of a TV set is supplanting time that in previous generations had been spent reading books and newspapers. For the most part, although it can be argued that the range of substantive offerings on TV today provides alternatives to Newton Minnow's "vast wasteland," the viewing choices made by most children and adults, combined with the fact that those born in the TV generations are forsaking reading, bodes poorly for the overall educational level of Americans, both formal and informal. Because the United States is the world's only superpower, a status some commentators consider threatened by lagging education levels, it is vitally important that our population be aware of issues that face our country and the world and that they develop the qualities of analytical and critical reasoning gained through reading. Although TV at its best can provide information and explain the complexity of issues, it does not give people the intellectual tools to address them.

There are defenders of TV viewing. Steven Johnson argues in his book, *Everything Bad Is Good for You: How Today's Popular Culture Is Actually Making Us Smarter*, that today's culture of TV, video games, and the Internet actually increases IQ and cognitive abilities. To some extent, present-day multitasking at the computer and the interaction involved in video games may well hone a variety of cognitive skills. But there are vast areas of analytic ability and deeper thinking that come, for instance, from studying works of history, fiction, and scientific theory. Equally important is reading factual material on what is happening in the world around us, which can only be obtained with any real degree of completeness and confidence in its veracity from books and periodicals.

As a technology, TV has provided avenues for us to become more educated. Many children are entering kindergarten more prepared than were their parents or grandparents, and many individuals with college degrees would not have them without telecourses. In this limited context of formal education, TV can be considered successful. However, despite such successes and the opportunities available through television, TV's larger impact often undermines its educational potential.

With a range of programming that permits people to avoid exposure to new subjects and with the substitution of viewing for reading, we may well have a less educated population that tends to seek only information that reinforces previously held views. With the computer either supplanting or being united with television, the choice of watching will only become even more tailored to individual likes and dislikes. The early hope that television will help us become an increasingly sophisticated population would appear to be farther from fulfillment today.

Notes

1. *Technical Report of the 1991 School Utilization Survey.*
2. See Rautiolla-Williams, "The Howdy Doody Show."
3. Huston et al., *Big World, Small Screen*.
4. Anderson and Wright, "The Markle CTW Recontact Study."
5. See "Supervising Student Teachers by Videoconference."

Chapter 12

Doctors and Patients: Television and Medicine

To say that there have been many changes in the field of medicine over the past fifty years would be a gross understatement. Change has occurred in technology, medications, and the nature of the workforce and of specialization. For example, according to the Department of Health, Education, and Welfare and American Medical Association (AMA) statistics there were 208,997 active physicians in 1950, or 1.35 per thousand people in the population. By the year 2000 the number of active physicians had risen to 737,504, or 2.64 per thousand, a growth of over 500,000 physicians or 95 percent in physicians per thousand. In addition, the nature of the physician population has changed insofar as in 1950 women doctors were the exception rather than the rule. According to the AMA, as late as 1970 women only accounted for 7.6 percent of the physician population, but by 2002 they accounted for fully 25.2 percent, and women are continuing to grow as a factor in the medical ranks. The Association of American Medical Colleges reports that in 2003 medical school applications from women exceeded those from men for the first time ever.

Just as television has exposed the public to various aspects of the criminal justice system, it has given similar exposure to the field of medicine. From *Medic* to *ER* the public has gotten a variety of views of what it is like to practice medicine and/or work in a hospital. There is a cable medical channel that presents a variety of medical topics to a general audience on a daily, full-day schedule, and many mainstream news programs now include a regular medical feature. Finally, television hums with a large daily dose of ads for prescription and non-prescription medicines, both inform-ing and confusing the public and changing the doctor-patient relationship.

According to a 2002 Kaiser Family Foundation poll, 49 percent of adult Americans cite TV as their primary source for health information. Since the Food and Drug Administration began to allow detailed adver-tising of prescription medicines on TV in 1997, the growth of such advertising has been explosive. A 700 percent increase in advertising expenditures for prescription drugs was reported between 1996 and 2000, most of which was for television ads.[1] This has led to a new behav-ior, with one in eight Americans having requested and received a pre-scription from their physician for a drug they heard about on television.

In addition to TV broadcasts to a general audience, closed-circuit tele-vision is being used in a variety of ways in medical education and con-sultation, extending the reach of those who are expert in their fields. Miniaturizing television has allowed the doctor to view what is going on inside the body as it is happening without exploratory surgery. Given this variety of television-related developments, it is clear that television has had a profound effect upon both the purveyors and users of the med-ical system.

Medicine in Drama and Comedy

Medic, which ran from 1954 to 1956 and starred Richard Boone as Dr. Conrad Styner, was the first medical drama with a tone of reality, which laid the foundation for many shows to follow. Because the show was shot in actual hospitals, the Los Angeles County Medical Association demanded control of the medical accuracy of every script, thus ensuring a realistic presentation of the practice of medicine. This sense of reality was carried through in creator James Moser's next show, *Ben Casey,* in which Casey's superior's frequent comment, "Ben Casey you know so much about medicine and so little about people," illustrated where the emphasis lay between technical and bedside manner skills. For millions, a "subdural hematoma" became as familiar as a "stomach ulcer."

Since 1952 there have been dozens of shows dealing with doctors, as well as with other aspects of medicine with which the American public had relatively little knowledge or even awareness. Among the most pop-ular of the medical shows over the past fifty years were *St. Elsewhere,* *Chicago Hope,* and *ER,* all of which portrayed the practice of medicine in a big city hospital. Each of these shows covered a wide variety of med-ical problems and the modern technology available to deal with these problems. But as is common in many TV dramas, the subplots focusing on relationships between characters and especially spectacular events began to take a central role, eventually turning many of these shows more into soap operas than attempts to accurately portray the practice of medicine within a big city hospital.

One very popular and long-running medical show was *Marcus Welby, MD* in which the main character was portrayed by the movie star Robert Young. In this show the relationship between doctor and patient took center stage over the disease itself. In contrast to Dr. Casey, Dr. Welby's role was not only that of a physician but also of a friend, counselor, and caregiver.

Perhaps the most popular medical show of all time was *M*A*S*H*, a show that achieved a delicate balance between its primary thrust as a comedy and the serious messages it attempted to deliver about life and moral behavior. The main characters (except Major Burns) were out-standing surgeons, and they often demonstrated this fact by saving lives or limbs in ways that required outstanding knowledge, imagination, and skills. But the practice of medicine that was depicted in this show was far from the type of reality shown in *Medic* or *Ben Casey*. The main characters were also rebels against authority, covering up their emotional vulnera-bility, but demonstrating that medical skill forgave the breaking of rules.

*M*A*S*H* was not the only comedy show built around doctors and the practice of medicine (for instance, *Becker* and *Empty Nest*), but although the others did not reach the popularity of *M*A*S*H*, they all portrayed physicians as medically competent and caring. However, *Scrubs*, which debuted in 2001, is a slapstick comedy about doctors and nurses in which all relationship to medical reality is discarded. Here the context is a hospital, but it could just as well be a hotel, a supermarket, or a city dump. The objective of the show is comedy, and any relation-ship between the actual practice of medicine and the practice as it is por-trayed is totally incidental. Similarly, *Diagnosis Murder*, another popular show set in a hospital, focuses on the solving of a crime and only occa-sionally is medicine a major part of the plot.

Thus, in providing the public with a view of the practice of medicine within a hospital setting, TV has taken a major turn. It began by provid-ing a great deal of realism and finding the drama within the patient's dis-ease and the doctors' efforts to control or cure it. Currently, the drama or comedy in medical shows is found more within the relationships among the characters, with the patient's problem only occasionally occupying center stage.

Before attempting to draw any conclusions from this trend, it is important to note another recent development in medicine-related dramatic programming: the forensic medicine show, exemplified by *Crossing Jordan* and *CSI* and their clones. These shows present an area of medicine of which few people had any knowledge or interest, but because of their dramatic content they have made pathologists and the work they do interesting to millions of people. In a like manner, *Third Watch*, and to a lesser extent *ER*, have made the job of emergency medical technician more visible to the American public.

Thus, TV drama has provided average Americans with a far more intensive look at medical practice than they have ever had before. Sometimes that look is realistic and other times it is not. What might the outcomes of this exposure have been over the last half-century? Little systematic research has been conducted on this broadly defined subject, but one incident reported by the Mednews Web site is worth noting. In an *ER* episode a teenager is diagnosed with human papillomavirus (HPV), a common sexually transmitted disease. Surveys before and after the show indicated that the number of people who were familiar with HPV doubled and the number able to describe it tripled, suggesting that millions of people first learned about the disease from that show. Clearly, as cited above, people do get information about health issues from watching television.

Other possible effects are less well documented, but certainly worthy of speculation. For one, after viewing heroes like Drs. Welby, Quinn, or Pierce, a person might not be very happy with a doctor who, because of the pressures of managed care, spends little time with him or her. Thus the patient may be more ready to sue if the outcome is not entirely positive. In fact, this issue began to be seriously discussed within the medical profession in relation to the show *Marcus Welby, MD*. The effect of watching such shows on the behavior of actual patients toward their real doctors became such an issue within the medical profession in the 1970s that it was the subject of formal sessions at professional medical meetings.

One characteristic that has been notable in almost all the medical dramas is the presence of women physicians, who appear in numbers similar to their male counterparts in almost all current medical shows, such as *ER* and *Grey's Anatomy*. In addition, a number of women have been cast in roles of superior skills and stature. For instance, *Chicago Hope's* Dr. Kate Austin was a cardiothoracic surgeon who certainly held her own among the very strong male personalities. Dr. Kerry Weaver rose from the position of resident to head of the hospital in *ER*. In a different context, *Dr. Quinn—Medicine Woman* portrayed an early female medical pioneer in a way that would make any woman proud to follow in her footsteps. It seems highly likely that the significant increase in women applicants for medical schools noted earlier has been stimulated or reinforced by viewing large numbers of highly capable women depicted as physicians on TV.

Finally, it is interesting to note that, concurrent with the popular dramatic shows dealing with forensic pathology (*CSI, CSI Miami, CSI New York, Crossing Jordan*) there has been a rise in the number of students choosing pathology residencies within the past few years. There has been a very significant rise in the numbers choosing residencies in emergency medicine since *ER* went on the air in 1994, although that specialization had been increasing in popularity since the mid-1980s. Television images may well have significant influences on the choice of specialties within medicine, as well as on the choice of medicine itself.

Medical Reality Shows

The wide variety of medical-related dramas and comedies are not the only source of information about medicine on commercial television; these shows are merely the source that reaches the most people. Another class of programs comprises realistic shows, such as *Trauma: Life in the ER, The Residents: Circle of Life*, and *Untold Stories of the ER*, which take the audience into an actual emergency or operating room as a procedure is being performed. These shows do not have the smoothness and polish of the dramas, but they certainly do provide a first-hand look at what goes on in many critical medical situations.

Even more informative than the realistic shows are medical documentaries, which are often aired by the major networks. These shows explore particular medical problems, such as rising health costs, a specific disease such as the SARS epidemic in 2003, or another medical-related topic that might be sufficiently newsworthy to occupy an hour or sometimes even two of prime time. These shows are normally well researched, often present different opinions about the issues involved, and are designed to be informative rather than merely entertaining. A compressed version of the full documentary format is a fifteen- to thirty-minute segment on one of the news magazine shows, such as *60 Minutes, Dateline NBC*, or *20/20*.

The nightly local and network news broadcasts often feature medical stories as one of a number of lifestyle issues that have received coverage in recent years, mainly as a reaction to twenty-four-hour cable news channels that "scoop" the networks on hard news. Almost as a general rule now, local stations and networks have a doctor on the staff who supplies medical information in local or national news shows. On New York's WNBC channel, for instance, Dr. Max Gomez has a regular feature in which he has a few minutes to cover some information that has just appeared in a medical journal, a drug recall, or other subjects pertinent to the health concerns of the viewing audience. Other local channels around the country may have someone they call upon to comment on a significant current medical story, such as a shortage of flu vaccine. And, of course, if the medical story is big enough, both the local and national news shows, as well as the news-only channels, may do a feature on it, including interviews with doctors, research scientists, public health officials, or drug company executives, depending upon the nature of the story. In addition, medical societies may produce and distribute health-related video news releases (VNRs) to local stations, as did the American Society of Anesthesiologists in distributing a VNR on pain medicine to over 700 stations nationwide.

Finally, there is a medical channel on cable television that presents all types of medical content throughout the day. This content may range from a round-table discussion, such as how the government can best ensure the universal availability of health care, to a program comparing different weight-reduction diets, to an examination of the efficacy of drugs for reducing cholesterol.

All the above sources present medical and health issues from the standpoint of providing health information, not selling a product. Thus, from a pure exposure perspective, the American public has a much greater opportunity today to be informed about medical issues. It would be ludicrous to believe that people fail to act upon this information. More likely, when people hear things that are relevant to their own health, at least some discuss those issues with their doctors and are better equipped to ask intelligent questions when their doctor recommends a particular course of action. One downside of all this input is that the headlining of simplified news about initial research findings may be misleading and may cause either anxiety or hope where neither is actually warranted.

Advertisements/Infomercials

In the early years of television, over-the-counter remedies were among the many products advertised. Who from that era can forget the black-and-white commercials for Alka-Seltzer intoning "Plop, plop, fizz, fizz, oh what a relief it is"? Of course as television matured, the ads got slicker and covered a wide variety of pharmaceutical products, even including such things as tampons, which had previously been strictly taboo. Yet, even though the tube promoted more and more products, the relationship between the manufacturers and consumers did not change. The same over-the-counter drugs advertised on TV had previously been advertised in print media with the same messages and descriptions.

Starting in 1983, however, this relationship *did* change as drug companies were allowed to advertise prescription drugs directly by name (without citing their benefits) to the general public. In 1997, the FDA rules were again changed to allow prescription drugs to be advertised along with their benefits as long as certain conditions were met, including listing their potential side effects. This change caused an explosion in prescription drug advertising.

Traditionally, the marketing of prescription drugs was aimed at the physician and was delivered only through technical and professional media. He or she was then left with the decision of what drugs would be appropriate for what patients. Many would argue that these decisions were also influenced by free trips given to physicians to attend seminars in beautiful vacation resorts or even research grants they obtained. Regardless of inducements, however, of the millions of prescriptions written each year, most were based on the physician's understanding of a new drug's advantages and disadvantages and the patient's particular needs.

Now television has inserted itself between the doctor and patient and added an additional set of influences to the decision. Unlike the medical documentaries or news items, these commercials advertising prescription medication exist to convince people to take a specific course of action. A patient who is suffering from a particular set of symptoms watches attractive, happy models enjoying life free from those symptoms, because they are taking the targeted prescription drug. Yes, the words that are most often spoken or just scroll across the bottom of the screen warn of significant and sometimes life-threatening side effects. But given the power of visual images, the person watching is not attending to the words, but more to the happy people in the pictures who demonstrate how much the drug can help.

Influenced by the ad, the patient now goes to the doctor with a strong desire to take the medicine and improve his or her life. The doctor may disagree because of the drug's side effects or because of the belief that the benefits have been oversold, especially for this particular patient with his or her idiosyncratic makeup and medical history. There is now a chink in the relationship between the two; if the patient becomes adamant, the physician is put in the dilemma of either prescribing the medication or losing the patient. In fact, many doctors admit giving in rather than arguing. In a study reported by the American Academy of

Family Physicians, the authors noted that when a patient requested a specific drug from their physician, that request had a profound effect on the course of treatment. Thus, television has introduced a significant new dimension to the doctor-patient relationship, clearly one that has the potential for changing that relationship.

Further, because many prescription drugs can have devastating side effects, massive advertising increases the probability that large numbers of people will suffer those effects before greater controls are put on the use of the drugs or they are pulled from the market altogether. Such was the case with the use of Cox 2 inhibitors (Vioxx, etc.) from which many people died of heart attacks within a relatively short time. Had the advertising been less intense, many fewer people would have been taking the drugs before their danger was uncovered.

The use of television commercials to guide people toward specific products that are claimed to improve their health reaches some type of apotheosis in the many health-related infomercials aired almost any place on the dial. These programs are most often aired late at night, in the early morning, or on weekend mornings, but are liable to be found some place on the TV spectrum at almost any time. Infomercials are extended programs (usually either a half-hour or an hour) that are designed to sell a product touted to have a significant health benefit. The products involved are usually some type of vitamin or herbal combination, a salve or cream, a miracle diet, or an exercise machine. The results promised are usually nothing short of miraculous, including the disappearance of the symptoms of aging, the promise of youthful and unlined skin, or the amazing development of sculptured bodies with only a few minutes of exercise a day. The FDA does not regulate these commercials nor the non-prescription vitamins or other treatments offered in them, nor is the rigorous research required for prescription medications required for these products. Thus, with these infomercials, television now provides the modern version of snake oil salesmen the ability to give their pitch not just to a few people at a time, but to thousands at any time of day.

TV Technology in Teaching and Medical Practice

The use of television, especially closed-circuit TV, has made the factor of distance almost irrelevant in the education of doctors and the treatment of patients. For instance, Johns Hopkins' Web site indicates that their "faculty and administrators are available to deliver live lectures" via video teleconferencing technology, which include a fifteen-minute question-and-answer period. In addition, "international physicians can request a videoconference session with a colleague at Johns Hopkins to discuss, in real time, challenging patient cases, treatment protocols, or research ideas." Certainly Johns Hopkins is not the only medical institution offering such services, and video teleconferencing has become a standby at major medical institutions across the country. In fact, googling "teleconferencing" with "medical school" results in 343,000 hits referring not only to programs in the United States but also to programs within and between nations around the world.

In addition to being used in teaching medical students, interactive video technology has also been used to evaluate these same students. In a pilot program conducted in Texas, family medicine preceptors were, from their offices, able to observe students in other locations conducting interviews and examinations with patients who gave the same set of answers concerning their symptoms and medical history. Afterward they were able to have a dialogue with these students as they made their case presentations. Again, this is a method of shrinking distance to enhance the medical education process.

A very different type of shrinking involving television lies at the very forefront of medical practice. It goes back to the book and subsequent movie, *Fantastic Voyage,* by the well-known science fiction writer Isaac Asimov. The plot of the novel involved the discovery of a process for making large items small by shrinking their atoms. But the scientist who is key to the furtherance of this technology was suffering from a life-threatening blood clot deep in his brain. A multidisciplinary team and a submarine were miniaturized to the degree that they could travel through his circulatory system and break up the clot before it completely cut off blood supply to a critical area of his brain.

When the book was written in 1966, the entire plot was clearly science fiction, but today there is an element of reality in it. We still cannot shrink people small enough to travel through the human body, but we have been able to shrink a television camera to a small enough size that it can make the journey to various parts of the body. In 1957, developments in fiber optics led to its successful use in a gastroscope, a flexible tubing that is inserted down the throat into the stomach. What is seen at the working end of the gastroscope is displayed on a television screen so that the physician conducting the test can "see" what is inside the stomach. This new technology was followed by developments in colonoscopy that did for studies of the lower bowel what the gastroscope did for the stomach.

Concurrent with the development of fiber optics for diagnosis, the video miniaturization technology was turned toward the practice of surgery. Scores of operative procedures have now been developed whereby a laparoscope, which transmits TV images, is inserted through a very small incision while surgical instruments are inserted through one or more other incisions. The use of the laparoscope eliminates the need for large incisions and results in less time under anesthesia and a dramatically shorter recovery time.

Finally, an even more incredible step was taken in 2000, when Professor Paul Swain of the Royal London Hospital announced the development of a "capsule endoscope," which is swallowed by the patient like any other medication. The difference is that this capsule contains a tiny video camera that takes and transmits images to a portable recorder strapped to the patient's waist as the capsule progresses on its way through the intestinal tract.[2] Now, without the physician being present, television is able to record what is happening within our bodies and perhaps point the way for life-saving treatment.

The Physician's Role

Some of the many effects of television on medicine are clearly established, whereas others lie more in the realm of possibility. These influences include the following: the knowledge or misconceptions that the patient brings to the doctor-patient relationship, the expectations the patient has of the doctor, the attractiveness of medicine as a profession and of its subspecialties as a career choice, and the new technologies available to diagnose and treat disease. Before the age of television, doctors were clear authority figures in the community, dispensing pills and advice without being challenged. Today, even though there is much greater knowledge and many more tools available to the physician, he or she is challenged much more often in the choice of medication or of a procedure. TV has made people seemingly more aware of the medical options while revealing the human frailties of doctors. It has thus clearly changed the place of the physician in society and in many ways made the job considerably more difficult.

Notes

1. See Malone, "TV Remains Dominant Source for Medical Information."
2. BBC News, "Video Pill's 'Fantastic Voyage.'"

Chapter 13

Criminal Justice: Television and the Law

Clearly, the enormous amount of crime and violence portrayed on TV is indisputable. The American Medical Association has determined that by age eighteen a child brought up in a home with a premium cable channel or a VCR will have seen 32,000 murders and 40,000 attempted murders.[1] Although movies had previously made images of violent crime familiar to viewers, they probably did not see them more than once a week and possibly much less frequently. Television has made violence daily and pervasive in our lives.

Has TV turned the country into a mass of potential killers? According to the U.S. Department of Justice Bureau of Justice Statistics, the homicide rate rose significantly from the mid-1960s to the mid-1970s and remained at that level through the 1980s, possibly lending support to that argument.[2] However, the murder rate declined almost steadily during the 1990s, a time when TV content and channels were being added at a prodigious rate, but the economy was very strong. More surprising, it has continued to decline in the first years of the twenty-first century, even though the unemployment rate rose from 2001–2003. To get a feel for the magnitude of the decline in violent crimes since the 1970s, consider this statistic: the total number of serious violent crimes, including rape, robbery, aggravated assault, and homicide, dropped from 3.6 million in 1973 to 1.7 million in 2002, clearly a very significant decline.

But just as it is clear that television has not raised the violent crime rate, there is a good deal of research that links children's viewing of violence on TV to negative outcomes. In a very comprehensive review of that research, Professor John Murray of Kansas State University indicates that the evidence linking the viewing of violence to aggressive behavior is very strong both in laboratory and field studies. But for the most part these studies deal with aggressive childhood and adolescent behavior, not later criminal behavior. Interestingly, most of the violence to which young children are exposed is found in cartoons, rather than in the explosion of evening shows involving crime. Many of us think of cartoons primarily as being light and funny, but careful examination shows that they are full of violence, which young children may well perceive more seriously than adolescents or adults.

Two recent studies, both of which followed individuals for a number of years, have some frightening results that point to TV violence as a causative factor in later violent behavior. L. Rowell Huesmann and his colleagues describe the results of a study that followed 329 people over fifteen years. It demonstrated that children exposed to violence on TV were much more likely to be convicted of a crime later on and also tended to exhibit more violent behavior toward their spouses. Another study, conducted by Jeffrey Johnson and his colleagues, followed 700 youths over seventeen years. This study "showed a definite relationship between TV viewing habits and acts of aggression and crime in the later life. All other possible contributing environmental elements, such as poverty, living in a violent neighborhood, and neglect, were factored out of this study."

But is the influence of TV in the area of crime totally negative? Criminals in TV dramas are much more likely to be apprehended and punished than in real life. U.S. Department of Justice Bureau of Justice statistics indicate that, of all serious crimes reported in 1980, arrests were made in only 13 percent of the cases.[3] This compares to statistics derived from TV crime dramas reported by the University of Central Florida[4] in which 79 percent of the perpetrators of serious crimes were caught, killed, or punished, and only 5 percent were clearly successful. Thus television may act as a deterrent to some potential criminals if that's where they get their knowledge of arrest and conviction statistics and they do not relish spending time in jail.

Another possible, and subtler, effect of TV may be increasing the desirability of careers in the criminal justice system. There has been a dramatic rise in the number of people graduating from law school since the 1950s when television began to be a regular part of most households. According to the various Statistical Abstracts of the United States, in the year 1960 9,314 people graduated from law schools; by the year 1980 this number had risen to 35,647 and, by 2000, to 38,152. Other careers in the field of criminal justice are also receiving increased interest from college students. Mark Clayton's *Christian Science Monitor* article on a survey of college admission officers reported that, of the colleges experiencing an increased interest in a specific major, 60 percent reported the interest to be in criminal justice.

Portrayal of Crime in TV Dramas

Until recently in the overwhelming majority of TV crime dramas, the perpetrator is caught and punished, sending the message that such behavior will have dire consequences. Today's crime dramas portray a different reality. In reviewing *The Wire*, a cop show on HBO, A.O. Scott in a *NY Times Magazine* article observed, "It posits a universe of moral ambiguity that makes every other cop show, even *Law & Order*, look like *Dragnet*." In other words, in *The Wire* good is not always good, bad is not always bad, and the cases often remain unsolved. *The Shield* on FX cable goes as far as to portray the police squad as corrupt and vicious. Thus television's possible propensity to inhibit criminal behavior because of the negative consequences associated with that behavior is waning, as more shows do not associate the punishment with the crime. However, the decrease in serious violent crimes in the past decade would indicate that today's crime shows have not thus far led to increased criminal behavior.

Television's portrayal of criminals is unrealistic in another sense. The same University of Central Florida study mentioned above also provides information on who commits crimes in TV programs as compared to real life. Compared to actual FBI arrest reports, the criminals portrayed in television dramas are older and are more often white, middle or upper class, and operating from greed as a single motive. Thus, even though most crime is perpetrated by young people in depressed areas, TV portrays a different reality. Does this skewed portrayal stem from a belief that most viewers would not tune into shows about poverty and crime or that having more dramas about crime in poor areas would just reinforce class differences and the desire to remain separate?

Changes in TV Crime Shows

From its early days, television has had a fascination with fighting crime and from various perspectives. Early powerful dramas involved lawyers (*Perry Mason*, *The Defenders*), the police (*Dragnet*, *Kojak*), and even social workers (*East Side West Side*). Criminals were rarely made the heroes of these dramas, although occasionally the perpetrator was portrayed as a sympathetic character, really a good person at heart.

Over the years the number, tenor, and variety of programs have changed considerably. First, the number of crime-related shows has grown enormously. A count of the number of crime-related dramas (not including cartoons, which often portray criminally violent behavior) broadcast in a typical cable-served community (Sarasota, Florida) during one week in July 2002 yielded a total of 479, more than might have been shown in the first twenty years of network TV combined. In that week there were police dramas (*NYPD Blue*), crime documentaries (*American Justice*), court dramas (*100 Center Street*), real court cases (*Crime and Punishment*), and actual police chases (*Now See This*). Uncounted was the steady diet of violent crime on the myriad of news shows.

Second, the earlier shows portrayed each of the various types of crime-fighting professionals as doing his or her job in an honest and capable manner. Can any of us guess how many people may have been inspired to pursue a career in law or police work by the characters portrayed by E.G. Marshall, Raymond Burr, Telly Savalas, or Jack Webb? These people may have been disappointed when their ambitions took them into the real world of law or police practice, but their intentions would have been to pursue their fields as competently as their TV heroes. Beyond those who actually sought careers in law enforcement, the larger viewing audience saw these figures as role models.

Some of the later law programs, such as *Law & Order*, portray the same ideals, although even here the Assistant District Attorney (ADA) McCoy often faces moral dilemmas that are resolved in ways with which many people would disagree. Other recent shows portray lawyers in less idealistic terms. *Ally McBeal* usually dealt with civil rather than criminal cases, and it made the practice of law seem totally inane. In *The Practice*, which often dealt with cases of violent crime, the actions of the attorneys were sometimes shown as underhanded, as in the use of "plan B": this occurs when the defense counsel accuses an individual other than the defendant of the crime because there is no real evidence with which to defend the client, who may well be guilty. In *100 Center Street*, one of the stars of the show (thus a sympathetic, not sleazy character), while he was an ADA, changed his brother's computerized arrest record so that he would be able to get probation for a current offense. Even though the brother was fired, receiving some punishment for his offense, the ADA's action is one that would not have occurred on early TV. Finally, *Boston Legal*, which morphed out of *The Practice*, stars a totally unprincipled attorney who is a doddering egomaniac as the senior partner of the firm.

134

Criminal Justice: Television and the Law

So as with recent police dramas, current legal shows are more likely to present the potential flaws as well as the strengths of the legal profession and the criminal justice system. But such a characterization is also in line with many of the realities of our world today as opposed to fifty years ago. Real "perp walks" today too often involve CEOs and other executives of large, formerly respected businesses, priests who have been accused of child molestation, and political officeholders who have used their offices primarily as a way to enrich their bank accounts, and that doesn't even include reporters who are fired for plagiarizing their stories. Thus, although television may be painting a much less attractive picture of the behavior of the people involved in the criminal justice system, the view may well be closer to reality than the older view and may better prepare people who might be motivated to pursue careers within the system.

In the same way that the portrayals of both the police and the practice of law have changed, *The Sopranos* has changed the portrayal of the criminal. As mentioned earlier, except in circumstances where the criminal was innocent or perhaps driven to a crime for otherwise admirable reasons, he or she was not the hero of the show. Although the characters in *The Sopranos* are not always portrayed sympathetically, the criminals are the main players or stars and, in many ways, its heroes, just as the death of John Gotti, who committed many despicable crimes, was treated in the press as the death of a hero. This portrayal is quite different from the way that movies of an earlier era dealt with criminals. The Hays Office, the watchdog of morals in the movies between 1930 and 1966, introduced its Production Code, which mandated that the criminal had to have a bad end, no matter how glamorous his life.

In the past few years a new type of crime show has been introduced to the TV screen, focusing on the forensic issues in any crime scene. Beginning with *CSI*, followed by its clones *CSI Miami* and *CSI New York*, these shows have become enormously popular. Again, they open up an additional area of the criminal justice system with which relatively few people had been familiar. There are also reality forensic shows, such as *Forensic Files* or *Evidence* on Court TV, that provide less drama but deal with the same issues. Will we see more college students entering forensic careers? The *Christian Science Monitor* suggests this has already begun: "By far the hottest majors, however, appear to be criminal justice and forensic science—both fueled by a push for homeland security and pop-culture television shows, professors and students say."

A totally different crime genre emerged with the introduction of TV cameras into actual police and courtroom activities. Court TV is a cable channel in which most of the daytime programming is devoted to live coverage of actual court cases. In certain cases with wide popular interest (read O.J. Simpson), news channels have provided gavel-to-gavel coverage as well as incessant analysis of the case. Another type of reality crime show (*Cops!* and *Now See This*) provides actual films of police car chases and, in some cases, of police stopping and arresting evildoers.

A further addition to the reality lineup was *Law & Order, Crime and Punishment*. In this show, actual individuals involved in a criminal case are shown both in and out of court. Unlike Court TV, the film is cut and spliced to maintain interest and produce continuity of issues, as well as to avoid the inevitable long periods of inaction characteristic of an actual trial. The program is somewhat like a documentary, but its editing maximizes the dramatic content. Finally, there is the true crime documentary, such as *City Confidential, American Justice*, or *Cold Case Files*, which portray old cases that are sometimes solved, sometimes not.

Thus, as television has evolved, there are not only many more programs that deal with criminal content than there were in its early days but there are also many more *types* of such shows. Obviously, there would not have been this explosion in the variety and number of shows dealing with crime if people were not interested in watching them. Is it that people are interested in crime from the standpoint of learning how they might avoid the pitfalls in making an illicit buck? Obviously not, because we have not experienced a crime epidemic of massive proportions. More probably we enjoy seeing the guilty caught and punished, although some of the more recent shows seem to be getting away from that model and are still popular. Is watching such shows an outlet for our own aggressive urges that must be sublimated in a moral society, or do we just enjoy puzzles and like to solve the crime before the hero does? Or are we just interested voyeurs in a system that most of us will never have any contact with, but that involves so many heinous crimes and often famous people that day after day occupy the front pages of the newspapers and news shows both on radio and TV? As far as we know, no one has come up with anything close to a definitive answer to the question of why such a broad variety of criminal justice programming has gained such popularity.

Although watching all these programs dealing with crime has clearly given us a great deal of exposure to violence or other felonious behavior, it has had to have something of a consciousness-raising or educational influence upon us as well. How many of us have ever sat in a courtroom to watch a criminal trial? How many of us have walked inside a police station or talked to a detective? How many of us have discussed the strategy of how to pursue a trial with either a prosecutor or a defense attorney? The TV shows we watch give us a chance to look into the criminal justice world, one with which so many of us are completely unfamiliar. Whether the picture we get is largely realistic or totally misleading is another, and certainly important, issue.

As noted, the nature of the criminals and the likelihood of them being caught are portrayed much differently on TV than in real life. But regardless of how faithful each show is to reality, we probably get more instruction in individual rights and burden of proof issues from these programs than we did in our high-school history or civics courses. We might also get more of an understanding of the difficulties experienced by all the participants in the justice system.

TV Violence and the Encouragement of Violent Behavior

One of the main concerns evoked by the many TV shows involving criminal behavior is that individuals will be influenced to imitate that behavior in their own lives. And if the portrayal does not have much of an effect on the behavior of rational adults, might it have more influence on unstable adolescents? Unarguably, there have been individuals who have seen a crime on TV and attempted to imitate that crime. Would the shooting at Ft. Gibson, Oklahoma, have occurred if the slaughter at Columbine earlier the same year had not been given 24/7 coverage for many days? Probably not, but even if television did not exist, Columbine would certainly have been given very dramatic and extensive coverage in newspapers and on radio, as well as in newsreels in movie theaters. Who can say whether or not that coverage would have been sufficient to trigger the clearly irrational thinking that led the thirteen-year-old student in Ft. Gibson to shoot four of his schoolmates?

It is likely that "normal" adults view TV programs for just what they are, entertainment, and when our upbringing teaches us to eschew violence in our daily lives we do just that, not imitating what we see in programs we know are not a "real" part of our lives. Real crime and violence probably have much stronger roots in socioeconomic conditions than they do in television, but the research linking TV viewing to aggressive and even criminal behavior is certainly compelling. There is also the rare possibility that extended crime news coverage or even crime dramas may send someone with a tenuous hold on reality to act out his or her fantasies in a criminal manner, but that possibility could hardly be used as an excuse for censoring news or drama. Even though we do not have any real estimates on how likely it is that a child who is brought up in a loving environment with law-abiding and caring friends will adopt violent modes of behavior because of the violent TV he or she has watched, it is becoming clear that young children watching lots of violence on TV is not a good idea.

One measure aimed at reducing the amount of violence viewed by children is the 1988 introduction of the V-chip, which gives parents more control over what their children watch on TV by automatically blocking programs that parents find unacceptable. But the American Psychological Association and other informed and concerned groups have called for further measures to reduce and modify (e.g., have the punishment quickly follow the crime) the amount of violence to which children are exposed on TV.

TV and the Justice System

Before we begin to summarize the possible impact of TV on attitudes and behavior toward crime and the justice system, it is important to recognize that TV is primarily an entertainment medium, and any impact it may have on attitudes or behavior is a secondary effect for the vast majority of programming. Had the federal government wanted to, it could have been much more stringent in awarding and renewing licenses for use of the public airwaves. But the reality is that, with few exceptions, stations offer what people enjoy watching and what will bring them the greatest revenue.

On the positive side, television has certainly given us exposure to the many professions involved with law enforcement. There has been an increase in the number of law school graduates and a clear rise in enrollments in programs related to other aspects of criminal justice, especially forensic science.

Another clear trend has been for TV to present more of the darker side of the various parts of the criminal justice system and those who participate in it. Is TV leading us down a path for the sake of dramatic impact or reflecting a generally growing mistrust of authority that has taken place in our society? This mistrust has been based in reality, as presidents have lied to us (Gulf of Tonkin, Iran Contra scandal, "I did not have sex with that woman," and WMDs), our most respected companies have been exposed as acting totally in the self-interest of their leaders rather than of stockholders or the public (Enron and Worldcom), and police have acted like the vilest of violent criminals (the Abner Louima case in New York and the Rodney King beating in Los Angeles). Given the wide news coverage of these and many other instances of the despicable behavior of those in power, it is not surprising that at least some of the TV shows dealing with criminal justice have begun to show the players in a more venal and perfidious light.

What we can conclude is that TV has provided those generations that grew up with the medium an intensive and extensive view of how the players in the criminal justice system do their jobs, good or bad, and how that might affect them as Joe or Jane Citizen. However, although TV has produced a greater awareness of the criminal justice system and probably encouraged more individuals to enter careers within it, by projecting frequent violence the medium may also have increased the propensity for people to deal with their problems violently, rather than in more level-headed ways.

Finally, there is the question of whether the viewing of so much crime on TV distorts people's perceptions of how law enforcement professionals behave and their expectations of how they would be treated were they to deal with law enforcement officials. In the dramatic world of shows like *Law & Order* or *CSI*, not to mention *The Shield*, police customarily lie to those they are questioning in order to get them to provide information or confess. Although this is allowable behavior in actual interrogations, it can sometimes seem "over the top" to viewers who have no real contact with police, especially in the many instances where the police at first have the wrong suspect. In the real world of TV news, rarely is a positive story about a policeman's behavior featured, but a story like that of Louima or King that is replete with pictures of police misbehavior will be shown frequently all over the country. The day-to-day exposure to these glimpses of law enforcement may well have fostered an atmosphere of mistrust between the public and the law enforcement officials there to protect and serve.

Notes

1. See CyberCollege.com, "TV and Film Violence."
2. Bureau of Justice Statistics, "Homicide Trends in the United States."
3. Bureau of Justice Statistics, "Four Measures of Serious Violent Crime."
4. University of Central Florida, "Criminals in TV Entertainment."

Chapter 14

Financing the Game: TV and Professional Sports

Sports have been close to the American heart from even the time before we were a nation, with the early settlers engaging in a number of games for the sheer enjoyment of the participants and the entertainment of onlookers. For instance, they learned such activities as wrestling and archery from the native Indians; English settlers brought ninepins, which was a game similar to bowling, to America; and the Dutch brought ice skating.

Folklore attributes the invention of baseball to Abner Doubleday in 1839, but according to *The Concise Columbia Encyclopedia* Doubleday had nothing to do with it and it most likely evolved from the English games of cricket and rounders. Whatever its origin, baseball grew in popularity until, with the establishment of the National League in 1876, it became the first professional sport in the United States, paying its players and charging those who wanted to watch it being played. Baseball, of course, was followed into the professional ranks by many other sports, such as football, basketball, tennis, hockey, and soccer. These sports were developed as amateur contests and became standard fare from grade schools to colleges. Basketball probably had its strongest following at the high school level, whereas football became the strongest big-time sport at the college level. Well before the first truly professional football game was played in 1895, the first intercollegiate game was played at Rutgers against rival Princeton in 1869.

We have become used to large stadiums packed with tens of thousands of people watching these games. The smell of hot dogs and popcorn, the cheering of the crowd, the arguments over who's the better player, and the traffic jams getting out of the parking lot have all become a fixture of the American experience. But here, as in other aspects of American life, from the introduction of roller derby on black-and-white TV to the daylong spectacle of the Super Bowl in living color, the advent of television has changed that experience, some might say for the better, some for the worse. The following sections examine that influence in a variety of sports.

Football after TV

Television has probably had as much influence on football as on any professional sport, the most substantial influence being the money that television brought into it. Presently, we have the NFL with two conferences and a total of thirty-two teams as opposed to the one league with thirteen teams that existed in 1950 when the Los Angeles Rams became the first professional football team to have all its games televised.

Seeing the potential for substantial increases in income from TV, a number of entrepreneurs established the American Football League in 1960, which struggled for survival until it signed a five-year contract with NBC for $36 million in 1964. This contract gave each team $850,000 per year, which was just under what the NFL teams were getting from CBS. The rest, as they say, is history. Because the AFL was now able to compete for players on a much more equal basis and TV was able to enhance the enjoyment of the game itself, the number of fans grew rapidly, and the NFL began to view the AFL as much as an opportunity as it was a threat. This led to the establishment of a Super Bowl contest between the winners of the two leagues in 1966 and then to their merging at the beginning of the 1970 season. With the 1968 Super Bowl victory of the Joe Namath-led Jets over the heavily favored Baltimore Colts, the AFL's credentials as a professional league were firmly established.

The nature of football, with periods of intensive action occurring at many places on a large field at the same time followed by periods of inaction, makes it exciting, but somewhat uneven and sometimes difficult for fans sitting in the stands to follow. If you're watching the ball carrier a considerable distance away, you might be fooled into following the wrong person by a fake or a reverse and miss a key block. If you're watching on TV, during the time that the pileup is being unraveled and the team huddles for the next play, you are probably seeing that reverse or the block replayed from a camera operator who is assigned to cover that aspect of the play. With its multiple camera angles, instant replay, slow motion, and ability to focus broadly or close, TV can provide a view of the game that may be more exciting and informative than that experienced by the fans at the stadium. In fact, many fans at the game carry portable TV sets for just those reasons.

Some of TV's other influences on football are also neither subtle nor unobtrusive. For instance, instant replay would not exist if there were not a TV tape to play back and review "instantly." We've put the last word in quotation marks because the review is by no means instant and usually takes a number of minutes. The NFL has experimented with different sets of rules governing instant replay in an effort to improve the accuracy of officials' decisions while keeping delays to a minimum. Whether instant replay has added to or subtracted from your enjoyment of the game is your decision, but it is certainly a change that TV has brought to the sport.

A consistently positive change that TV has brought to the viewing of the game is the superimposing of a yellow first-down line on the screen. This line gives a clear and immediate indication of whether a first down has been made on a play or how far the ball must be advanced for a first down. This view is even more accurate than one gets as a fan in attendance at the game because it is close up and is not distorted by the stadium fan's viewing angle.

Another change brought by football is the TV time-out. If a game is proceeding apace with too few natural pauses, such as time-outs called by the teams or official time-outs for measurement, scores, or changes of possession, the officials will call a time-out specifically to give the TV station an opportunity to air commercials. To the fan at home, nothing seems amiss because the dead time is filled by a commercial. To the fan at the stadium, however, it is a time when everyone is just wandering around having conversations with one another, and it just appears that the game has been suspended. After awhile one gets used to the process and knows what is happening, but such time-outs are clearly an annoyance to those who have paid high-ticket prices to watch a game, not inactivity.

The most notable TV influence on football is the coverage of the Super Bowl. The game has become primarily an entertainment vehicle and only secondarily a sports event. It has expanded into a bacchanalia week before the game and twelve hours of coverage on the day of the game. Both before the game and at half time, the most popular entertainers in the country put on elaborately and expensively staged musical numbers. Advertisers use the event to unveil new commercial campaigns, and there are actually industry awards for the best Super Bowl commercials. Indeed, the contract to telecast the Super Bowl is more valuable to a TV network than the contract to televise the entire regular football season.

143

TV has made football the most-watched professional sport in America. This is probably because of the ability of multiple cameras, superimposed first-down lines, and selective replays to provide the viewer with a fast-paced, exciting sport, with more access to what is happening on the field than if the person were actually in the stands. In an almost perverse situation, TV commercials even provide some entertainment during otherwise dull time-outs. Finally, and perhaps most importantly, TV makes the games available to an audience of millions rather than the thousands who can be fit into a stadium.

Going beyond TV's influence on sports is its impact on society. For many millions of people, TV changed Sunday from a family-oriented day to a sports-oriented day in front of the TV set, spent either alone or perhaps with friends. TV's revenues have enabled more teams to enter and survive in the NFL, thereby giving more fans home teams to root for and more opportunities to see games at a local stadium. And for millions of others, there are numerous games to choose from in the early and late afternoon as well as evening, especially those who have cable or satellite TV with a sports package. Thus, like it or not, for a large segment of society and for a good part of the year, TV has defined Sunday as FOOTBALL day.

Baseball in an Age of Action

TV has also directly affected America's national pastime because a major portion of its revenue comes from TV, and most people see the games on TV, rather than at the ballpark. Today, for all the major sports, the number of fans who watch the games or matches on television is much larger than the number actually at the ballparks. For instance, because the 2002 World Series involved two California teams, it had the lowest ratings since the earlier days of TV when there were many fewer sets. Despite this dearth of viewers, however, there was still an average of over 12.5 million homes tuned in to each game, as compared to an average of just under 44,000 fans who were able to watch each game at the stadium. Thus, for every fan who attended one of the series games, at least 284 watched on TV (if only one person watched it in each household).

Financially, it is just as important for the game to appeal to TV watchers as to those who actually show up at the stadium, because the income from TV is a major source of total team income. Thus, although baseball was conceived as a daytime sport and remained so for many years, since the age of television it has become overwhelmingly a prime-time nighttime sport to maximize TV audiences.

144

But even though it has been given prime-time viewing exposure, the number of viewers has been falling because of the game's inability to compete with other sports that provide more continuous action. Hockey, soccer, and basketball are sports with fairly continuous action and comparatively few pauses of any considerable length. Football has many pauses, but each play involves much movement and many exciting things happening at the same time, and the pauses are utilized to replay the previous action at various speeds and from various angles. Baseball telecasts frequently reshow a play, but there are still many long pauses between relatively infrequent actions.

TV has conditioned us (especially those who grew up with MTV) to look for flash, color, and pulsating sound, qualities that are typically lacking except for possibly a few minutes during a three-hour baseball game. Thus, as television has matured into its own individualized medium, baseball has come to fit less and less into its dominant characteristics. However, it's interesting to note that, although there has been a considerable decrease in baseball's TV audience, attendance at the ballgames has been rising considerably from just over forty-three million in 1980 to 62.6 million in 1997. It is still a sport that is usually played in pleasant weather, and the camaraderie and banter experienced at the ballpark are not normally experienced at home.

Thus, the advent of TV has had a lot smaller influence on baseball, which is still our national pastime in terms of actual total attendance at professional games, including minor leagues, even though it is far from our favorite TV sport. The sport, as displayed on TV, has not changed that much; what has changed is its financial structure.

The Growth of Stock Car Racing

Stock car racing is a relative newcomer to the arena of professional sports. This sport has a colorful history, having grown out of the problems of bootleggers during Prohibition in the 1920s and 1930s. The distribution of "moonshine" liquor required cars and drivers who could rapidly transport their goods from place to place without being caught by the police. The ability to elude the police meant the difference between money in one's pocket and a term in jail. The people involved in this business "souped up" their cars to the best of their ability and became quite skilled at driving the country roads at high speeds. Bootleggers then began to hold races to see who could drive the fastest, racing on Sunday afternoons and "delivering" on Sunday nights. This racing activity persisted even after the repeal of Prohibition in 1933, because the races remained popular and there was still a good deal of bootlegging due to the high taxes on whiskey.

William H. G. France and others established the National Association of Stock Car Auto Racing (NASCAR) in 1947. NASCAR now comprises ten divisions, but the most well known is the Winston Cup in which the best drivers compete. Although many people still have the image of NASCAR racing being a "redneck" sport limited to the backwoods of the southeastern United States, it has grown into the second most-watched sport on TV behind football. NASCAR has tracks in twenty-three cities around the country in the states of Nevada, Texas, California, Illinois, New Hampshire, Indiana, New York, Kansas, Arizona, Pennsylvania, and Michigan, as well as many southeastern states. Attendance at these events is enormous, with an average of over 150,000 people per Winston Cup event and a total attendance of 6.5 million people in the year 2000.

Bruce Martin, SportsTicker contributing editor, cites television's role in NASCAR's tremendous growth, arguing that CBS's flag to-flag coverage of the Daytona 500 since 1979 "has played a key role in elevating that event to status enjoyed by the Super Bowl and World Series." ESPN was the first station to carry the majority of the NASCAR races at a time when the major networks carried only a few of the better-known races, and this coverage was a big factor in the growth of ESPN as a viable cable channel (now multiple channels). But the growth of interest in NASCAR racing became irresistible to the larger networks, and in 2001 NASCAR signed a $2.8 billion, six-year contract with the FOX, NBC, and Turner networks. Motorsports Management International estimates that these races produce an annual national television audience of 300 million viewers, an audience that is growing considerably faster than any other sport.

Is Bruce Martin correct in attributing NASCAR's tremendous growth to television? It is certainly true that many more people now view the sport than would if it were not telecast, but that is true for all sports. And certainly, with television involved there are potentially more races, bigger purses, and more money flowing into the sport than anyone would have dreamed of fifteen years ago. But its enormous and rapidly growing popular appeal is what brought major TV coverage to the sport in the first place. NASCAR has those elements that make for excitement, continuous action, danger, and the ability to produce "stars" based on their skills. The fact that these elements lend themselves to television coverage is a clear plus and has resulted in the emergence of a new national sport that takes a back seat to no others.

Unlike television's influence on professional football in the form of TV time-outs, for example, there has been no similar impact on the conduct of the races themselves, and given the danger inherent in the sport, there are not likely to be. In addition, NASCAR, more than any other professional sport, provides opportunities for advertisers to show their wares. Although in every sport there may be signs plugging products posted around the stadiums, NASCAR provides the opportunities to place product logos on cars, equipment, and drivers' jumpsuits. Indeed, a NASCAR race is a brightly colored array of probably hundreds of product logos lighting up the TV screen. These endorsements and their display on TV are a large source of income for the people and organizations involved in the sport and help ensure its survival and growth. It appears that auto racing and television are perfect companions, giving the sport a venue for growing into an American favorite.

Multiplying Sports Coverage

In addition to the sports described above, basketball, hockey, tennis, golf, and wrestling are heavily covered on TV, with soccer and boxing less so. Basketball and hockey are natural events for TV, with quick action and lots happening around the field of play. Tennis tends to have some of these same qualities even though there are fewer people in the field of action. Each of these sports draws large TV audiences.

Surprisingly, golf, which has little of the action of these sports, is also a staple on TV, not because it draws a larger TV audience than some of the other sports, but because the audience it draws has a very high level of disposable income, a quality that is endearing to a number of advertisers of upscale merchandise and services. In some ways, golf has exercised more control over how TV has covered its matches than have other sports; this is particularly true in the coverage of the Masters tournament where the network is severely limited in many of its production aspects, even in how often and how many commercials it may air.

Before TV, golf in the United States was a spring through summer sport, but now the season has expanded. In addition, a number of special formats have been introduced, one being the Skins Game, which pits four very popular players against one another in a hole-by-hole competition. But for the most part, the game has been left intact, but made more exciting by using many cameras and switching every minute or so to where the most popular action is taking place, either live or through instant replay. The attendee at the match can only see a limited amount of the action by staying at one hole or by following a specific golfer. The TV viewers, on the other hand, see mainly the golfers who are among the top ten leaders, any outstanding shots, good or bad, and their most popular heroes (such as Tiger Woods) whether or not they are among the leaders.

Programming Our Lives

As a result, the main influence of TV has been to increase the popularity of the game and the number of golf courses in the country. Although there was some drop in the number of rounds played during the recession of the early 2000s, golf has grown from a sport that was very limited in public appeal in the 1940s to one with broad appeal to all segments of the population. The National Golf Foundation estimated that 26.2 million individuals over age eighteen played over 500 million rounds of golf in 2002. Most likely the exposure on TV has been a major factor in bringing people from all walks of life to participate in a sport that had previously been limited mostly to the more affluent.

TV has had a complex effect upon professional boxing, at first introducing more fans to the sport, but then possibly being a major factor in its decline. Boxing became very popular between the 1920s and the 1940s with boxers like Dempsey, Tunney, Louis, and Marciano becoming household names. Boxing was well suited for TV when it developed because the action was intense and took place in a limited amount of space, making it easy to cover. The icing on the cake was that there were one-minute breaks in the action that lent themselves well to commercials.

Thus, boxing became a very popular feature in the early days of TV, with the *Gillette Cavalcade of Sports* broadcasting a weekly bout for national TV. In the late 1940s and early 1950s, millions of people would go to their neighborhood taverns to watch the Friday night fights, because the taverns immediately installed TVs, recognizing their appeal, and most people did not yet own a TV. However, the rise of television viewing was accompanied by a decrease in attendance at local bouts, resulting in the closing of many of the clubs that served as the base of development for young fighters. Whatever the dynamics, interest in the sport as a TV attraction declined rapidly to where only championship bouts were covered. Today, boxing tends to be covered by some type of premium or pay-TV arrangement.

So in its early days, TV significantly raised the popularity of boxing, and boxing, in turn, increased the popularity of TV. But with the widespread proliferation of TV and the decline in boxing's popularity, other sports are featured in the numerous sports bars, and boxing is no longer a major element of network programming.

Wrestling, which is more an entertainment than a sport, also increased in popularity enormously in the early days of TV because it had some of the same qualities as boxing: it takes place within a limited space and has relatively continuous action. In the days of black-and-white TV one could watch a wrestling match almost any night of the week, and wrestlers like Gorgeous George and Antonio Rocco received tremendous newspaper coverage. Wrestling is no longer a feature on network TV, but still receives some of the highest cable TV ratings of any type of programming.

Soccer is something of an enigma; even though it's the most popular sport worldwide, its history as a professional sport in the United States has been checkered. Relatively few Americans realize that soccer has been played as an amateur, semi-professional, and professional sport in the United States since the nineteenth century. However, in this country it was mostly viewed as an ethnic sport and not consistently embraced by the majority of the population, even though America entered the first World Cup in 1930. Because soccer—known as football outside the United States—is so popular worldwide, there have been a number of professional leagues established in this country, including the North American Soccer League, which in 1985 brought Brazilian soccer star Pele out of retirement to provide it with immediate TV pizzazz.

But attempts at establishing a profitable professional soccer league in the United States have not been as successful as in other sports. According to *Media Life* magazine, in 2002 TV viewership of most Major League Soccer (MLS) matches in the United States was only about 200,000, which compares to millions for a football game or auto race. Just as baseball has shrunk in TV popularity, but grown in actual attendance, soccer has failed to make it on American TV, but grown as a participative sport. Thanks to Pele and the introduction of soccer to the TV audience, the sport has enjoyed enormous participation in the United States, with more children currently playing in organized little league soccer than in little league baseball.

The Olympics

The Olympic games have always had a broad following around the world. Television has greatly enhanced the reach of the Olympics, and every two years either the winter or summer games garner a tremendous audience. How many of us would know a luge from a loge if it were not for television? Thus, perhaps the most potent outcome of the interaction of TV and the Olympics has been to popularize, at least to some extent, some sports that have not had very much exposure in the United States. In no instance has this been as true as in the competition of figure skating in the winter games. This event had achieved wide popularity even before the advent of television, perhaps reaching its zenith when Sonja Henie, the Olympic gold medal winner in 1928, 1932, and 1936 became a movie star on the basis of her popularity on the ice.

Television, however, has had perhaps as much of a positive impact on the sport as it did on football. Because the TV production crew is aware

149

of each skater's program in advance, the director can use the camera to provide wide shots as well as tightly focused shots to the skater's best advantage. Also, while the judges are making their decisions, TV can replay the highlights of the performance, whether good or bad. Based on its TV coverage the sport has gained enormous popularity, and it is a rare weekend in the winter when there are not at least two or three skating programs, whether competitions or exhibitions, on both network and cable TV.

Women's Professional Sports

One aspect of figure skating is that the women's competitions are at least as popular as the men's, if not more so. Thus, in figure skating, television has created a platform for women to compete professionally for large international audiences. But this is not the only instance in which television has been instrumental in providing a platform for women's professional sports. The Women's National Basketball Association began playing in 1997, with TV contracts that significantly improve its chances of survival over time. Not as successful was the Women's United Soccer Association, which began play in 2001, also with TV contracts, but was not able to survive. In tennis, the women's matches have perhaps become as popular as the men's, and the women stars are probably more popular as celebrities.

Sports Finances

In each of the heavily covered sports there has been an explosion in player salaries (or winnings), in some ways made possible by court rulings against the antitrust nature of league practices, but actually made financially feasible by TV revenues. For example, even with the free agent clause in effect, no player would be able to command an $11 million dollar annual salary if there were no TV revenues. It is highly unlikely that in the absence of TV, any current professional team could pay its player-related expenses and not go into bankruptcy within a short period of time. Even in the individual sports, for example, the winner of today's Master's golf tournament will go home with more purse money than Sam Snead won in his entire career.

This raises the question of the effect that all this money has had on how individual players play the game. In some sports, such as tennis and boxing, the individual player uses all his or her skill and wiles to win the match, and the issue of individual versus team effectiveness is moot. In others, like football, and to a lesser degree, hockey, teamwork is clearly the critical factor, and individual assignments are more defined, giving the individual less ability to "hot dog." Although basketball is also characterized by teamwork and many set plays, the opportunity for one individual to work the ball until he can shoot, no matter how difficult the shot, is clearly present. Given the small number of players on the field and the millions of salary dollars riding on individual statistics, a *Harvard Magazine* article by Craig Lambert suggested that the team sport of basketball has been deteriorating to one of five individuals on the court. This article further hypothesizes that this change in the nature of the sport is why arenas that had been sold out for years are now experiencing thousands of unsold seats at every game. To the extent that this is true, basketball, like boxing before it, may find itself a victim of its own success on television.

The Demand for Thrills

It is clear that television has had a very strong influence on the development of sports in the United States, including what sports we watch, how we watch them, and even what the rules are for the contests themselves. Certainly, without television, our choice of what games we would be able to see and be able to play would be severely constricted, except for boxing, in which there might be more matches today if not for TV. Further, television, in creating a certain mode of interaction with its viewers, has created a dichotomy between those sports we like to watch on TV and those sports we either participate in or attend in person. Television is a communications medium and as such has certain technical and financial requirements. These include lots of action, the ability to replay key events as well as fill dead time, and the ability to air commercials relatively frequently without losing out on the action. Those sports best fulfilling those requirements have become our favorites for TV viewing, whereas those that lack those requirements may still be very popular, but not necessarily as TV staples.

TV has had a profound impact on the way we view the world around us, and our changed perception also affects our relationship with the sports we watch. Viewers seek thrills through ongoing action and the rush of heightened drama. As a result, and with the urgings of sponsors who demand ratings, the pace and performance of the contests themselves have changed. Rules of the games, such as those of basketball, have been changed to promote high scoring. Football goalposts were moved back to the rear of the end zone to make field goals more difficult and encourage touchdown efforts.

Yet, continuous activity in itself is not the key to ratings success, as illustrated by the failure of soccer to command an American viewing audience. Those games are low scoring and the player performances exemplified by subtle skills rather than sudden outbursts. Those come with the infrequent shots to score, most of which fail. Thus, announcers in other cultures scream "Goal! Goal! Goal!" when a shot succeeds, and even the missed shots receive continuing replays on the postgame highlight shows. That's not enough for us. Soccer does not provide the kind of tension the American TV audience demands.

Television creates much of the drama of sports through its presentations, especially the commentary provided by announcers and background analysts who outline and rehash plays and hype tension with enthusiastic energy. They, as much as the players and coaches, give excitement to the final two minutes of a football game, which—with timeouts and stopped clocks—can actually last fifteen or twenty minutes.

Not only has TV changed the nature of many sports and the way we watch them but our viewing of sport has—more significantly—changed the way we engage with much of the world around us—personally, occupationally, socially, and politically. Ironically, when the late historian Daniel Boorstin, in his 1961 book *The Image*, argued that what he called pseudo-events had taken over much of public life, he saw sports as providing a refreshing antidote of spontaneity, one area that could not be manipulated. Now, a half-century later, the forces that have made so much of politics, commerce, and entertainment artificial have infiltrated sports. Of course, outcomes are still surprises and the core drama is genuine. Yet the audience has come to accept the hyped atmosphere and contrived urgencies and has come to expect equivalent thrills from elections, business deals, holiday events, and even daily life.

Part IV

Our World

Chapter 15

Broadcast Cultures: TV in the World

Live TV in the United States went coast to coast for the first time more than a half-century ago with the November 18, 1951, broadcast of CBS's *See It Now*. The technology that made it possible was a coaxial cable of layered copper wires buried in the ground. The media celebrated this connection as a high point of unified communication, perhaps not with the pomp of the golden spike that joined the transcontinental railroad but as an event of major significance. From our perspective today, transcontinental TV may seem a primitive achievement, as blurred and deficient as the grainy gray pictures displayed on the screens of the 1950s, but then it represented an important human accomplishment. We have come a long way, no doubt far beyond the imaginations of those who watched that first intercontinental broadcast.

Now images of the entire world are available in seconds. No place is too remote for live broadcasting, even if only via a jerky camera phone. We have seen the earth from outer space and have seen the landscapes of the moon, of Mars, and beyond. We can view the bottoms of the oceans, the peaks of Everest, and the inner recesses of the human body. Very little is beyond the access of the camera, and very little can be considered strange territory.

Satellites and the Internet

Satellites and the Internet have not only made an abundance of programming available to people throughout the world but they also provide

155

access to broadcasts originating from areas thousands of miles away. For some time Americans have been able to purchase satellite dishes capable of tuning into signals from across oceans. Now some U.S. cable companies, aware of the growing potential market of immigrant populations eager for programming from their home countries, are offering programming packages in targeted areas. For example, Cablevision's packages include programming in Russian, Korean, Hindi, Chinese, Japanese, Portuguese, German, and Italian. Domestic Spanish channels are widely available. A few broadcast channels provide occasional programs in a variety of languages. Those with broadband Internet connections can watch programs from dozens of nations on their monitors, much of it especially created for the Internet. Any limitations on offerings result from viewer interests, not technology. The availability of this linguistic variety no doubt contributes to the changes that have moved U.S. society from a melting pot to a multicultural potpourri.

Europeans with cable or satellite connections can choose among programs originating from throughout the Continent in several languages. *The New York Times* reported in May 2004 that Singapore Telecommunications is leading a consortium of telephone companies in a project to install more than 9,300 miles of fiber optic cable that will link Europe, Asia, and the Middle East. Access will be extended to what are now underserved parts of the globe.

Television, even before the installation of that cable, exists as a global phenomenon, penetrating to remote villages with power generators. Each year, it is growing in the reach and range of its offerings. Now TV is a dominant and universal source of entertainment; often the same programs are dubbed into many languages or presented in local iterations of their formats. It serves as a consumer marketing force both through the actual commercials shown and through the lifestyles portrayed on its programs. What dominates are the objects that people wear and decorate with, what they drive, where and how they live. This increased desire for consumption is also a political influence, especially when combined with news reports that provide additional information about the economic and social limitations of the viewer's society. For the majority of the world's population, television has changed what people know, what they want to possess, what they want from their leaders, what they believe, how they think, and how they spend their time.

What the World Watches

In 2002, shortly after the beginning of a new millennium, the earth was home to nearly 1.5 billion TV sets for 6.1 billion people. There were almost twice as many TV sets as telephones in the world. In the United States, more than 98 percent of homes have at least one set. The 1997 TV density per population ranged from one set per every 1.3 people in the United States and approximately one set for every three people in European countries to extremes like one set for every 200 people in Angola and one for every 503 in Ethiopia. Most likely, today there is greater TV density per population in the poorer nations.

In 1997, India, for example, had one set for every forty-four people. Yet, given the country's population and its potential as a market for both commercial and non-commercial broadcasting, the availability of programming is burgeoning. Even villages that were just hooked up to electricity are receiving cable and satellite broadcasts. In 2000, India had fifty cable channels, such as Sony, Star, Zee, and ETC, with the expectation that the number will grow to 120 by 2010. Much of the programming is foreign, supplied by Disney, ESPN, the Hallmark Channel, and other channels familiar to people in the United States. But the number of Indian-language programs is increasing.

American programming, or local variants, still clearly dominates throughout the world. For example, an analysis of one day of programming in May 2004 on Malaysian TV found that most of the programs featured Western actors in shows such as *Third Watch, Mutant X*, and *Jake 2.0* and only a few local shows. In contrast, in the same month, one Nigerian channel offered an evening lineup of locally produced programming, including dramas about the intrigue and subterfuge surrounding a woman's inheritance, a village girl trying to escape marriage to an unpleasant rich old man, and another young woman whose stepsister and stepmother set out to frame her for fraud.

Although these stories focused on contemporary African themes, they shared a common concern of TV dramatic programming in most places: a focus on human dilemmas and, in these particular examples, women in distress. Nigerians with satellite reception were far from limited to these local choices. In addition to other African channels, they could watch British and French channels.

A Monday evening's viewing in Botswana was decidedly American, going from *Robocop* to *Sesame Street* and the *Flintstones*, and then to such soap operas as *Passions* and *The Bold and the Beautiful. Dikgang*, a local program, preceded *Oprah Winfrey* and *Hughleys*, with a show from the Christian Broadcasting Network in between. Local news came before *FBI Files*, followed by *Forever* and the British *BBC News*.

Whatever local programming variations exist in the world, they tend to assume certain basic formats. For news programming, anchor people sit at credenzas with footage projected behind them or expanding to the

157

full screen. Game shows and Reality TV follow the same formats. Dramas, whether soap opera or crime shows, have similar rhythms, whatever the culture, costuming, or language. Occasionally, a unique show appears directed to local tastes. For example, the French are attracted to intellectual discussions among a group of men and women sitting in a room. Austrian TV on Saturday nights may show a lederhosen-clad oompah band performing in a local beer hall.

Attempts to Censor and Control

Knowledge—whether authentic, exaggeration, or misinformation— invariably has consequences that sometimes are manifested in political pressures. When a nation's television offerings deny its citizens opportunities to view the range of programs found throughout the rest of the world, that country is usually a closed society obsessed with controlling what its citizens can see and know.

Authoritarian governments have been well aware of the dangers TV presents to their control. For example, to maintain the system of apartheid, South Africa did not allow television broadcasts until 1976. Those in charge wanted to keep people in distinct categories in which they accepted their limitations because they were ignorant about how other groups, especially the white majority, lived. TV was seen as providing too much information about the privileged. Writing for *The Atlantic* about the situation during the years he grew up in that country, Rob Nixon noted,

> In this context official hostility to television made perfect sense. The state recognized that TV's market-driven voracity would show scant respect for the jigsaw of militarily enforced ethnic boundaries. [Albert] Hertzog condemned TV on these grounds: "There is no more powerful medium for dismantling the population groups' sense of identity." As one of his parliamentary colleagues put it, rather more emphatically, "Television, like communism, promotes sameness."

In contrast, most blatantly repressive regimes seek to promote an unthinking sameness in their people. The actions of North Korea exemplify this control. That country allows TV sets in homes, but restricts programming to patriotic fantasies and suppresses news of the country or the world. Most of its airtime features endless shots of the Dear Leader, Kim Jong Il. Other programs glorify the army and excoriate North Korea's enemies—South Korea, the United States, and Japan. It's hardly a matter of viewer choice. Both TV sets and radios are pretuned and locked in to the government's official broadcast outlets. Trying to switch stations is a crime. It is no wonder that in 1999, the country had fifty-five sets per 1,000 people compared with 361 in South Korea.

Other governments, like that of China, use more selective controls, offering a host of broadcast outlets and a variety of programming; yet China controls what gets in from outside its borders. For example, it denied access to the British-based Star satellite stations until Star agreed to drop BBC news from its offerings. When it entered the World Trade Organization, China limited foreign access to its radio, film, and TV sector and forbade foreign investment. As James Kynge wrote in the December 31, 2001, issue of *The Financial Times*, "Beijing saw the media as too sensitive an area to be formally thrown open to foreign capital as part of its WTO succession deal."[1]

It remains to be seen how much longer the Chinese government will be able to maintain control over the media in the face of social and political pressures and technological advancements. But governments are not wrong when they believe that the media, and perhaps television especially, can undermine their authority. In Shakespeare's time, the number of stationer's companies—those who were allowed to print documents—was limited to three to facilitate supervision and censorship. When the Soviet Union existed, it attempted to place strict limits on the use of copying machines. Part of that system's collapse can be attributed to the ultimate failure of such controls and its people's growing exposure to the outside world through the media.

The end of Soviet communism, however, has not meant the end of attempts to limit what the Russian people can see on TV. The post-Soviet Russian government took control of the ORT channel, the only one that broadcasts to all of the country's eighty-nine regions. In many other countries the media are puppets of the state, which is why during revolutions and rebellions one of the first strategic goals becomes occupation of the TV broadcasting station.

The strongest force that threatens such political censorship is the existence of cable news networks with international exposure, such as CNN and BBC World. Because of technological limitations or porous borders not all governments have China's ability to block these services. With exposure to cable news, more people than ever before share an awareness of what is happening around the globe.

Although many applaud this information explosion, critics voice several areas of concern. These news sources come from the West and, therefore, cannot avoid a built-in pro-Western bias. Al Jazeera, the Arabic-language satellite network, is one attempt to provide an alternative voice, although many in the West accuse it of having its own bias. Some fear that these worldwide news channels will damage local cultures, in contrast to those who applaud the potential of an electronic linkage bringing about a universal mass society with a shared consciousness.

What People Want and What They Can Get

The threat to local culture arises less from news than from the programs, mainly American, watched by so many. In addition to the fact that TV viewing in itself can occupy much of people's time, taking them away from traditional activities, what they see can change their values and expectations. That is a primary reason why American clothing, foods, logos, and sport and film stars have become objects of desire in even remote lands.

Another problem in an age of unprecedented sharing of information may be a TV version of the digital divide that is now seen between those with and without access to computers. For television, this divide translates to those who own or do not own sets, and it is the range of programming available to those who do own sets that is key. As the above figures for TV set penetration indicate, the differences between the affluent and poor nations are dramatic. In a globalized world, whether that transformation is positive or negative, those denied access are handicapped. Although the poor no doubt will acquire more sets in time, that may not be soon enough for them to gain the information that will help compensate for extreme contrasts in economic realities and potentials. For the technologically advanced, the convergence of television broadcasting and computers no doubt will grow even faster than will the number of basic TV sets among the poorer peoples.

TV access also has economic consequences. Consumer wants result from both viewing commercials and exposure to the products used by performers in the shows themselves as aspects of the lifestyles depicted. Marketing specialists covet the potential sales to the vast worldwide audience that will crave American goods. But even though American products now dominate commercial TV, other industrial nations envision new outlets for the cars, electronics, clothing, and other goods that they produce. Here again, the poorer nations are likely to be left behind, wanting to buy and having little to sell.

Now that cell phones are beginning to offer video cameras as well as still cameras and wireless broadband access is becoming more widespread, it's not difficult to imagine a future in which billions of people in the developed areas can watch TV wherever they are. With satellite signals, many of their choices probably will be international programming.

TV in the future will continue to shrink the world, certainly economically if not politically.

Accuracy and Validity

Now that hundreds of millions of people spend so much time viewing programming from throughout the world but primarily originating from the United States, the issue of their cultural knowledge becomes more crucial. The material objects of the societies they see on TV shows—homes, furniture, landscapes, food, cars, clothing, and the like—certainly exist. But what about their context? Much of TV programming, especially situation comedies, emphasizes the extremes and often the totally fictitious. How accurate are the impressions we get of other societies, and what are the consequences of those impressions?

In the final years of the communist bloc before the Berlin Wall fell, its propagandists tried to convince people that American TV documented the decadent West as a place of criminals, gunfire, murders, and mayhem. We had a different perspective, of course, and for the most part so did East Germans who had access to West German TV or Russians who could watch the then-popular *Dallas* from Finland. What they saw was affluence, as represented by large and lavish homes, flowered landscapes, shiny cars, and fancy clothes. The screen revealed circular drives lined with Cadillacs and Mercedes. Who cared if the characters driving them were thieves and murderers? These *Dallas* fans halfway across the world named their children Sue Ellen, Pam, and Jock and longed for that abundance. If this was decadence, they wanted in.

Although Iron Curtain viewers did see plenty of crime and violence, they found a more compelling reality in the TV image of the American lifestyle. With their everyday experience of long queues for half-empty store shelves, cramped apartments, and toxic dumps, the landscapes of Texas and California, the shops of Rodeo Drive, the high-rise luxury of New York, and the actors' wardrobes revealed actualities once beyond their imaginations. Most immigrants, who endure unbelievable hardships in journeying to the United States, either legally or illegally, come not for the abstract concept of freedom but for the economic opportunities implied in the U.S. television shows that are shown throughout the world. When once verbal rumors of "streets paved with gold" circulated among the hungry and deprived, now clear pictures of affluence project into city slums and village hovels on every continent.

American viewers may be surprised that someone would be so naïve as to assume that the scene on the screen is real. The wealth depicted, they know, is just a prop. But are we so different from those who transform their TV experience of America into instant anthropological analysis? Don't we do the same when we see TV depictions of other cultures? Our impressions of other lands are no different in kind. We come to think that there is nothing out there but Russian mafia, Arab terrorists, slave labor, starving children, or illegal aliens crammed into cargo cases or crawling across sun-baked fields to cross a border. Is that the whole picture? Other than an occasional import of a British drama or comedy, U.S. TV is totally void of an English-dubbed drama or comedy produced in Russia or in Mexico that might give a richer view of family life in those countries.

Pictures can be riveting, especially when they appear in vivid color and come to life on a screen. They convince because they seem so real, sharp, clear, and concrete in their detail. For the majority of viewers who lack the actual experiences of place with which to contrast the pictures, the image imprints because it fills a vacuum.

TV brings us the world. The spread of lightweight cameras and the opening of borders leave few places that cannot be photographed and transmitted by beams bounced off satellites. Without rising from our easy chair we can witness the Great Wall of China, kangaroos hopping across the Australian Outback, the Eiffel Tower, or reptiles slithering along the banks of the Amazon. We can watch insects breed in close-up, lions stalk for prey in slow motion, and flowers bloom in time lapse.

Are we watching the world or the TV version of the world—cropped, selected, re-paced? Some may argue that this is a useless question. We can't go everywhere. We can't experience everywhere first hand. Do we have an alternative to television cameras and editors who package the choices for us? Are misconceptions and illusions about places in the world preferable to no conception at all?

The answer is neither obvious nor easy. It can be argued that exposure to America, distorted as it was, hastened the downfall of communism. But what if the people and the places in the camera become Others, human beings made strange by their garb or their food choices or their religious ceremonies and the Other becomes the enemy? Misinformation and misunderstanding then escalate into hostility.

Can pictures lie? Of course they can. Even an unadulterated shot can give a wrong impression because of the time span it covers and because of all of the information it omits. One way to gauge their accuracy is to measure the moving images against the perspective of the printed page, preferably a number of pages and from a variety of commentators. Most people, of course, won't take the time to do that, and even some who do will not be able to suppress the vividness of the picture. When they finally travel to a place they have already seen on TV, many will measure the actuality against the scenes in their memory and end up seeing what they expected to discover. TV can overwhelm what our eyes witness and our mind knows. It has that much power.

People can acquire significant amounts of information from TV, but the question becomes, what do we really know?

Note

1. Cited in Hughes, "Written Testimony."

Chapter 16

Multiplying Channels: Proliferation and Fragmentation

As the commercial possibilities of television began to be contemplated in the late 1930s, it was clear that the problems of distribution would have solutions similar to those of radio, rather than those associated with the distribution of electricity. The TV signal was broadcast over the airwaves, and with the construction of a reasonable number of towers to project or transmit the signal all but the most remote locations could receive coverage with a relatively modest capital investment. Thus, there was no need to give broadcasters exclusive rights to a geographic market as was done with utilities that supplied gas and electricity. Stations that obtained licenses were free to compete for viewers against other stations in the same broadcast area, just as radio stations had done.

This situation led to a great disparity in the number of stations available in different homes, depending on where they were located, but the free market system very quickly spread TV coverage across the country. In very remote areas there may have been no TV available in the 1950s, and in other rural areas one or two stations may have been broadcasting. In contrast, in New York, seven stations began competing with one another from the earliest days of TV.

Reaching an Audience

But technology soon began to remove the limitations on the number of stations that could be received in any one location. When cable became an alternative form of getting television into the home, governments reverted to the electricity model of distribution, with contracts being negotiated at the local rather than at the state level. The companies were not guaranteed a certain level of profit, but rather were contracted to pay the municipality a certain percent of their revenues. Thus, of all the markets served by cable, the vast majority are monopolies, as were the utility companies. The success of this distribution system is demonstrated by the fact that from 1970 to today, the number of households receiving cable TV has increased from less than four million to approximately seventy million, with a large number of current households receiving digital transmissions.

The latest innovation in broadcasting signals is satellite transmission, and although it is still a young technology by comparison, it reached more than seventeen million households in 2002. Furthermore, satellite is able to provide almost universal coverage to the country and through hundreds of channels, because satellites employ only digital transmission. Satellite transmission also bypasses the question of local monopolies because there is no need for wiring infrastructure. As a result, it offers competition to cable TV for viewers who want a wide range of choices.

Multiplying Channels

The growth of cable and satellite transmission was paralleled by the growth of additional channels that were more focused in their offerings and had to compete to be picked up by cable (and then satellite) companies, because they did not broadcast directly over the airwaves to the viewing public. HBO, which showed relatively recent movies, was the first channel to be made available exclusively through cable, followed in 1976 by Ted Turner's WTBS and the Christian Broadcast Network's CBN (later named the Family Channel). WTBS, a local channel in Atlanta that owned the Atlanta Braves of the National League and the NBA's Atlanta Hawks, used these franchises to broadcast games nationally through cable. The first true sports channel, the Sports Programming Network (later called ESPN), began in 1979 and the first news channel, CNN, also a Turner enterprise, began in 1980. Interestingly, the development of these cable channels and the growth of cable itself were co-dependent; the more programming of interest that could be offered over cable, the greater the potential growth of the cable company itself. This proliferation of relatively narrow content channels (today some systems offer over 200) has led to a number of interesting developments, not all of which were either anticipated or desired.

Multiplying Channels: Proliferation and Fragmentation

With the expansion of program availability, the TV audience has become much more fragmented. In 1990, 55 percent of the total viewing time of the American public was spent watching the broadcast network affiliates. Nine years later that figure had dropped to 46 percent, with the greatest gains being made by the basic cable networks, such as TBS and Discovery, whose viewing time increased from 21 to 41 percent during the same period. One could argue that less concentration of programming has to be a good thing because that leaves many more choices for us all. It's not that simple, however, because the more stations that compete for available advertising dollars, the greater the pressure on operating budgets that are used to produce programming worth watching. In addition, the existence of so many channels creates an imperative to find content to fill the multiplying broadcast hours.

One unanticipated development, which was heartily welcomed by the owners of shows and movies, is that the shelf life of many types of programs has been increased significantly. Old sitcoms, dramas, game shows, movies, and cartoons have found an active second life on a variety of cable channels. One piece of evidence that children and young adults are watching reruns of shows from the 1950s is that advertising for today's products is using references to yesterday's shows. In 2002, Old Navy was using the images and theme song of *Green Acres* to advertise its jeans and the images and theme song of the *Partridge Family* to sell its Rugby shirt line.

By watching the reruns one gets a chance to compare the practice of medicine at *Saint Elsewhere* with that in *ER* (similar) or the practice of law by Perry Mason with that in *Boston Legal* (very different). Archie Bunker seems to be as funny to a younger audience as he was to their parents. This expanded shelf life provides a greater choice of programming for the public and an abundance of riches for those who have rights to these old shows, but equally important, it supplies the younger generation with a vision (no matter how real or distorted) of their parent's world. This vision is further enhanced by the History Channel, which is prone to running many hours of programming each week on events that have occurred in the past sixty years, especially the battles of World War II.

Changes in Programming

The pressure on operating budgets is one of the reasons why a season of network shows now consists of twenty-two original episodes and reruns, rather than the thirty-nine episodes it once did. However, while the networks have reduced the number of original episodes of comedy and drama offered, the slack has begun to be picked up by cable stations.

For some years, cable stations such as HBO, TNT, TBS, USA, and A&E have been developing and airing original programs, including half-hour comedies, hour-long dramas, movies, and biographies. In 1999, HBO became the first cable channel to develop a series, *The Sopranos*, that outdrew the leading network series. HBO has also developed several other popular series, including *Sex and the City, Six Feet Under*, and *Curb Your Enthusiasm*, as well as a number of original movies or miniseries. Because premium cable channels have an economic model based on fee income that frees them from sponsor and, to a lesser degree, rating pressures, they have more freedom and resources to develop programming that is outside the norm. Also, because they are not using the public airwaves, they are not subject to the same restrictions on what type of material they can air. Clearly the early examples of this newly found freedom have provided the viewer with an increased emphasis on sex and violence. Depending upon one's point of view, this development has either liberated television writers to express their art without undue governmental interference or it is a sad commentary on the uses of increased artistic freedom.

In 2002, for the first time in TV history a comedy/drama series, *Monk*, was developed by USA, a non-premium cable channel, and rerun a few days later each week on ABC, one of the major networks. In 2004, *Sex and the City* finished its six-season run on HBO, and content-censored reruns began to be aired on TBS, a non-premium cable channel. Perhaps these are harbingers of a future where many stations develop a few costly shows that are later rerun by other cable or network stations, which helps cover the original development cost.

For the present, however, the shrinkage in the number of people watching any particular channel means smaller revenues for product development, resulting in fewer new shows or in more shows that cost little to produce. As noted earlier, because reality shows have low production costs but are still able to attract viewers, they have multiplied like rabbits. For those who do develop new dramatic or comedy shows, primarily the broadcast networks and a few of the cable networks, there are fewer viewers who will watch any single program or series, putting greater pressure on advertising dollars. In addition, the networks' desperation to keep running any show that is drawing a large audience has led to the stars demanding enormous salaries, which again raises the cost per show.

As discussed earlier one response to this situation is a decrease in the number of programming minutes and an increase in the number of advertising minutes in each show. The trend has become quite evident in recent years. More and more our lives are subject to sophisticated exhortations to buy products and services, whether or not we perceived a need for them before watching the commercials. It's a stretch, but this may be one of the significant causes of the rise in consumer debt, which has grown approximately $700 billion from August 1995 to August 2002. Because, for the most part, these years were times of high employment at higher wages than ever before, it's clear that people have stampeded to buy things that they could not afford out of their current income.

Effects on Our Interests

The proliferation of narrow interest stations suggests another possible impact that television has had upon our society. It is entirely possible that in its first fifty years TV has run full cycle from broadening our views of the world to narrowing them. With so many channels of specialized material available, people may only be watching programs with the same type of content and/or the same point of view. If one likes sitcoms, one can tune them in from morning till bedtime, or the same with sports (even individual sports), drama, nature, fashions, "talking heads," and a number of other subjects. The relative decline in network viewing demonstrates that people are tuning in to these more focused sources of programs.

Even in the domain of news coverage, the all-news stations tend to emphasize the editorial side in addition to straight news reporting, and they have their own political and social biases. As mentioned earlier, a 2004 Pew Research Center study shows that Fox News and CNN tend to attract the majority of their viewers from opposing halves of the liberal/conservative spectrum. If people limit their viewing to just one of these stations, they will not tend to be exposed to forceful arguments for opposing views. Thus, the narrower one's viewing pattern, the more one's views and perceptions are reinforced and the less worldly and broad-minded one becomes.

Choice and Fragmentation

Cable and satellite now send out even more broadcast choices over the airwaves, depending on how much people are willing to pay. At one point, 500 channels was held out as the goal of future TV, and many laughed. Today about 200 channels are offered, and that number will probably grow in the near future. In addition, digital TV offers a number of specialized video magazines and several dozen music choices, with only text on the screen.

Even with 200 channels, including the all-movie channels, the options may be overwhelming for the majority of viewers. Just taking the time to find out what is on TV costs many viewing minutes. The process of selection requires several steps: remembering programs of interest, narrowing them down, and finally picking one. Many may consider that too great a burden and just stick to what is familiar. A study conducted by *The Economist* in 2002 ("Power in Your Hand") revealed that most people watch a small range of programs in the same categories: "Together, the broadcast networks (NBC, CBS, ABC, Fox, the WB and UPN) and the top ten cable channels grab about 90% of the audience, a figure that has remained steady for several years." Most viewers stay within an average of fifteen channel choices.

So far, *The Economist* concludes, choice has not led to excessive viewer fragmentation. However, the limited list of the familiar fifteen may vary greatly from person to person. Some devote the great majority of their viewing time to sports, to just golf, to the several history channels, to the game show channel or the cooking one, to shopping, to all news, or to old-time TV. Because most American homes are connected to cable or satellite and most have several TV sets, even one for each family member, it's not much of a stretch for each person to have his or her own relationship to the world of television.

Yet beyond all the TV choices, we also have the Internet. Some studies have shown that young people, especially, spend many hours on the computer and watch that much less television. Adolescents are drawn to the computer by its capacity to do instant messaging with friends, play video games, and download music. Will such behaviors continue as they mature and become working adults? Even if they return to spend more time watching TV, we have seen that their years of playing action games and multitasking have given them different expectations for activity and color on the television screen.

They could also turn from broadcast and cable networks to Web-based TV; that is, independent stations that stream their programming over the Internet. According to an article in *The New York Times* in July 2004, over 100 such stations were in existence, "covering every imaginable interest." Five are devoted to classic movies and TV shows. At present, the audiences are miniscule. But the potential exists for anyone to become a broadcaster if they have the hardware and programming knowledge.

If convergence of the computer and TV achieves consumer acceptance, the future will see the two blur even more. It would become common to watch television programs over the Internet and switch back and forth from them to games and e-mail and news and information. In such a case, the choices will be endless and the issue of differentiating what is TV from what is Internet will become insignificant.

TV—An Addiction?

A final side effect of the proliferation of TV channels and programming may be the development of an actual TV addiction, aspects of which have been studied by many researchers. Robert Kubey and Mihaly Csikszentmihalyi discuss this research and its implications, as follows:

> Psychologists and psychiatrists formally define substance dependence as a disorder characterized by criteria that include spending a great deal of time using the substance; using it more often than one intends; thinking about reducing use or making repeated unsuccessful efforts to reduce use; giving up important social, family or occupational activities to use it; and reporting withdrawal symptoms when one stops using it.

Most of us exhibit at least some of these characteristics, at least some of the time, and do not consider ourselves addicted to television. But considering that the average viewing time per household is in excess of six hours per day, it is not surprising that the authors reported on studies in which some subjects clearly demonstrated most of these characteristics. What's more, although study subjects (otherwise known as people) report feeling relaxed and passive when turning on a TV set, the feeling of relaxation leaves when it is turned off, but the feeling of passivity and a difficulty in concentrating remain. Such feelings are not experienced after engaging in sports or an active hobby.

Thus, television has provided us with one more behavior, like gambling or overeating, which can become compulsive, especially considering that we encounter its influence not only in our homes but also throughout our day. As we travel, the children can watch TV tapes in the rear seat of the car; we can watch a movie as we fly cross-country; and as we sit in a cab crawling our way through rush-hour traffic, we may be watching commercials, which add to the bottom line of the cab company. Because TV input is so ubiquitous, the study suggests that it is allowing us little control and thereby is diverting us from other, possibly more socially desirable or healthful pursuits. Worse, a recent study reported in *The Lancet* found that children who watched "the most TV between ages 5 and 15 were more likely to be overweight, have heart and respiratory problems, have higher cholesterol, and smoke at age 21." Clearly, addiction to TV can have very deleterious consequences.

The proliferation of programming and a myriad of choices give addictive personalities more opportunities to retreat into their obsessions. For others who limit their TV time, this choice enables them to indulge specific interests. The public has become a collection of viewing minorities ignorant of each other's TV world, united only by occasional events, such as a Super Bowl or an Olympics.

Chapter 17

Nothing Out of Range: The Prevalence of TV Cameras

Although our discussion has focused primarily on the influence of broadcast TV on our lives, television cameras that are not owned by TV stations are assuming a large and growing presence; in many ways these cameras affect us more directly and intimately than does broadcast TV. One of the characteristics of technologies in the latter half of the twentieth century is a very rapid shrinkage both in size and price. In the late 1940s, one might have paid $500 or more for a television set with a seven-inch (yes, *seven*) screen. In 2003 dollars, that $500 would be worth more than $5,000. Although the screen was only seven inches diagonally, the set was a console that was more than three feet high off the floor and more than two feet wide. But as manufacturers began to sell millions of TVs every year, their size began to benefit from miniaturization and the price dropped precipitously. Today's tabletop TV with a twenty-seven-inch screen is roughly two feet by two feet and can be purchased for less than $200—what a difference. But almost more important than the shrinkage in size and price of the TV set is the shrinkage in the TV camera, and therein lies the tale of a new age.

Personal TV

Back in the 1940s, the first TV cameras were very large and very expensive, and clearly for use by professionals only. But as with other technologies, as they became widely adopted the price dropped rapidly. Equally important, their size shrank so that they are now not only affordable but also highly portable for vacations, family get-togethers, sporting events, and the like. They have become ubiquitous in office buildings, stores, banks, airports, schools, hospitals, and other strategic locations. Finally, cell phones have now incorporated cameras so that they can transport wireless video around the globe in seconds.

TV has clearly become a medium on which amateurs can record, store, and display major events in their lives, such as birthdays, weddings, anniversaries, family reunions, births, and the first steps and words of their children. What was once a collection of photo albums or a box stuffed with photographs has now become a shelf lined with TV tapes or, more recently, digital disks. Of course the current Medicare generation may have had home movies to pass on to their progeny, but relatively few of that generation owned movie cameras, and the film, if not already converted to another medium, is rapidly decaying. For future generations it will be a common experience to see their parents, grandparents, or even earlier generations moving and talking, thereby providing a much fuller picture of what their lives were like. TV is providing us with a tie to our personal past as never before, and with DVD technology we can expect the disks to last a very long time.

Amateur/Professional TV

The proliferation of TV cameras in the hands of amateurs has also added to the footage seen on network and cable television; in fact TV stations often seek out individuals who were in a position to use their personal cameras when a newsworthy event occurred in their area. One incident captured by an amateur that was very widely displayed on television was the beating by several Los Angeles police officers of a handcuffed Rodney King after a car chase. There were also amateur tapes of the 9/11 terrorist attacks and its immediate aftermath that were shown repeatedly on network and cable TV. Probably the most-noted movie film shot with an amateur camera, which became familiar to almost everyone in America because of its repeated showing on television, was the Zapruder film showing the 1963 assassination of President John F. Kennedy. Such filming was an exception at the time. Now hundreds of video cameras are present at every presidential motorcade.

Professional TV cameras have also captured many unplanned pictures. Some of the most memorable include the shooting of Lee Harvey Oswald by Jack Ruby, the assassination of presidential candidate Senator Robert Kennedy during a campaign stop in Los Angeles, and the attempted assassination of President Ronald Reagan outside the Washington Hilton.

Nothing Out of Range: The Prevalence of TV Cameras

Of the live situations that were captured in a planned way by professional TV cameras, the trial of O. J. Simpson became the longest piece of sensational history we lived with, as it dominated our TV sets for the better part of a year. Whether caught by an amateur who happens to have a camera at a crucial time and place or by a news crew sent out by a TV station, the proliferation of TV cameras means that we are now likely to see most newsworthy events as they occur, giving us a box seat to history that few people ever had before.

Going from one extreme to another, there is also a program called *Funniest Home Videos* and a knock-off, *Funniest Pets*, that regale us with outrageous events, either staged or occurring by accident, as backyard video enthusiasts ply their hobbies. *Candid Camera*, a show aired in the early days of television, staged events to show us how funny it can be when people are faced with strange events. The proliferation of personal video cameras has given us an opportunity to see, on the one hand, key events in history and on the other, how humorous people can be in their daily lives.

Surveillance TV

The increased availability of TV has also enriched our lives and made them easier. When we've put the baby down for a nap in a second-floor bedroom, we no longer need to run up periodically to check whether the child is still asleep, under the covers, or in any distress. Now we can have a TV camera tuned on the baby while we are downstairs doing the taxes, fixing dinner, or handling any of dozens of other tasks while a nearby monitor allows us to see and hear any problem that might arise upstairs. Additionally, when we go to the theater at night and leave the baby with the sitter, we can record the sitter's activities to assure ourselves that our child is getting the attention he or she needs and that our house has not become a venue for a teenage party. Finally, by sending computerized video over the Web, we can share the excitement of the child taking its early teetering steps with grandparents who live across the country.

Stationary or revolving cameras keep watch not only over babysitters and pets but also many aspects of our lives. Should we walk into a jewelry store or any other shop selling expensive merchandise, the chances are high that our movements will be recorded on a TV tape or disk. The same would happen if we walked into a bank, made a deposit at an ATM machine, boarded a bus, or sat down at a casino table. Our struggles with navigating our way through an airport are likely to be captured at many points, as are our efforts to find our way through a hospital. Many office buildings will take our picture upon our entering as well as when we get to the floor we are visiting, and many people who live in apartment houses can now see the person ringing the bell downstairs, rather than just talking to him or her.

A 2003 *New York Times* article by Andrea Elliott highlighted the extremes to which a department store like Macy's goes to reduce loss through shoplifting, which amounted to $15 million in 2002 in their flagship Manhattan store alone. Shoplifters are subject to holding cells, body searches, handcuffs, interrogations without legal representation, and the immediate payment of penalties. The entire shoplift prevention effort rests primarily on TV surveillance cameras, 300 in the Manhattan store, connected to dozens of monitors watched by security workers, who can even "follow" a suspect with the use of a joystick that controls the movement of the camera. For better or for worse, we are clearly not unobserved when we wander the aisles of a department store inspecting the goods and making our purchases.

According to a CNN article by Steve Irsay, the International Association of Police Chiefs claim that more than 200 local and state law enforcement agencies use some type of surveillance technology. In addition to law enforcement agencies, other groups are also installing TV cameras in an effort to reduce crime. In August 2002, a *Seattle Post-Intelligencer* article by Phuong Cat Le reported on the plan of Seattle's Pioneer Square Community Association to use TV monitoring of public areas in an attempt to "reduce crime and make neighbors feel safer." According to CNN.com, probably the most televised city in the world is London, where "the British government has installed 1.5 million surveillance cameras and the average Londoner is taped more than 300 times a day."

In today's atmosphere of heightened sensitivity to security needs, many believe that the TV camera is becoming an indispensable weapon in combating crime and terrorism. Others argue that the costs in the loss of privacy are too great, hearkening to the image of *1984* where one never escaped being viewed by Big Brother. For the most part, the millions of cameras taping the movements of individuals conducting their daily activities are taping individuals guilty of no more than jaywalking. Yet, if saved, analyzed, and organized, those tapes have the potential to provide the government (or anyone with whom the government cared to share them) with a detailed picture of the habits and daily activities of each of us, a prospect that would be abhorrent to many.

A possibly stronger argument against the widespread use of surveillance cameras is that there has been no clear evidence that their proliferation reduces crime. One study in England found that, of twenty-four cities using surveillance cameras, thirteen experienced reduced crime, in seven there was no effect, and in four, crime actually increased significantly. In March 2002, the UPI reported, "crime is soaring across the country [England]." In London, where there are more than 1.5 million surveillance cameras, the murder rate is increasing at a record pace. The number of street robberies, the very crime that closed-circuit TV is supposed to be most effective at deterring, will reach 50,000 this year. Detroit abandoned its surveillance camera system after fourteen years because the mixed results could not justify the ongoing personnel expenses required to keep the system operative. This leads to the final point: the purchase, installation, and maintenance of the cameras are very costly, to which must be added the cost of the people to monitor the cameras. Clearly, the use of TV surveillance by law enforcement has grown enormously, but the jury is still out on whether resources expended in buying, placing, and monitoring cameras are well spent or could provide greater dividends if applied to other aspects of the law enforcement process.

The proliferation of privately owned portable and surveillance cameras has, however, had a clear impact on police procedures, especially in urban business areas, but also even at isolated gas stations and convenience stores on country roads. Collecting tapes in the vicinity of a crime scene has become as common a practice as taking witness statements or collecting other forensic evidence. Throughout the country, perpetrators are being tracked down and ultimately convicted on the images obtained from non-governmental cameras in the vicinity of the crimes. Indeed, in the July 2005 London subway bombings and attempted bombings, the rapid identification of the perpetrators and co-conspirators was attributed to initial identifications on multiple videotapes. Although the American Civil Liberties Union and other organizations have registered strenuous objections to the proliferation of government-owned surveillance systems, the growth of private surveillance cameras continues to accelerate, and there seems to be no sign that their use as an important weapon in law enforcement will abate.

Related to surveillance is another use of TV in the criminal justice system, namely in producing a visual and auditory record of the interrogation of suspects. The use of TV to film the interrogation ensures that the person being interrogated cannot falsely claim that he or she was the victim of excessive force or coercion. In addition, the police involved in the interrogation know that if they use techniques that will not stand up in court, any results they get will be useless, thereby encouraging them to pursue activities that will ultimately lead to a conviction.

TV Conferencing

TV conferencing is rapidly expanding for a number of reasons. For one, the price of setting up a TV conference has dropped dramatically. The cost of TV camera equipment has decreased significantly, broadband communication has become much more available at reasonable prices, and the use of the Internet can bring the costs of a TV conference down to where friends in different parts of the world might just get together for a chat.

Given the greater availability and lower costs of TV conferencing, it has become a very popular vehicle for cost cutting in companies hungry to find any way to add to the bottom line. Meetings that only a few years ago would involve tens of thousands of dollars in travel to get people from diverse locations together in the same room for a few hours can now be accomplished at a small fraction of that cost, with much less disruption to the participants' schedules. As noted previously, doctors from all over the world can discuss the diagnosis and possible courses of treatment for a particularly difficult case. Without leaving her office in London a doctor can examine the x-rays, CAT scans, or MRIs of the patient in question in Los Angeles. The patient might even participate in the conference, answering questions that any of the participating physicians might have.

Social Engineering

While TV cameras have been used for some time to identify drivers who fail to pay tolls on entering a bridge or tunnel, that ability is now being combined with economic theory to reduce the enormous amount of traffic congestion in central London. Considering that scarce resources are highly valued in the free marketplace and considering that on-street parking space is a rare resource in central London, a bold traffic control program based on the availability of TV surveillance cameras was initiated in February 2003. People who drive into the ten square mile area of central London have to prepay a daily fee of approximately $8.00. This is designed to reduce the number of cars that drive into the central city, and the revenues will be used to improve the mass transit alternatives. The entire system relies on the presence of hundreds of TV cameras that photograph the license plates of cars entering the area and then compare them with a database of those who have paid the required fee to enter the area. A stiff fine is levied on those who drive in without paying. A Cybercast News Service (CNS) news report by Mike Wendling indicated that the program has been quite effective by decreasing traffic levels by 16 percent, exceeding the 10 to 15 percent reduction estimated by its developers. This same report indicated that average speeds had increased from eight to eleven miles per hour in the zone, reducing average journey times by 13 percent.

Here, the TV camera is being used in a massive experiment to change individual behavior for the common good. In a way, the surveillance cameras in Macy's are being used in the same way. The lower their losses through shoplifting, the lower prices they will be able to offer to the honest customer. However, there is a difference in the two situations insofar as those commuting into London are fully aware that if they don't pay the toll they will be caught by the camera and fined. The objective there is not to collect fines, but change behavior, with the TV camera being used to reinforce that change. Although most people are generally aware that there are surveillance cameras in stores, relatively few are aware of the extent to which a store like Macy's goes to apprehend and extract payment from shoplifters. Given London's successful application of TV surveillance, it might well be in the interests of retail establishments to publicize their efforts to discourage those who might otherwise think that it is easy to shoplift and not get caught. Perhaps that is why Macy's opened up their entire operation to the *New York Times*, which devoted more than a full page to the story, including photos of the control room, resembling what most of us would imagine the war room at the Pentagon would look like, and a cell with handcuffs attached to a table bolted to the floor.

Finally, in October 2003 Nokia announced that they were launching a television cell phone, and other manufacturers quickly followed. Although small TV sets have been available for some time, these new phones easily fit into a pocket or a pocketbook. With this step we proceed to the ultimate prevalence of TV, having it wherever and whenever one wishes. Now TV will have the power to turn our attention from other pursuits while we are at work, commuting, jogging, attending class, eating out, or merely sitting on a park bench communing with nature.

It's a Televised World

The prevalence of TV has clearly changed our lives insofar as it has made us both viewers of history as it happens and the object of viewing in our day-to-day activities. On the positive side, it has given individuals and society's institutions powerful tools with which to accomplish their daily activities more effectively, from keeping in touch with the folks back home to catching suspected terrorists. It has also made us a part of history as we wept when Walter Cronkite announced that President

Kennedy had died or cheered as Astronaut Neil Armstrong stepped on the moon, taking "one giant step for mankind." The Los Angeles Police Department went through a major reorganization because of the Rodney King incident, and the world watched in horror as the tanks rolled against the people in Tiananmen Square. Given the ubiquity of surveillance cameras coupled with the large number of personal TV cameras in use and the ability of cell phones to take and project a video, it will be the rare future event that will not be captured on TV.

On the negative side, there are serious civil and privacy rights issues stemming from the widespread use of cameras in public places and places of employment. There are also serious doubts as to whether the large expenditures for widespread TV surveillance produce results that are worth anywhere near their cost.

Chapter 18

The Future of TV: Technology, Content, Effects

Much is possible. What will result is unpredictable. A variety of new technologies already exist, with others close to realization. A number of these would transform television as we have known it. However, in recent years, several new advances have been made available to viewers with great fanfare and large investments, but the public has responded with indifference. Essentially, the future depends on what people decide they really want.

Public rejection of new or advanced technologies happens frequently enough to make manufacturers realize they are taking big gambles when they invest in them. Consider the disappearance of Betamax videotapes despite that system's vaunted technical superiority to VHS. The failure of mini-compact disks and laser disks for video are further reminders that the buying public can be indifferent to new technologies.

At times, the innovations may be far ahead of buyer interest. When personal computers first became compact enough to fit into living rooms and dens, they found a place in only a small minority of homes. The commonly given reason for not buying a computer is summed up in this question, why should I buy an expensive device to write letters and organize my recipes? The World Wide Web (WWW) changed all that. Accessing the Internet before the WWW was too complex for most users. The easy navigation and search ability of the Web provided by search engines and especially the ubiquity of e-mail made a home PC essential for a good percentage of American families, enabling them to keep in touch with far-flung family members, shop, do homework assignments, download music, and find information.

Much Is Possible, But Not Always Accepted

The picture phone represents a technology at the edge of a long-delayed breakthrough. Bell Laboratories developed a prototype more than a half-century ago. They were not cheap. But if there had been interest, mass production and economies of scale would have led to a price drop, as they did for television sets. However, people did not see any real advantage to picture phones, even in recent years when both size and cost were greatly reduced. Today computer services offer the capability of video e-mail, with a small camera pointed at the sender. Few take advantage of that opportunity. Now cell phones that take and transmit photos and video are being heavily marketed in print and on commercials. In the first half of 2003, ElectricNews.net reported that cell phone digital cameras outsold both film and digital camera sales. In fact, according to *Forbes*,[1] "Investment bank UBS forecasts camera phone sales will rise to 44 percent of all mobile phones sold in 2004. Research group Gartner says global handset sales could grow to 580 million units in 2004." Finally, people want to send photos over the phone.

Probably the costliest rejection of new TV technology thus far relates to the attempts to interest test populations in interactive television; that is, the ability to "talk" back to the set by pressing buttons that would convey votes and choices or could select camera angles. Each involved a trial in one or more communities that possessed demographics of interest to the sponsoring company, and each was launched with massive publicity. Although each of the trials received national news coverage at its inception, each, like General McArthur's "old soldier," just faded away with minimal coverage of the actual results, which were obviously disappointing to the sponsor. Some digital cable TV systems do allow viewers some choice of perspectives for sporting events and give them the ability to call up information, such as batting averages or yards gained. But only a committed handful of viewers use these tools. As Philip Swann of TVPredictions.com asks, "Do couch potatoes really want to interact with their TVs? For instance, why would anyone interrupt their favorite show to order a character's dress or shoes? Or, why would you order a pizza on your television when you can simply pick up the phone?"

A distinction may be made, however, between active interactive TV and passive interactive TV like that offered by video on demand. In the active version, the viewer engages in a continual relationship with the set, making frequent choices. What can be considered passive interaction is the occasional choice of a program or movie that once selected allows the viewer to just sit back and watch. In one sense, such a choice is just a variation of choosing a channel.

On the Horizon

Yet certain inevitable developments are already on the way. No doubt the nature of the TV picture itself—the screen that we watch on—is already in the process of change. Relatively thin plasma or LCD screens that can be hung from a wall like a painting have been increasing in sales despite their high cost compared with cathode ray tube sets. For those who like big screens, these flat screens allow size without bulk. They also provide a wider aspect ratio than standard sets, meaning the ratio of width to height. For years, that has been 4:3; the new screens are 16:9. The new ratio is similar to that of movies shot for wide theater screens, which must be truncated at both ends to fit onto the typical TV screen. These sets also fit into the marketing concept of the home theater, an integrated combination of screen, surround-sound speakers, receiver, music player, and more that can, in some affluent homes, become the rationale for a dedicated entertainment room.

Picture quality also will improve with the higher pixel density of high-definition television (HDTV). In 1997 the U.S. Congress mandated that all new sets should be equipped for HDTV by May 1, 2002, and that non-HDTV broadcasting be phased out. But as a result of resistance by both broadcasters and viewers, Congress had to back off and change both the deadline and the HDTV-only mandate. Because HDTV sets cost much more than regular TVs, viewers saw no reason to make obsolete those they already owned. In turn, broadcasters were unwilling to send out HDTV signals to only a limited number of receiving sets in homes. Now both types of signals can be transmitted, and a growing number of programs offer the HDTV option, especially on digital cable systems. It is inevitable that future TV watchers will enjoy larger, wider screens and clearer pictures.

When to Watch—TV and Time

How people will watch is another matter with an uncertain outcome. Will they continue to adjust their lives to the schedules of the networks and cable channels, sitting in front of their screens during the times programs are broadcast? Or will they watch at their convenience? Changing viewing habits is not just a matter of adapting to new technologies; it means a reorientation of our relationship with leisure time as we perceive it.

Conditioned from years of experience, people plan their viewing evenings around the schedule grid, timing trips to the supermarket, newspaper reading, phone calls, and bathroom breaks according to the boundaries of their favorite shows. They rarely think that such behavior is unique in human history. Television has—following radio—altered our personal relationship with time.

Digital video recorders (DVRs), a new recording technology, are much simpler to use than VCRs or DVD recorders and much more flexible. Users can program them to record individual shows or weekly broadcasts of the same show. The storage unit holds thirty hours or more of programming, with easy retrieval of the viewer's choice. Some recording services using DVRs charge a small monthly fee. Purchasers of such systems swear by them, often claiming that the devices have transformed the nature of their TV watching. As yet sales of DVRs have not skyrocketed, but cable and satellite providers have taken note of the technology and have begun offering them on a rental basis. As a result, the adoption of the technology is progressing more rapidly. Whether the devices will eventually become commonplace or remain an interesting but unsuccessful gadget remains to be seen.

Several other alternatives also allow watching when the viewer wishes, though the choices are much more limited than those possible with VCR, DVD, or hard disk recording, which can copy anything that is broadcast. More and more, shows past and present are being released on prerecorded DVDs, which are commercial-free and available for frequent viewing. Entire seasons of certain programs can be purchased. They take their place in personal DVD libraries along with DVDs of movies. Shown on the same screen, TV shows and films lose their distinction as different sources of entertainment.

Digital cable's on-demand menu has become another option for self-timed viewing. But, thus far, only a handful of broadcast TV shows can be seen this way. The premium cable channels like HBO and Showtime offer a much fuller set of past and present shows, along with some movies, for a small monthly fee. On-demand also presents many movies, current and old, for rental at costs similar to that of a video store. On-demand is at an early stage, and the number of TV shows available may increase. Unlike prerecorded DVDs, of course, what can be watched depends on the menu for any given day.

In addition to the convergence that has existed for several years, the sale of shows for downloading began in 2005 with Apple's introduction of an iPod that displayed TV programs on its small but clear screen. Only a limited number of shows were available initially. Soon after, perhaps in response, Warner Brothers announced plans for an Internet service that would offer 4,800 episodes of 100 old TV series at no cost, to be supported by advertising. In 2006, both CBS and NBC will, for a small fee, enable downloads of recent broadcasts.

Yet the existence of DVDs, on-demand, and TV downloads blurs the distinctions among TV shows, movies, and the Internet. Conceivably, people could spend most of their viewing time alternating between cable and satellite movie choices, on-demand, DVDs, and the computer. Sponsored television shows that are broadcast at a specific fixed time, a format that people have watched for decades, could become merely occasional choices for many people.

New Convergences

Potentially, an even more radical shift in viewing technology could result from a merger of the personal computer and the television set, but it has not yet happened. A decade or so ago, the buzzword was "convergence," a merging of all home media, including telecommunications and music players. It did not catch on, probably because the technology of the time was not up to the theoretical promise of the concept. Attempts to offer e-mail and Web browsing through television sets failed for lack of interest, perhaps because, as computer prices came down, using an inexpensive computer for those purposes was simpler and provided many more options. It also left the TV set free for watching shows.

The introduction of broadband and wireless home networks (wi-fi) presents a range of interesting possibilities in TV viewing. Broadband refers to the means of access to the Internet through DSL or cable modems, rather than by dialing up through a modem attached to standard telephone lines. The top speed of such dial-up modems is 56 kilobytes per second. Broadband access can be 100 times as fast. For example, downloading a six-megabyte movie preview at the highest dial-up speed could take fourteen minutes compared with fourteen seconds via cable broadband.

Programming Our Lives

The distinction between the personal computer and the television set may disappear in the near future as companies compete to offer the device preferred by the multitudes. Will hardware manufacturers, chip makers, or software writers prevail? Given this competition for ascendance in providing "the digital home," *The Economist*[2] in July 2004 noted that "Intel's vision is that consumers will start to use their PCs at home to download, store and manage files, songs, and games, in order to transmit all this fun stuff wirelessly to TV screens and stereo speakers throughout the house." No matter which technology prevails, the magazine concludes, "The one thing that all companies seem to agree on is that households will be connected to the internet via a broadband link that is always on, and that the content will be shared wirelessly between rooms within the home. The upshot is that there need not be any single device inside the home that becomes a central media hub."

Therefore, broadband offers possibilities that could transform home viewing. Although some future technological enhancements will be necessary to achieve that transformation, a number already exist. People can now buy movies for downloading over the Internet the same way they do music, both responses to earlier illegal file sharing. Movies can be viewed on computer screens or networked to much larger TV screens. Already hundreds of old TV shows are stored on the Internet. What of new ones? Will individuals and small groups be able to bypass the airwaves or typical cable or satellite stations and broadcast directly on the Internet, with TV parallels to the many Internet-only radio stations? Some broadcast stations already make their programming available on the Internet, free or at low cost. Some TV programs already offer expanded coverage on their Web sites, including even the opportunity to ask questions and make responses. In essence, the computer has provided a form of interactive TV for a national audience.

The integration of broadband and wireless home networks enhances the relationship of the computer to the TV set. Inexpensive devices already exist to facilitate wireless transmission from the computer to the television screen and from a TV set to a computer monitor. Family photos stored on the computer can be shown on the TV screen. The music library downloaded to the computer can be played on stereo speakers connected to the TV set in a home media center. And the shows and films already on the Internet can be seen in a similar manner. Of course, most home computers play DVDs, and some can record them.

Unlike previous attempts to merge computers and TV, the new availability of thin LCD monitors and the expansion of computer manufacturers, such as Dell and Gateway, into TV monitor manufacturing and marketing have made public acceptance more likely. Dell advertises

"Watch TV while you work!" A FAQ on its Web site offers this definition of an LCD TV:

> An LCD TV is a combination PC and TV monitor. It offers standard analog VGA (PC) input to connect with your computer. You can mount it on the wall or under a cabinet to take advantage of its space-saving flat screen, but it must be viewed head-on for best picture results. HDTV (high-definition television) and progressive scan support allow the LCD TV to function as your television screen.

Again, the question is not so much what can be done as what people want to be done. In essence, consumer choice for media entertainment has never been greater. Consumers have to decide which technologies to adopt, if not immediately, then in just a few years.

Where to Watch

TV screens are virtually everywhere. Outside the home, we find them in stores, waiting rooms, airplanes, stadiums, parks, beaches, automobiles, offices, bars and some restaurants, and even outer space. Already hardware adaptation makes possible viewing TV on computers, though that has not been a popular choice so far. For example, people in businesses for which access to breaking news is vital can have an all-news or business channel broadcasting in a corner of their PC screens. Widespread watching that turns the entire computer monitor into a TV screen would be the next step of TV's growing omnipresence.

In fact, viewing on computers is already happening as one aspect of the technology of placeshifting. A device such as Slingbox attached to a home TV set uses a broadband Internet connection to transmit from the home screen to a remote receiver anywhere another high-speed connection is available. That receiver can be a desktop or laptop computer, a handheld PDA, or even a cell phone.

In addition to taking still photos, some of the latest cell phones can function as TV cameras. They also serve as TV receivers, with the cell network providers offering the ability to watch programs on the tiny screens. One can even imagine clothing wired for reception through special wraparound optical devices. Such technology already exists for computers and virtual reality. Three-dimensional TV broadcasts are not far in the future, if that is what people want.

If, at some point, three-dimensional TV becomes more than a technological diversion for museums and amusement parks, the word "viewer" would no longer be appropriate. We would be living in the created worlds of the programs, perhaps even participating as television merges with virtual reality.

Potential Effects

The extreme possibility of three-dimensional (3D) TV has, of course, the greatest likelihood for bringing about dramatic changes in the way we live. With the screen separated from us, no matter how large it is or how sharp the images, television is still a phenomenon outside us, part of an environment that can divert our attention if the cat runs across the room or someone asks a question. Usually we sit passively, often engrossed but not immersed. Even with an option to communicate via e-mail while we watch, we are engaging with something out there. A technology that allows us the illusion of participating in what was once called television would transform the way we think about the tangible world and the illusory.

Virtual reality systems already allow individuals wearing headsets over their eyes and what are in effect computers on their body or stored in special clothing to live alternative realities in holographic space. The visuals are not yet nearly as clear and precise as the real world around us or the pictures on a two-dimensional TV screen because of the current limitations on computer power. Yet experts predict that such power will exist within a decade.

Television sets in the living room accentuated the effects of radio by further limiting the amount of conversation and human interaction. The presence of sets in many rooms keeps people physically apart. The plethora of specialized programs allows people to separate even more by indulging a limited set of interests. The introduction of 3D TV would cross another threshold. That is, if people choose to want it.

Even if the future continues to provide TV on screens we just watch, we may still be changed in less dramatic ways. The flexibility to watch what we want when we want could heighten our expectations for the availability of individual choices in other areas.

Perhaps the most significant changes will affect our relation to the political system and the way our society is governed. Surveys tell us that young people watch much less news than their elders. If this trend continues for future generations and today's young continue to avoid the news as they age, the majority of Americans will know little beyond the headlines. The growing diversity of TV choices, not to mention the Internet, has the potential of exacerbating fragmentation into interest groups, leading to a large number of uninformed people who care about only a few issues with limited comprehension of the more complex contexts. Like viewers with choices over what they watch and when, they will care about only what they want.

Such a prediction may be dire, and, if we are fortunate, it will not be realized. Yet the age of television in the past half-century has coincided with a decline in the percentage of people who vote and who engage in the political process. Certainly, other forces have played a role in those changes, but TV already has played a central part in determining who we are, how we act, and how we engage with the world. New technologies are likely to continue TV's role.

Notes

1. See "Global camera phone sales rise five-fold in 2003."
2. See "Life in the Vault."

Conclusion

Chapter 19

American Life after Sixty Years of TV

From roughly the middle of the twentieth century to the beginning of the twenty-first century, Americans have undergone a dramatic transformation in the way they think, the way they act, the way they engage with the world around them, and the way they seek gratification. Concurrent with these changes, television has gone from a curiosity that was owned by a privileged few to the country's most dominant force for communication and entertainment, reaching into more than 100 million homes, three-quarters of which have more than one set. Almost everyone in the United States now has access to TV.

Other than the hours we work and sleep, TV viewing is the most prevalent single activity in our lives. The impact of all these hours can in no way be neutral. Marshall McLuhan was right in claiming that the medium was the message, but we can't overlook the multiple submessages contained within that larger message. TV is almost impossible to avoid. It bombards and overwhelms. TV has given us a radically different relationship to information and the world beyond our lives. It has changed how we relate to that world around us, what we think about other people both near and distant, what we expect for entertainment and amusement, what we want, and what we think we need. TV has changed our buying habits, our politics, and our expectations of how we should live. This book has tried to explore some of the changes that have taken place in our society and to speculate on what role television might have played in causing those changes.

America in the 1940s

Possibly the best way to understand the changes that have taken place in the past sixty years is to draw a picture of what America was like in the 1940s, at the dawn of the TV age. Educationally, the primary goal was to obtain a high-school diploma, with relatively few graduates aspiring to a college degree. Other than the dislocations caused by World War II, typical families consisted of a father, mother, and children living under the same roof, with the mother working full time at running the household and taking care of the children. Most people lived either in towns and cities or on farms, close to where they worked, with very little in the way of suburbs around the cities. According to the 1940 census, only twelve states had more than 50 percent of their population in urban areas; of those, seven were just slightly more than 50 percent.[1] The cop on the beat was someone you looked up to, someone who could be relied upon for support in a variety of ways. Children were taught to be seen and not heard and by and large were expected to do various chores around the house. Their friends were from the neighborhood and the school, and their parents were not involved in their daily play. Companies tended to be loyal to their employees and employees to their companies. Boastfulness was frowned upon, and the guiding philosophy tended to be "let your actions speak for themselves," rather than "blow your own horn because no one else will." Possibly the major aspiration of teenage children was to follow in their parents' footsteps, whether it be to the local factory, college, or motherhood. For the most part, if girls wished to pursue any type of work activity (usually until they got married), there were three appropriate positions to aspire to—nurse, teacher, and secretary. To a large extent, the races were separate, with little opportunity for African-Americans to attain anything more than menial positions in a white man's world. At the extreme, there was a core of race hatred that was typified by the Ku Klux Klan. The European immigrants who had come to this country earlier in the century, including the Irish, Italians, and Jews, had now established themselves and were integrated into many aspects of the economy, but still felt some stigma of societal exclusion. Because poverty rates had fallen dramatically after the Great Depression, most people had a roof over their heads and enough food to eat to avoid starvation or serious medical problems. And if one did have medical problems, there was a friendly, affordable doctor to take care of you, or a free clinic if you couldn't afford the doctor. People tended to live in the same home or vicinity for most of their lives and had many friends and connections to their community; statistically, migration rates declined dramatically following the Great Depression.[2] It was a period that was in no way idyllic, but it did seem to be a kinder, gentler era, perhaps because people's lives were more self-contained within families and localities.

The event that unleashed major changes in this era was World War II. Millions of young men had been away from their homes and their jobs fighting the war and were returning to resume their lives. Because, in many cases, marriage and/or children had been put off because of the war, there began an enormous baby boom. Also, because the government was offering the returning GIs an opportunity to go to college, many who would never have considered that route now went to university on the GI Bill. With so many families being formed and expanded, housing development, which had been put on hold for four years, became a critical need. A family of builders named Levitt used production-line methods to build Levittown, a development of over 17,000 homes in former potato fields of Long Island. This began a mass movement toward home ownership, not inside existing towns, but outside of them in areas that were called suburbs. Meanwhile, many of the women who had replaced the soldiers in their jobs in factories and service industries liked the idea of earning an independent living and pursued both education and careers toward that end.

Generally, then, the period after World War II was a time of expansion—expansion of the population, expansion of opportunities, expansion of the middle class, and expansion of home ownership. Thus, television became a fact of life at a time of considerable upheaval, when long-established patterns of behavior were changing and people were reaching out for new possessions and new ideas. A better match could not have been planned.

I Want It—Now!

The growth in population and its increasing affluence stimulated a strong desire for material possessions. The advent of television was the perfect vehicle to reinforce those urges and to provide a visual smorgasbord of products to satisfy them. A basic consequence of these combined forces has been the expectation of immediate gratification. Much of our gratification comes through the possession of the products TV lures us with hour after hour, both in ads and in programming. TV makes us want, and we want it now, not as rewards to be earned after decades, but as entitlements, which are deserved right away. The development of credit cards that were themselves heavily promoted on television removed one more barrier in the way of instant gratification. We could have it now and pay later.

The more and more of expected possessions finds a parallel in the more and more of TV channels now available through cable and satellite, with fifty movies being broadcast at any hour and dozens of football games, pro and college, to watch. If you like sports, you never have to do without. A choice of contests is on twenty-four hours a day. If you want the news, you have constant access to capsule reports that predigest and summarize. This drive for more and more has expanded from TV to compact music players that store thousands of tunes and to the Internet with its billions of choices at the click of a mouse.

The remote control signifies how little effort we're willing to expend to achieve diversion. The remote facilitates channel surfing, the elimination of viewing boredom. If one program doesn't grab your attention, switch to another and then to another until you find one worth watching. We're attuned to sensory energy—flashing colors, rapid movement, disorienting camera angles, and pulsating sound. The remote serves as a tool to ensure stimulation; it is a weapon of the impatient.

Equal Rights

Although the experiences during and shortly after World War II clearly set off a quest for physical possessions, they also ignited another more meaningful quest, the fight to obtain equal rights by those who had been treated as second-class citizens. Beginning with Rosa Parks' refusal to give her seat to a white man in a bus in Montgomery, Alabama, the civil rights movement found its voice under the leadership of Martin Luther King, a doctor of theology and Baptist minister who was deeply impressed by Mahatma Gandhi's principles of nonviolent protest. During the ensuing years television became an important player in this movement, for it was able to bring into the majority of homes unforgettable moments of cruelty and oppression experienced by black Americans merely because of the color of their skin. Such scenes included Sheriff "Bull" Connor of Birmingham ordering firemen to turn their hoses on the well-dressed, well-behaved men, women, and children as they marched, and then having his policemen club them and releasing police dogs to attack them. Another unforgettable visual event was that of a petite black girl named Elizabeth Eckford being blocked from entering Central High School in Little Rock, Arkansas, and being

196

menaced by an angry mob threatening to lynch her while Arkansas National Guardsmen stood by and watched silently. These scenes, and many others in the 1950s and 1960s, had a major impact on the conscience of America and led to a series of federal and state laws barring discrimination in many aspects of society, such as jobs and housing. Would the change in America's psyche have occurred without the impact of watching these events while sitting in the comfort of one's own home? Possibly, but if they did, it probably would have taken much more time and even more misery.

Another group discriminated against—in some ways more subtly and in some just as blatantly—were women, regardless of their color or nationality. Their experiences in the working world during the war probably laid the foundation for the movement, but the first volley in the coming gender conflict came in 1963 with the publication of *The Feminine Mystique* by Betty Friedan. The book was prompted originally by the responses she obtained from her 1957 survey of her fellow graduates of Smith College on their post-college experiences and satisfaction with their lives, and then by more extensive research among women. Friedan's thesis was that "women are victims of a false belief system that requires them to find identity and meaning in their lives through their husbands and children." This began a long process of enlightenment and change in which Friedan and Gloria Steinem were the torches that led the way.

Television did not play as big a role in this movement as it did in the fight for racial equality, but it did have its place. There were fewer instances that would draw cameras to news in the making, the most memorable perhaps being the burning of bras as a symbol of emancipation. However, the women's movement did become news, and as such spokespersons like Friedan and Steinem were frequent guests on news and talk shows. Without this type of exposure it would have been much more difficult to get the message across to the tens of millions of women who may have felt dissatisfied with their lives, but had not been able to articulate what that dissatisfaction was and why it had come about. Once again, television served as a conduit for social change, spreading the ideal of equality in a democratic society.

Growing Up Is Different

Whether because of the basic need for enough income to support a family or the desire for a better material life, working mothers have become the norm, rather than the exception—a trend described by Eduardo Porter in his 2006 *New York Times* article. With this shift in roles, mothers had less time to devote to their children, and often whether the child was with a sitter or the harried mother had to perform household chores that might otherwise have been done during work hours, watching television became the child's activity. For young children, the potential effects of watching TV include a form of addiction and the poor school performance turned in by many of the children who watch many hours of TV each day. Three new studies reported in the *Archives of Pediatrics and Adolescent Medicine* find that too much television time can lower test scores, retard learning, and even predict college performance.[3] Yet if the amount and type of television watched are supervised properly, it can help prepare children for their entry into a successful educational experience and help them broaden their horizons throughout their school years.

Children in the 1940s and 1950s engaged in more spontaneous physical activity than the children of today. Writing in the *Boston College Magazine* in 2004, sociologist Juliet Schor notes, "Children born in the late 1940s and afterward had a more carefree, play-oriented upbringing with less family responsibility than the generations that preceded them." Now, children are more likely to be in an organized league, be it soccer, baseball, or football, but the actual time they spend practicing or playing the game is far less than the almost total immersion in play experienced by children in the 1940s and 1950s in the daylight hours, weekends, and summers. Because of the distance between houses, today children frequently have to be chauffeured to "play dates" with school friends, but more often than not these involve indoor activities, rather than energy-absorbing outdoor games. Add to that the time spent watching television, playing video games, and working on a computer (with its video screen), and it appears that today's child devotes much less energy to active play. The very significant growth in obesity is a subject of major concern in this country and one that will significantly exacerbate the national health care problem. Is it not reasonable to suspect that at least part of that problem begins in childhood, with so much time being spent in TV screen activities rather than in outdoor, physically demanding activities?

The Kaiser Family Foundation's 1999 study, *Kids & Media @ The New Millennium*, found that children aged eight to thirteen devote four hours a day to watching TV and videotapes and five-and-a-half hours a day to involvement in all media combined. All this passive watching does stimulate the desire to possess the products advertised on television, including foods that contribute to obesity. Children, like their TV-watching parents, have become fixated on brands and possessions.

Shifting Values

Much has been written about the effects of TV violence on youthful behavior, with an ongoing debate over whether watching those hours of death and gore has desensitized young people. The test most often used to measure such a consequence is overt action, such as the number of kids beating or shooting other people. Certainly the violence at Columbine and other schools was shocking to the nation. But an equally important measure of its impact is how society as a whole reacts to violence of people against each other. Here the outcome has been mixed. On the one hand, we have become so desensitized to violence that the daily reporting of a shooting or other form of mayhem hardly grabs our attention for the few moments it takes to report the story. We've seen it before and we'll see it again. On the other hand, the video of Rodney King being beaten by Los Angeles policemen created a good deal of revulsion and led to a call for reform of police leadership and training. Perhaps that's because what we saw on the screen was "real," a scene captured by an amateur video camera. Yet, the news camera scenes of death and destruction throughout the world tend to be shrugged off after an initial grimace. Certainly, it is hard to believe that the vast amount of violence portrayed on television does not either make violence more acceptable as a form of dealing with problems, especially to children, or else desensitizes us to all the negative aspects of violence.

The issue of behavioral changes caused by TV watching transcends just violent programming and crime statistics and is more a general issue of deteriorating norms in people's interactions. Simple actions like showing respect or caring for the needs and values of others seem to have declined in frequency to the point where they are rarities rather than expected behavior. TV, as it has evolved over its half-century, seems to be more and more seeking the sensational to stimulate a jaded audience and in doing so has created situations wherein people clearly show disdain rather than respect for others. We see this phenomenon most especially in Reality TV, where participants are humiliated and degraded, or in the makeover shows, where being ordinary is treated as something to be ashamed of. Even on TV sitcoms, children have evolved from objects of love and pride to little more than inconveniences who are due little, if any, respect. The result of TV viewing today may not be the overt commission of criminal acts, but rather the growth of an uncaring and unfeeling society, one in which people are so focused on achieving their own gratifications that they look at others as objects of diversion and amusement. A tragedy such as 9/11 can, of course, change that focus for a time. Still, the underlying detachment dominates.

199

Programming Our Lives

Another arena in which television has had a significant impact on what we consider to be right or wrong is sexual behavior. In the past sixty years we have gone from movies in which even a husband and wife could not be shown in the same bed to *NYPD Blue*—which ended more often than not with two unmarried people in bed and a clear shot of partial nudity—and an abundance of more or less explicit sexual programming on cable. We can't say that television created the porn revolution, because in many ways movies led the way. But television quickly jumped on the bandwagon and is continuing each season to extend the limits of what is acceptable. Furthermore, television, unlike movies, brings previously unacceptable sexual activity into the home, which automatically gives it more of an imprimatur of the "norm."

Impatience and Simplification

Despite its important role in furthering the breakdown of racial barriers and limitations on women's lives, not to mention opposition to the war in Vietnam, television on balance has done more to gloss over social and economic difficulties and pander to our wish to avoid complexity. The felt needs for instant gratification of our desire for possessions and entertainment has led us to seek simplification in other parts of our lives, and again television has been there to meet our needs. We see the results in our politics, where the sound bite dominates. Few viewers are willing to sit still for a lengthy discussion of an issue, especially one fraught with ambiguities that require deliberation. Instead, they settle for quick opinions encapsulated in a catchy sentence that is as much slogan as information. Presidential election debates limit answers to ninety seconds and responses to sixty, the average times for a report on the news. Candidates are evaluated not on their substance, but on their ability to deliver a zinger that will resonate like the catch phrase of a successful commercial.

Television itself cannot be dismissed as inherently shallow. Over the years there have been many excellent gripping dramas, classic comedies, and unforgettable reporting of national tragedies. TV has proved to be an effective educational tool. TV technology now permits us to experience aspects of much of the globe, outer space, and even the depths of the oceans. These high points, however, have often been eclipsed by the choice of the lightweight and the sensational. It can be argued, of course, that as a species humans throughout our history tend to avoid intellectual and perceptual effort, gravitating toward the easily grasped, even if that is superficial. Television, however, facilitates this tendency because it provides so much so effortlessly. We don't even have to turn a page or get up from our chair, or open our mouths, or our minds.

Television offers us so much that we can access passively with minimal effort and engagement, and therein lies its main shortcoming. For many it is an addiction; for many more it is an escape, an excuse to withdraw from active engagement with the fullness of life. We can mourn the lost opportunities of the medium, the failure to seize its potential to inform and enrich. But we doubt that potential can ever be achieved.

Expectations beyond Our Imaginings

Has television jaded us? In many way it has, certainly in our expectations of the entertainment we want any time of the day and certainly in the escalating measure of what it takes to shock us. We doubt that the future can reverse these trends. In fact, it promises even more access via our computers, in our cars, and even over our cell phones and other portable devices. In contrast to the hundreds of sources of information we have today, we probably will have thousands in the future. And the medium will become more personal, open to individual choices often transmitted to small groups and, perhaps, even individuals. Television will be everywhere.

For those of us who were present for the first half-century of TV, what exists today has far transcended our most futuristic fantasies. Our wildest guesses for what the next half-century will bring no doubt will be just as inadequate. But one thing is sure: For the indefinite future, our lives will continue to be filled with and changed by what we now call television.

Notes

1. See the University of Virginia Library, "Historical Census Browser."

2. For more detail, see Rosenbloom and Sundstrom, *The Decline and Rise of Interstate Migration in the United States.*

3. See Parsons, "Television in a Child's Bedroom May Hurt Performance in School."

References

Preface

Minnow, Newton N. *Equal Time: The Private Broadcaster and the Public Interest*. New York: Atheneum, 1964.

Introduction

About.com. "The History of the Motion Picture" *Inventors*. http://www.inventors.about.com/library/inventors/blmotionpictures.htm.

Bowman, Darcia Harris. "Television's Influence." *Education Week* 23, no. 43 (July 28, 2004): 10.

Elliot, Victoria Stag. "TV-Free Week Gets Support of Physicians." *American Medical News*, May 5, 2003. http://www.amednews.com.

Horton, Gerd. "Radio Days on America's Homefront." *History Today* 46, no. 9 (1996): 46–53.

Nielsen Media Research. "Nielsen Reports Americans Watch TV at Record Levels." http://www.nielsenmedia.com/newsreleases/2005/AvgHoursMinutes 92905.pdf.

Ramonet, Ignacio. "The Power of Television Pictures." *Communication and Information in the Knowledge Society*. http://www.unesco.org/webworld/points _of_views/200202_ramonet.shtml.

Chapter 1

CAMagazine.com. "TV Viewers Like Multitasking." http://www.camagazine .com/index.cfm/ci_id/20806/la_id/1.htm.

References

eMarketer. "Net Most Popular Media to Use While Watching TV." April 28, 2003. http://www.emarketer.com/eStatDatabase/ArticlePreview.aspx?1002200.

Chapter 2

Barry, Ann Marie Steward. *Visual Intelligence: Perception, Image, and Manipulation in Visual Communication.* Albany: State University of New York Press, 1997.

BBC News. "Watching TV 'is bad for children.'" April 6, 2004. http://news.bbc .co.uk/2/hi/health/3603235.stm.

Christakis, Dimitri A., Frederick J. Zimmerman, David L. DiGiuseppe, and Carolyn A. McCarty. "Early Television Exposure and Subsequent Attentional Problems in Children." *Pediatrics* 113 (April, 2004): 708–713.

Dancyger, Ken. *The Technique of Film and Video Editing.* 3rd ed. Boston: Butterworth-Heinemann, 2002.

Elias, Marilyn. "Short Attention Span Linked to TV." *USA Today,* April 5, 2004.

Hartmann, Thom. *Attention Deficit Disorder—A Different Perception.* Rev. ed. Grass Valley, CA: Underwood Books, 1997.

Healy, Jane M. "Early Television Exposure and Subsequent Attention Problems in Children." *Pediatrics* 113, no. 4 (April 2004): 917.

Johnson, Steven. *Everything Bad Is Good for You: How Today's Popular Culture Is Actually Making Us Smarter.* New York: Riverhead, 2005.

Moyers, Bill. *The Public Mind: Illusions of News.* Directed by Richard M. Cohen. WNET/New York and WETA/Washington. Alexandria, VA: PBS Video, 1989.

Strong, Colby. "Is Excessive Television Viewing in Children Linked to ADHD?" *Neuropsychiatry Review* 5, no. 3 (May 2004). http://www.neuropsychiatryreviews .com/may04/npr_may04_excessiveTV.html.

Chapter 3

Doherty, Thomas. "Assassination and Funeral of President John F. Kennedy." Museum of Broadcast Communications. http://www.museum.tv/archives/ etv/K/htmlK/kennedyjf/kennedyjf.htm.

Entertainment Weekly. "The Assassination and Funeral of John F. Kennedy." *Television Top 100: The 1960s.* http://www.ew.com/ew/fab400/tv100/60s_p2 .html.

JFK: Breaking the News. Directed by Hugh Aynsworth. KERA-Dallas/Fort Worth. November 19, 2003.

Lucyfan.com. "In Loving Memory: Milton Berle (1908–2002)." http://www .lucyfan.com/miltonberle.html.

"Power in Your Hand: A Survey of Television." *The Economist,* April 13, 2003: 4.

Smith, Terence. "Presidential Ultimatum: Reaction." *Online News Hour.* Sept 21, 2001. http://www.pbs.org/newshour/bb/media/july-dec01/bush_9-21.html.

References

U.S. Census Bureau. "50th Anniversary of 'Wonderful World of Color' TV." *U.S. Census Press Releases*, March 11, 2004. http://www.census.gov/Press-Release/www/releases/archives/facts_for_features/001702.html.

U.S. Census Bureau. "USA." *State & County QuickFacts.* http://quickfacts.census.gov/qfd/states/00000.html.

Chapter 4

Watt, Ian. *The Rise of the Novel: Studies in Defoe, Richardson and Fielding.* Berkeley: University of California Press, 1957.

Chapter 5

Greene, Bob. "Was It Real for You, Too?" *New York Times*, July 23, 2005: A13.

"Reality TV World." http://www.realitytvworld.com.

Reiss, Steven and James Wiltz. "Why American Loves Reality TV." *Psychology Today*, 34, no. 5 (September 1, 2001): 52–55.

Salamon, Julie. "When Group Therapy Means Coming Clean on TV." *New York Times,* June 22, 2004: E1.

Chapter 6

Cinema Laser. "Jerry Springer—Too Hot for TV 2000: Welcome to the Hellenium." http://www.thecinemalaser.com.

Felluga, Dino. "Modules on Baudrillard: On Simulation." *Introductory Guides to Critical Theory*. West Lafayette, IN: Purdue University, 2003.

Robinson, Bryan. "Plaintiffs Rest After Amedure's Father Accuses Jones Show of Destroying Both His Son and Jonathan Schmitz." *Court TV Online*, April 27, 1999. http://www.courttv.com/archive/trials/jennyjones/042799_pm_ctv.html.

Rostow, Ann. "Court Reverses 'Jenny Jones' Ruling," *PlanetOut.com Network*, October 23, 2002. http://www.planetout.com/news/article-print.html?2002/10/23/1.

Chapter 7

"The Harder Hard Sell: the Future of Advertising." *The Economist*, June 24, 2004: 84.

Ives, Nat. "Rain or Shine, Win or Lose, This Ad Is Just for You." *New York Times*, June 28, 2000: C1.

Poniewozik, James. "This Plug's for You." *Time,* June 18, 2001: 63.

Robins, J. Max. "Ad Nauseam: Commercials and Promos Are Growing at a Sickening Rate." *TV Guide*, January 24, 2004.

References

Walker, Chip. "Can TV Save the Planet?—Television Is Spawning Worldwide Consumer Culture." *American Demographics*, May 1996: 42–47.

Chapter 8

Alter, Jonathan. "The Lessons of Oprahland." *Newsweek*, October 2, 2000: 32.
Campaign Media Analysis Group. "Politics on TV." http://www.politicsontv .com.
Druckman, James N. "The Power of Image: The First Kennedy-Nixon Debate Revisited." Paper presented at the annual meeting of the American Political Science Association, Boston, MA, August 28, 2001.
Jones, Tim. "Inside Media: Study Finds Little Political Discourse on Local TV." *Chicago Tribune*, February 8, 2001: 2.
Kaid, Lynda Lee. "Political Processes & Television." *Television: The Great Equalizer?* Museum of Broadcast Communications. http://www.museum.tv/debateweb/ html/equalizer/essay_polyprocesstv.htm.
Library of Congress. "The Great Debates of Nixon and Kennedy." *America's Story from America's Library.* http://www.americaslibrary.gov/cgi-bin/page.cgi/jb/ modern/debates_1.
Media Literacy Clearinghouse. "Political Ad Spending on Television Sets New Record: $1.6 Billion." http://medialit.med.sc.edu/election_ad_battle_smashes _record.htm.
Reece, Bonnie B. "Advertising." Chana High School, Auburn, CA. http://www .puhsd.k12.ca.us/chana/staffpages/eichman/civics/elections/3/advertising1 .htm.
Rich, Frank. "Paar to Leno, J.F.K. to J.F.K." *New York Times*, February 8, 2004: 2.1.

Chapter 9

Baker, James A., Thomas M. Defrank, and James A. Baker III. *The Politics of Diplomacy: Revolution, War and Peace 1989–1992.* New York: Putnam Publishing Group, 1995.
Dobbs, Michael. "The Day Adlai Stevenson Showed 'Em at the U.N." *The Washington Post*, February 5, 2003: C1.
Hallin, Daniel. "Vietnam on Television" *The Encyclopedia of Television.* The Museum of Broadcast Television. http://www.museum.tv/archives/.
Marks, Peter. "Even in College, the Vice President Was No Boob About the Tube." *New York Times*, July 16, 2000: 4.7.
Zunes, Stephen. "The US Invasion of Grenada: A Twenty Year Retrospective." *Global Policy Forum.* http://www.globalpolicy.org/empire/history/2003/10 grenada.htm.
Zwick, Jim. "Political Cartoons of Thomas Nast." *Political Cartoons and Cartoonists.* http://www.boondocksnet.com/gallery/nast_intro.html.

References

Chapter 10

Ainsworth, Diane. "Whistle-blower Lowell Bergman: An Insider's View of '60 Minutes.'" *News*. Berkeleyan Home Search Archive. http://www.berkeley .edu/news/berkeleyan/2000/06/07/bergman.html.

Althaus, Scott L. "American News Consumption during Times of National Crisis." *PS: Political Science & Politics*, September 2002. The American Political Science Association Online. http://www.apsanet.org/imgtest/AmericanNews Consumption-Althaus.pdf.

Baker, James A., Thomas M. Defrank, and James A. Baker III. *The Politics of Diplomacy: Revolution, War and Peace 1989–1992*. New York: Putnam Publishing Group, 1995.

Fairness and Accuracy in Reporting. "Media Giants Cast Aside Regulatory 'Chains': FCC Should Resist Attempt to Gut Ownership Restrictions." http://fair.org/index.php?page=1659.

Gannett Company, Inc. "Gannett on the Go." http://www.gannett.com.

Journalism.org. "The State of the News Media 2004." http://www.stateofthe newsmedia.org/2004/index.asp.

Marro, Anthony. "Review of *News and the Culture of Lying*, by Paul H. Weaver: The Free Press." *Columbia Journalism Review*, November/December, 1994: 71–75.

Newspaper Association of America. "Circulation and Readership." http://www .naa.org/artpage.cfm?AID=1610&SID=1167.

Newspaper Association of America. "Trends & Numbers." http://www.naa.org/ Trends-and-Numbers.aspx.

Pew Research Center. "News Audiences Increasingly Politicized." *Survey Reports*, June 8, 2004. http://people-press.org/reports/display.php3?ReportID=215.

Pew Research Center. "Self Censorship: How Often and Why." *Survey Reports*, May 25, 2004. http://people-press.org/reports/display.php3?ReportID=39.

Program on International Policy Attitudes (PIPA) "Misperceptions, the Media and the Iraq War." *World Public Opinion*, October 2, 2003. http://www.world publicopinion.org/pipa/articles/international_security_bt/102.php?nid=&id =&pnt=102.

Strupp, Joe. "New 'E&P' Poll Reveals Very Active Readership." The TechnoMetrica Institute of Policy and Politics. http://www.tipponline.com/ articles/00/ep092500.htm.

Chapter 11

Anderson, D. N., A. Huston, and J. C. Wright. "The Markle CTW Recontact Study: Initial Findings." In *A Communications Cornucopia: Markle Foundation Essays on Information Policy*, edited by M.E. Price and R.G. Knoll. Washington, DC: Brookings Institution Press, forthcoming.

Carnevale, Dan and Jeffrey R. Young. "Telecourses Change Channels." *The Chronicle of Higher Education*, July 13, 2001: 29.

References

Freed, Ken. "A History of Distance Learning." Media Visions. http://www.media-visions.com/education.html.

Gibson, Kristin. "Formative Research at the Children's Television Workshop." *Encyclopedia of Educational Technology.* http://coe.sdsu.edu/eet/articles/tv research/index.htm.

Huston, Althea C., Edward Donnerstein, Halford Fairchild, Norma D. Feshbach, Phyllis A. Katz, John P. Murray, Eli A. Rubinstein, Brian A. Wilcox, and Diana M. Zuckerman. *Big World, Small Screen: The Role of Television in American Society.* Lincoln: University of Nebraska Press, 1992.

Johnson, Steven. *Everything Bad Is Good for You: How Today's Popular Culture Is Actually Making Us Smarter.* New York: Riverhead, 2005.

National Endowment for the Arts. *Reading At Risk.* Washington, DC: NEA, 2004.

National Institute on Media and the Family. "Media Wise." http://www.media family.org/kidscore/index.shtml.

Rautiolla-Williams, Suzanne. "The Howdy Doody Show." Museum of Broadcast Communications. http://www.museum.tv/archives/etv/H/htmlH/howdydoodys/howdydoodys.htm.

"Supervising Student Teachers by Videoconference." *The Right Angle* 7, no. 1 (Spring/Summer 2004). Purdue University School of Education. http://www.soe.purdue.edu/alumni/right_angle/rightangle2004-7.pdf.

Technical Report of the 1991 School Utilization Survey, Study of School Uses of Television and Video 1990-1991 School Year. Washington, D.C.: Corporation for Public Broadcasting, 1992.

Wright, J. C. and A. Huston. *Effects of Educational Television Viewing of Lower Income Preschoolers on Academic Skills, School Readiness and School Adjustment One to Three Years Later.* Lawrence, KS: University of Kansas, 1995.

Zill, Nicholas and Elizabeth Davies. *Public Television Children's Programs: Are They Helping Young Children Get Ready for School?* Rockville, MD: Westat, Inc., 1994.

Chapter 12

American Academy of Family Physicians. "Study: Patients' Drug Requests Have 'Profound Effect' on Physicians Prescribing for Depression." http://www.aafp.org/x34119.xml?printxml.

American Medical Association. "Women Physicians Congress (WPC) Statistics and History." http://www.ama-assn.org/ama/pub/category/171.html.

Association of American Medical Colleges. "Applicants to U.S. Medical Schools Increase." November 4, 2003. http://www.aamc.org/newsroom/pressrel/2003/031104.htm.

BBC News. "Video Pill's 'Fantastic Voyage.'" http://news.bbc.co.uk/1/hi/sci/tech/762415.stm.

Malone, M. E. "TV Remains Dominant Source for Medical Information." *Boston Globe*, March 12, 2002.

Newton, Dale A. and Martha S. Grayson. "Trends in Career Choice by US Med." *JAMA* 290 (2003):1179–1182.

References

Turow, Joseph. "Marcus Welby, M.D." Museum of Broadcast Communications. http://www.museum.tv/archives/etv/M/htmlM/marcuswelby/marcus welby.htm

Turow, Joseph. "Medic." Museum of Broadcast Communications. http://www.museum.tv/archives/etv/M/htmlM/medic/medic.htm.

Chapter 13

Bureau of Justice Statistics. "Four Measures of Serious Violent Crime." http://www.ojp.usdoj.gov/bjs/glance/cv2.htm.

Bureau of Justice Statistics. "Homicide Trends in the United States." http://www.ojp.usdoj.gov/bjs/homicide/homtrnd.htm.

Clayton, Mark. "Major Trends." *The Christian Science Monitor*, November 19, 2002: 11.

CyberCollege.com. "TV and Film Violence." *Critical Issues in Film and TV.* Updated March 12, 2006. http://www.cybercollege.com/violence.htm.

Huesmann, L. Rowell, et al. "Longitudinal Relations between Children's Exposure to TV Violence and Their Aggressive and Violent Behavior in Young Adulthood: 1977–1992." *Developmental Psychology* 39, no. 2 (March 2003): 201.

Johnson, Jeffrey G., Patricia Cohen, Elizabeth M. Smailes, Stephanie Kasen, and Judith S. Brook. "Television Viewing and Aggressive Behavior during Adolescence and Adulthood." *Science* 295, no, 5564 (March 2002): 2468–2472.

Murray, John P. "Impact of Televised Violence." School of Family Studies and Human Services, Kansas State University. http://www.k-state.edu/humec/fshs/faculty/lifespan/murray/impact.htm.

Scott, A. O. "Working the Beat." *New York Times Magazine*, July 20, 2003: 7–9.

University of Central Florida. "Criminals in TV Entertainment." http://pegasus.cc.ucf.edu/~surette/tvent.html.

Chapter 14

"Baseball." *The Concise Colombia Encyclopedia*, 3rd ed. New York: Columbia University Press, 1994.

The Baseball Archive. "Major League Attendance 1990–1994." http://www.baseball1.com/bb-data/bbd-at9.html.

Blondin, Alan. "Number of Golf Rounds Falls throughout Country." Myrtle BeachOnline.com. http://www.myrtlebeachonline.com.

Boorstin, Daniel. *The Image*. New York: Vintage, 1961.

Lambert, Craig. "Has Winning on the Field Become Simply a Corporate Triumph?" *Harvard Magazine* 104, no. 1 (September–October 2001). http://www.harvardmagazine.com/on-line/09014.html.

References

Martin, Bruce. "Auto Racing Note." *Slam Motorsports*. November 11, 1999. http://www.canoe.ca/StatsRAC/BC-RAC-LGNS-TVFTR-R.html.

Motorsports Management International. "Motorsports Racing Series." http://media.corporateir.net/media_files/irol/99/99758/reports/electronicannual.pdf.

Packman, Tim. "Networks looking to maintain, increase in 2002." NASCAR.com, January 5, 2002. http://www.nascar.com/2002/NEWS/01/05/tv_2002.

Chapter 15

Africa Magic, May 2, 2004. http://www.africamagic.co.za/

Belson, Ken. "New Undersea Cable Project Faces Some Old Problems." *New York Times*, May 10, 2004: C4.

Hughes, Lyric. "Written Testimony before the U.S. China Economic and Security Review Commission." China Online, Inc. January 18, 2002. http://www.uscc.gov/textonly/transcriptstx/teshug.htm.

International Telecommunication Union. "ITU Launches New Development Initiative to Bridge the Digital Divide." June 16, 2005. http://www.itu.int/newsarchive/press_releases/2005/07.html.

Mander, Jerry. "TV and Computers: Who Benefits Most." *Resurgence* 208. http://www.resurgence.org/resurgence/issues/mander208.htm.

Peale, Cliff. "Overseas Sales Have Big Impact Back Home." *The Cincinnati Enquirer,* October 5, 2003. http://www.enquirer.com/editions/2003/10/05/biz_pgcincy.05.html.

"TV Guide." April 2004. http://www.CCTV.com (China).

"TV Guide." *Metropolis Japan Today*, April 30, 2004.

Chapter 16

Hancox, R., B. Milne, and R. Poulton. "Association between Child and Adolescent Television Viewing and Adult Health: A Longitudinal Birth Cohort Study." *The Lancet* 364, no. 9430 (July 17, 2004): 257–263.

Kubey, Robert and Mihaly Csikszentmihalyi. "Television Addiction Is No Mere Metaphor." *Scientific American,* 286, no. 2 (February 23, 2002): 74.

Pew Research Center. "News Audiences Increasingly Politicized." *Survey Reports*, June 8, 2004. http://people-press.org/reports/display.php3?ReportID=215.

Strover, Sharon. "United States: Cable Television." Museum of Broadcast Communications. http://www.museum.tv/archives/etv/U/htmlU/united statesc/unitedstatesc.htm.

Swann, Phillip. "Perspective: Interactive TV: Clearing the static." CNET News.com. May 13, 2002. http://news.com.com/2010-1071-911827.html.

References

Chapter 17

Barnes, Johnny. "Surveillance Cameras in the District of Columbia." Statement before the Subcommittee on the District of Columbia of the House of Representatives Committee on Government Reform, March 22, 2002.

CNN.com. "Smooth Start to London Traffic Tax." CNN.com, World. February 17, 2003. http://www.cnn.com/2003/WORLD/europe/02/17/london.traffic/.

Elliott, Andrea. "In Stores, Private Handcuffs for Sticky Fingers." *New York Times*, June 17, 2003: 1.

Irsay, Steve. "Surveillance Cameras Play Increasing Role as Investigation Tool." CNN.com Law Center. October 21, 2002. http://archives.cnn.com/2002/LAW/10/21/ctv.cameras/

Le, Phuong Cat. "Surveillance Planned for Pioneer Square." *Seattle Post-Intelligencer*, August 20, 2002. http://seattlepi.nwsource.com/local/83376_cameras20.shtml.

Webb, Al. "Smile, You're on Candid Camera." http://www.shagmail.com/sample/living.html.

Wendling, Mike. "'Congestion Charge' Cuts London Traffic; Businesses Upset." Cybercast News Service (CNS). http://www.conservativenews.org/ViewForeignBureaus.asp?Page=%5CForeignBureaus%5Carchive%5C200306%5CFOR20030606c.html.

Chapter 18

Balint, Kathryn. "Not ready for Prime Time: With Little High-Definition Programming, Consumers Find Little Reason to Invest in HDTV." *The San Diego Union-Tribune*, June 3, 2002. http://www.signonsandiego.com/news/business/20020603-9999_mz1b3primeti.html.

Bass, Steve. "TiVo, PVRs, and Other Things TV." *PC World*, July 14. 2004. http://pcworld.about.com/news/Jul142004id116647.htm.

Gleeson, Frances. "Camera Phones Outsell Digital Cameras." ElectricNews.net. September 22 2003. http://www.electricnews.net/news.html?code=9375927.

"Global camera phone sales rise five-fold in 2003." March, 29, 2004. Forbes.com. http://www.forbes.com/business/newswire/2004/03/29/rtr1314928.html.

Gnatek, Tim. "Internet TV: Don't Touch that Mouse!" *New York Times*, July 1, 2004: G5.

Hansell, Saul. "Internet Service to Put Classic TV on Home Computer." *New York Times*, November 14, 2005: C1.

"Life in the Vault: The Digital Home." *The Economist*, July 1, 2004: 72.

Mossberg, Walter S. "Device Lets You Watch Shows on a Home TV, TiVo From Elsewhere." *The Wall Street Journal*, June 30, 2005: B.1.

"Power in Your Hand: A Survey of Television." *The Economist*, April 13, 2003: 4.

Swann, Philip. "What Interactive TV Needs." http://www.TVPredictions.com.

"Television's Next Big Shift." *The Economist Technology Quarterly*, March 11, 2006: 16.

References

Wagner, Jim. "iTV: The Next Killer App?" Internetnews.com. July 16, 2004. http://www.internetnews.com/infra/article.php/3382491.

Chapter 19

Johns Hopkins School of Public Health. "Television In The Bedroom May Hurt Child's School Performance." July 4, 2005. http://www.jhsph.edu/public healthnews/press_releases/2005/borzekowski_tv.html.

Kaiser Family Foundation. "Kids & Media @ The New Millennium." November 15, 1999. http://www.kff.org/entmedia/1535-index.cfm.

Parsons, Tim. "Television in a Child's Bedroom May Hurt Performance in School." *Johns Hopkins Gazette*, July, 11, 2005. http://www.jhu.edu/~gazette/2005/11jul05/11teevee.html.

Rosenbloom, Joshua L. and William A. Sundstrom. *The Decline and Rise of Interstate Migration in the United States: Evidence from the IPUMS, 1850–1990.* October 18, 2002. http://aghistory.ucdavis.edu/Sundstrom.pdf.

Schor, Juliet, "America's Most Wanted: Inside the World of Young Minds." *Boston College Magazine*, Fall 2004. http://www.bc.edu/publications/bcm/fall_2004/ft_schor.html.

University of Virginia Library. "Historical Census Browser: State Level Results for 1940." Geospatial and Statistical Data Center. http://fisher.lib.virginia.edu/collections/stats/histcensus/php/state.php.

Index

Index

Index

Index

Index

Index

Index

Index

Index

About the Authors

WALTER CUMMINS is Professor Emeritus of English at Farleigh Dickinson University's College at Florham and Editor Emeritus for *The Literary Review: An International Journal of Contemporary Writing*. He is the coauthor of *The Literary Traveler* with Thomas E. Kennedy and the author of the story collections *Witness* and *Where We Live*. He serves on the editorial boards of *Web Del Sol*, *Tiferet* magazine, and the Fairleigh Dickinson University Press.

GEORGE GORDON has pursued a distinguished career as a partner of Hay Management Consultant and president of its Research for Management Division. He was also a member of the faculty of Rutgers University and a board member of a number of organizations. Over fifty of his articles and speeches have appeared in numerous business magazines, professional publications, and books. These span such publications as *Academy of Management Review*, *Directors and Boards*, *Research-Technology Management*, and *International Journal of Business*. His previous book, *Managing Management Climate*, was coauthored with Walter Cummins.